INFORMATION AND SOCIETY

[Essays in the Memory of Prof. P. Gangadhara Rao]

L.S. Ramaiah

N. Guruswami Naidu

T. Ashok Babu

B. Ramesh Babu

K. Ramanaiah

Ess Ess Publications

4837/24, Ansari Road, Darya Ganj,
New Delhi-110002

First Published 1997

ISBN : 81–7000–219–2

Price : Ess Ess Rs.800/-

Published by :
Ess Ess Publications
4837/24, Ansari Road, Darya Ganj,
New Delhi - 110 002
Phone : 3260807

Laser Typesetting :

CINOGRAPHICS
E-41, New Multan Nagar
New Delhi
Phone : 5583866

Printed at : Salasar Imaging System

Prof. Parvathaneni Gangadhara Rao
(1929-1990)

Foreword

I am extremely glad to write the foreword to the book **'Information and Society'**, a Festschrift presented to the departed soul of Prof. Parvathaneni Gangadhara Rao, the former Head of the Department of Library and Information Science, University of Madras, a prestigious institution in the south and if not in India. In this connection, we must remember a quotation -

The three things that make every man great, every nation great-

1. Conviction of the powers of goodness.
2. Absence of jealousy and suspicion.
3. Helping all who are trying to be and do good.

Prof. Rao is an embodiment of all these qualities of a great man. We all knew Prof. Rao as a Head of a teaching department. But he is a multi- faceted personality

- associated with professional journals,
- reviewer of books,
- adjudigator of theses,
- short story writer in Telugu,
- lyric writer in Telugu,
- a screenplay writer of Telugu movies,

and above all a great humanitarian and a lover of books. Prof. Rao is to be remembered for bringing the library education from the portals of closed circles to the doorsteps of the common. In a Festschrift, it may not be possible to represent all the areas, in which Prof. Rao has done considerable work. On the whole, this Festschrift was prepared on a broad- based theme INFORMATION AND SOCIETY.

Information is the key for the development of society and individual. Gradually, the society is being changed from feudalist to democratic and from democratic to information society. With this impact, information is being developed and elevated as economic commodity to act as catalytic agent in bringing about the desired social and economic change in a society. In a changing information society "Knowledge and Information foster innovation, policy and decision making and execution action". In the coming few years, we are entering in a new society. In this situation this memorial volume will give more new thoughts.

As President of Prof. P.G. Rao Memorial Committee, I am highly indebted to all the professional colleagues for the contribution of valuable papers, which enabled us to bring out this volume. I am grateful to all the donors for liberal donation, and particularly to Smt. P. Padmavati Gangadhara Rao for her munificient donation for Prof. P.G. Rao Memorial Fund which enabled us to institute -

1. Prof. P.G. Rao Award for the best library and information educationalist / scientist, at Potti Sree Ramulu Telugu University, Hyderabad, from 1996 onwards. (Prof. L.S. Ramaiah was the First Awardee).
2. Prof. P.G. Rao Gold Medal for the First Class First student in the University of Madras from 1996-1997 onwards.
3. Also planning to institute a prize of scholarship in the Z.P. High School, Punadipadu, where Prof. P.G. Rao had his early education.

The royalties received on this Festschrift will be credited to the **Foundation for Information and Communication**, a voluntary organisation started in this year, to cherish the ideas of our great professionals.

I must be grateful to all the professionals and non-professionals for making a great success of this great project.

Tenali
Dt: 30-05-1997

V. Venkatappaiah
President
Prof. P.G. Rao Memorial Volume Committee

Contents

Introduction

This man of little learning grows old like the bull
His flesh grows, his wisdom increases not.

– Dhammapada

You cannot step twice into the same river.

– Heraclitus

(Late) Parvathaneni Gangadhara Rao was Professor of the prestigious Sarada Ranganathan Chair in Library Science in the University of Madras from 1979 till his retirement in 1989. He was a multi-talented man. He was a great teacher, researcher, guide, examiner, editor and a creative writer. He was a man of simple living and high thinking. He had a wide circle of friends both in the profession and outside. During the IASLIC Annual Seminar at Lucknow in 1995, at an after dinner walk on the campus of Lucknow University, three of us viz. L.S. Ramaiah, Dr. Ramesh Babu and Mr. T. Ashok Babu, fondly remembered Prof. Gangadhara Rao and his contribution to the LIS profession. It was decided then and there to do something permanent in his name to make him alive in the hearts of his friends, colleagues and students. We later in consultation with the sane advice of Dr. Velaga Venkatappaiah and Prof. N. Guruswamy Naidu, a Committee was constituted to chalk out a plan of action. The results of the coordinated efforts are, the institution of a Gold Medal in the University of Madras, an Annual Award in Potti Sriramulu Telugu University, Hyderabad and this Memorial Volume. We feel that it is a fitting tribute to our departed friend and fellow professional.

Prof. Gangadhara Rao had believed strongly throughout his life that information is the strongest weapon against intolerance and ignorance. Right to information and free access to information to common man should be a matter of constitutional obligation. Information to society is like what is oxygen to an individual. Without libraries and information centres and access to information the individuals will become moribund and the society will stagnate. Information is essential today for growth in any field, let it be culture, science, economy or anything. Hence the title, *Information and Society*, which is chosen for this Memorial Volume is very apt and reflect the ideas and ideals of Prof. Gangadhara Rao.

There are 45 articles in 13 sections in this book. The sections are: (I) Libraries and Information, (II) Classification: Some Reflections, (III) Academic Libraries: State-of-the-Art, (IV) Libraries and Distance Education, (V) LIS Education: Challenges and Changes, (VI) LIS Profession and Professionalism, (VII) LIS Management, (VIII) Information Resources: Caring & Sharing, (IX) Technical Report Writing and Standards, (X) Information Technology, (XI) Information Superhighways, (XII) Internet and WWW, (XIII) Prof. Gangadhara Rao: Bio-Glimpses.

Each section deals with a particular aspect of information and developments in the field. The authors who are mostly senior professionals ably dealt with the subjects combining both theory and experience. The merit of these articles is their originality.

The book begins with an article by Rabindranath Tagore, which was his address to the *All India Libraries Association* in 1929. It was originally published in *The Indian Library Journal*, not easily available to the professionals due to the passage of time. In order to remind ourselves with the great thoughts of *Gurudev* on libraries, it is reprinted here. The Nobel Laureate said that librarians should not look for the quantity of library collections but for the quality and use of them. His message is still valid to the professionals even today.

The editors have taken care to include articles which have dealt with both the traditional subjects as well as the modern Information Technology. The various sections clearly indicate the nature, and focus of the articles and their relevance in this volume.

In India, information and knowledge, is concentrated by and large, in the hands of powerful and rich people.

This shakle is to be broken and the flow of information and knowledge to the downtrodden, disadvantaged and illiterate people living in the rural India at the grass root level should be ensured. For the last three quarters of a century, people in India due to the Freedom Movement and democratic form of government were politically awakened inspite of illiteracy. More importance was given to the flow of political information by the press, radio, and TV. Information and Knowledge in the fields of Agriculture, Education, Industry, Business were playing a second fiddle. They are most important for the social development and for the creation of societal prosperity. Large sections of people in the rural areas waste most of their leisure time and energy on unproductive activities due to lack of access to productive information. The infrastructure facilities created through the governmental planning are not used to the maximum extent in the villages due to lack of proper access to information. Education and access to information to rural people through community information centres alone can transform our villages from poverty to creators of National Wealth. Modern Communication Technology (MCT) and Information Technology (IT) should be used to create the superhighways, superbazars and markets of information. This alone will close up the gap between the information rich and information poor and enable every citizen of India to think globally and act locally.

JAI HIND

Hyderabad **L.S. Ramaiah**

01/07/1997

ACKNOWLEDGEMENTS

This volume in memory of Prof. P. Gangadhara Rao is the outcome of joint efforts of his colleagues, friends and students. Hence, it is a book of all of us. Since the name and work of Prof. Rao was familiar to all senior persons in the LIS profession, the task of the editors has become easier in getting a quiet good number of papers for publication in this volume.

At the outset, we express our deep sense of gratitude and thanks to Mrs. P.L. Padmavathi Gangadhara Rao and their son, Mr. Eswara Prasad and their daughter Ms. Sai Lakshmi for their consent and help in bringing out this volume of papers. Our sincere thanks are also due to all the members of the Memorial Volume Committee and particularly to Dr. Valga Venkatappaiah, a walking encyclopaedia of Library Science in India, and to Prof. N. Guruswamy Naidu, Professor, DLIS, Sri Venkateswara University, Tirupati for their constant advice and suggestions at every stage of this work. All the authors of papers in this volume cooperated with us by sending their papers promptly and according to the time schedule set out by the editors. Hence we express our thanks to them. Further, our special thanks are due to Dr. Grace B Agnew, Assistant Director, Atlanta-Fulton Public Library, Atlanta, USA, Dr. Daniel Gervais, Assistant Secretary General, International. Confederation of Authors, Paris and Dr. Anand P. Srivastava, Former Librarian, University of Delhi, for their permission to publish their articles in this volume.

As every beautiful building needs an Architect and an Engineer to design and build, every book needs an author and a publisher to publish it. The credit of designing and publishing this book beautifully goes to Shri Sumit Sethi of Ess Ess Publications, New Delhi, who has already published a large quantity of literature in the field of Library and Information Science. We express our whole hearted thanks to him and wish him all success in his endeavours.

Editors

PROF. PARVATHANENI GANGADHARA RAO MEMORIAL VOLUME COMMITTEE

President

1. Dr. Velaga Venkatappaiah
   H.No. 4-22-27
   Ithanagar
   Tenali-522 201

Vice-Presidents

2. Prof. L.S. Ramaiah
   University Librarian
   Ramesh Mohan Library
   C I E F L
   Hyderabad-500 007

3. Dr. Abbas Ibrahim
   Information Scientist
   Secretary General
   Database Society of India
   143/1, Peters Road
   Madras-600 086

4. Mr. S. Koteswara Rao
   University Librarian (Retd.)
   Nagarjuna University
   Nagarjuna Nagar
   Guntur-522 510

5. Dr. B. Ramesh Babu
   Reader

Dept. of Library & Information Science
University of Madras
Madras-600 005
Organising Secretary

6. Mr. T. Ashok Babu
Scientist/RCI
DRDL Library
Hyderabad-500058

Joint Secretaries

7. Dr. D. Chandran
Lecturer
Dept. of Library & Information Science
S.V. University
Tirupati-517 502

8. Mr. L. Venkatesware Rao
Lecturer, LIS
Sir CRR College
Eluru
West Godavari Dist. (A.P.)

Members

9. Prof. Amitabha Chatterjee
Professor
DLISC
Jadavpur University
Calcutta-700 032

10. Prof. M.R. Chandran
University Librarian
S.V. University
Tirupati-517 502

11. Dr. V. Chandrasekhara Rao
Reader
Dept. of Library & Information Science

Dr. B.R. Ambedkar Open University
Jubilee Hills
Hyderabad-500 033

12. Prof. K.S. Deshpande
Ramachandrakrupa
Malmaddi
Dharwad-580 007

13. Dr. Darothy Issac
University Librarian
Osmania University
Hyderabad-500 007

14. Dr. P. Eswara Prasad
245 Stevens Avenue
Jersey City
New Jersey-07305

15. Dr. S.R. Gupta
Reader
Dept. of Library & Information Science
University of Delhi
Delhi-110 007

16. Dr. Harish Chandra
Librarian
I.I.T.
Madras-600 036

17. Prof. S.R. Ijari
Professor
Dept. of Library & Information Science
Karnataka University
Dharwad-580 003

18. Prof. S.S. Janardhana Rao
University Librarian

Dr. V.S. Krishna Library
Andhra University
Waltair-580 003

19. Prof. C.R. Karisiddappa
Professor
Dept. of Library & Information Science
Karnataka University
Dharwad-580 003

20. Prof. P.N. Kaula
President, ILA
C-239, Indiranagar
Lucknow-226 016

21. Prof. M.B. Konnur
University Librarian & Head
Dept. of Library & Information Science
University of Poona
Pune-411 007

22. Prof. Krishna Kumar
Professor
Dept. of Library & Information Science
University of Delhi
Delhi-110 007

23. Prof. P.S.G. Kumar
Head, Dept. of Library & Information Science
and University Librarian
Nagpur University
Nagpur-440 001

24. Prof. N. Laxman Rao
Professor
Dept. of Library & Information Science
Osmania University
Hyderabad-500 007

25. Dr. Manorama Srinath
Reader
Dept. of Library & Information Science
University of Madras
Madras-600 005

26. Mr. T. Muthuswamy
Secretary
Tamilnadu Library Association
8/2 Brindavan Street
Chennai-600 033

27. Dr. V. Nagarajan
Professor
Dept. of Adult & Continuing Education
University of Madras
Chennai-600 005

28. Dr. Paul Mohan Roy
Professor (Retd.)
Madurai Kamaraj University
Madurai-625 021

29. Dr. V. Pulla Reddy
Reader
Dept. of Library & Information Science
S.V. University
Tirupati-517 502

30. Mr. A. Ragavaiah
Ithanagar
Tenali-522 201

31. Mrs. D. Rajeswari
Assistant Librarian
Sri Padmavati Mahila Visvavidyalayam
Tirupati-517 502

32. Prof. E. Rama Reddy
University Librarian
University of Hyderabad
Hyderabad-500 046

33. Prof. A.A.N. Raju
Professor
Dept. of Library & Information Science
Osmania University
Hyderabad-500 007

34. Prof. K. Sarada
Professor (Retd.)
Dept. of Library & Information Science
Andhra University
Waltair-530 003

35. Dr. M. Sankara Reddy
University Librarian
Sri Potti Sriramulu Telugu University
O.U. Campus
Hyderabad-500 007

36. Mrs. Ravi Sarada
Secretary
A.P. Library Association
Vijayawada-520 010

37. Mr. A. Satyanarayana
Director
Directorate of Public Library
Govt. of A.P.
Hyderabad-500 012

38. Mr. B. Satyanarayana
Dy. Librarian
J.N.T.U.
Hyderabad-500 028

39. Mr. I. Satyanarayana
Lecturer in LIS
ANR College
Gudivada
Krishna Dt. A.P.

40. Prof. N.R. Satyanarayana
Professor
Dept. of Library & Information Science
University of Lucknow
Lucknow-226 007

41. Prof. P. Soma Raju
Professor
Dept. of Library & Information Science
Andhra University
Waltair-530 003

42. Mr. A. Srimurugan
Head
DLISC
Madurai-Kararas University
Madurai

43. Mr. C. Srinath
Dy. Librarian
University of Madras
Madras-600 005

44. Prof. C.P. Vashishth
Professor
Dept. of Library & Information Science
University of Delhi
Delhi-110 007

List of Contributors

1. Mr. J. Abraham
Assistant Librarian
Gandhi Gram Rural Institute
Gandhigram 624 302

2. Dr. Grace B. Agnew
Assistant Director,
Atlanta Fulton Public Library
Atlanta, U.S.A.

3. Mr. M. Anjaiah
Lecturer
SDLCE
Kakatiya University
Warangal 506 009

4. Mr. T. Ashok Babu
Scientist / RCI
DRDL Library
Hderabad - 500058

5. Mr. G. Dhanasegaran
Assistant Librarian
Dr. T.P.M. Library
Madurai Kamaraj University
Madurai 625 021

6. Dr. Bipul Kumar Chakrabarty
Chief Librarian
National Institute of Fashion Technology
Karuangan, Manjusha Bhavan
Sector III, 1 B - 181
Salt Lake City
Calcutta 700091

7. Dr. Harish Chandra
Librarian
I.I.T.
Madras - 600036

8. Mr. J. Dominic
Assistant Librarian
Karunya Institute of Technology
Coimbattore - 641114

9. Mr. S. Ganesan
Dr. ALM Postgraduate Institute of
Basic Medical Sciences
University of Madras
Taramani
Madras - 600 113

10. Dr. Daniel Gervais
Assistant Secretary General
International Confederation of Authors
and Composers
Paris

11. Mr. G. Gopalakrishnan
Assistant Librarian
MIT, Anna University
Chrompet
Madras 600044

12. Dr. Abbas Ibrahim
Information Scientist
Secretary General
Database Society of India
143/1, Peters Road
Madras 600086

13. Pro. S.R. Ijari
Dept. of Library and Information Science
Karnataka University
Dharwad - 580 003

14. Mr. K. Kaliya Perumal
Assistant Librarian
Anna University
Madras - 600 025

15. Dr. B.V. Kannappanavar
Librarian
Sahyadri Arts College
Shimoga

16. Prof. C. R. Karisiddappa
Dept. of Library and Information Science
Karnataka University
Dharwad - 580 003

17. Mr. V. Kasi Rao
Documentation Officer
CLRI, Adyar
Madras - 600020

18. Prof. P.B. Mangla
Dept. of Library and Information Science
University of Delhi
Delhi - 110007

19. Dr. A.L. Moorthy
DESIDOC
Delhi - 110054

20. Dr. APSVVSNL Narasimha Raju
Reader, DNR College
Bhimavmaram-2

21. Smt. P.J. Nirmala
Assistant Librarian
Karunya Institute of Technology
Coimbatore - 641114

22. Mr. S. Palani
Dr. ALM Postgraduate Institute of
Medical Sciences
University of Madras
Taramani
Madras - 600113

23. Prof. N.B. Pangannaya
Dept. of Library and Information Science
Mysore University
Mysore - 570 006

24. Dr. N.R.V. Prabhu
Honarary Director
CRAIO
Madras - 600040

25. Dr. A.R.D. Prasad
Reader, DRTC
Bangalore - 560059

26. Dr. V. Pulla Reddy
Reader
Dept. of Library and Information Science
S.V. University
Tirupati - 517 502

27. Mr.. T. Rajendran
D.B. Jain College
Madras

28. Prof. A.A.N. Raju
Dept. of Library and Information Science
Osmania University
Hvderabad - 500007

29. Prof. L.S. Ramaiah
University Librarian
Ramesh Mohan Library
C I E F L
Hyderabad - 500007

30. Mr. K. Ramanaiah
Dy. Librarian
Kakatiya University
Warangal - 506 009

31. Prof. E. Rama Reddy
University LIbrarian
University of Hyderabad
Hyderabad - 500046

32. Mr. C.P. Ramesh
Assistant Librarian
Mysore University
Mysore - 6

33. Dr. B. Ramesh Babu
Reader
Dept. of Library and Information Science
University of Madras
Madras - 600005

34. Mr. Md. Gouse Riajuddin
Lecturer
Dept. of Library and Information Science
Nagarajuna University
Nagarjunanagar
Guntur Dist. (A.P.)

35. Ms. Sai Lakshmi Parvathaneni
C/0 Esware Prasad
245, Stevens Ave,
Jersey City
New Jersey - 07305

36. Dr. M.P. Satija
Reader
Dept. of Library and Information Science
Guru Nanak Dev University
Amritsar - 143005

37. Mr. B Satyanarayana
Dy.Librarian
J.N.T.U.
Hyderabad - 500028

38. Prof. N.R. Satyanarayana
Dept. of Library and Information Science
University of Lucknow
Lucknow - 226 007

39. Dr. Jagtar Singh
Reader
Dept. of Library and Information Science
Punjab University
Patiala - 147 002

40. Dr. Manorama Srinath
Reader
Dept of Library and Information Science
University of Madras
Madras - 600005

41. Dr. Anand P. Srivastava
University Librarian (Retd.)
University of Delhi
Delhi - 110007

42. Mr. M.S. Subramanian
Reader
Dept. of Library and Information Science
University of Madras
Madras - 600005

43. Dr. S. Sudarshan Rao
Reader
Dept. of Library and Information Science
Osmania University
Hyderabad - 500007

44. Dr. K. Sarada
Professor (Retd.)
Dept. of Library and Information Science
Andhra University
Waltair - 530003

45. Mr. S Swaminathan
Library Trainee
IIM
Bangalore

46. Smt. B.S. Swaroop Rani
Lecturer
Dept. of Library and Information Science
Bishop Herber College
Tiruchirapalli - 17

47. Rabindranath Tagore
Nobel Laureate

48. Dr. Mohamed Taher
Dy. Librarian
ASRC
Hyderabad - 500007

49. Prof. V.G. Talwar
Professor, DLISc
Registrar
University of Mysore
Mysore - 570006

50. Mr. K. Veeranjaneyulu
Asst. Librarian
College of Fishery Science
A.P. Agricultural University
Muthukúr
Nellore Dt. (A.P.)

51. Dr. V. Venkatappaiah
Chairman,. CSC Public Libraries ILA
4-22-27
Ithanagar – 522 201
Tenali, A.P.

52. Mr. P. Venkataramana
Technical Officer
Directorate of Rice Research
Rajendranagar
Hyderabad – 500030

53. Mr. L. Venkateswara Rao
Lecturer, LIS
Sir CRR College
Eluru, W.G. Dt. (A.P.)

54. Dr. Rama Vishwanatham
Asst. Reference Librarian
University of Illinois at Chicago
Library of the Health Sciences
1750 W Poek Street
CHICAGO, ILLINOIS – 60612

55. Dr. S.D. Vyas
Librarian
Banasthali Vidyapith,
Banasthali – 304002
Rajasthan

Section I
Libraries And Information

1

LIBRARY AND ITS USE

Rabindranath Tagore

[Rabindranath Tagore, as the Chairman of Reception Committee of *All India Libraries Association* prepared this speech. Due to his illness this speech was read out by Mr. Hirendranath Dutt. This speech had appeared in, *The Indian Library Journal,* Vol. II, Nos. 2, 3 and 4, 1929. The above title is given by the editors.]

Greed is one of the chief of man's internal enemies. Once he starts to gather and store, he becomes distracted with the obsession of Number, and tends to overlook the purpose of his accumulating. Whether it be the gathering of money to fill his own strong-room, or the gathering of men to enlarge his particular sect, the spirit of accumulation sweeps him along on its current, and its blind speed blurs the destination which was his objective, - his mind forgets that the value of any truth is not to be measured by its content of things.

Most libraries are possessed with this passion for accumulation. Three-quarter of their books do not come into use-their overgrown proportions even thrust into a corner the specially selected few that are meant for large riches is called a great man. When a millionaire comes into a gathering, all vie with one another to do him honour, - an honour not dependent on what he has to give, but merely on what he has. Much in the same way, the bigness of library is estimated by the number of its volumes. The facilities offered for their use that should have been its glory, are not deemed necessary for its pride.

The words that are owned by our language have two different repositories, - one is the dictionary, the other is its literature. It is useful to collect all the known words in a comprehensive dictionary, though comparatively but few of them are actually current. On the other hand the range of words found in literature, - which are living and therefore of which not one can be spared, - is ever so much less. And yet it has to be admitted that the value of literature is more than that of the dictionary.

The same truth applies to the library. That part of its contents which is for the purpose of extensive accumulation has its usefulness, but the other part which is for constant and varied use, gives it its significance. The average librarian, however, rarely takes thought or trouble to bring the largest number of books to the utmost use, because it is always easier to overwhelm the public mind with the mere display of quantitative abundance.

In order to bring a library into the fullest use, it is necessary that its contents should be clearly and specifically brought to notice. Otherwise it is difficult for the ordinary man to find his way about them, and the library is left as a city of vast accommodation that lacks sufficient means of communication. Those who frequent libraries on some special quest of their own, may manage to make a track for themselves by dint of their urgent pursuit. But the library itself should recognise its share of responsibility in the matter. Because it has the books, it is incumbent on the library to get them read, for then only it is justified. It is not enough that it passively permits visitors: its invitation should be active. For, as the Sanskrit proverb tells us: *tannashtam yannadiyate*, that which is not given is wasted.

The usual thing is for a library to say: *Here is my catalogue, come and select for yourself.* But in the usual catalogue there is no introduction, no invitation, no spirit of welcome. That library alone can be called hospitable which shows an eagerness to invite readers to the feast at its disposal, - it is such hospitality that makes a library big, not its size. That the readers make the library, is not the whole truth; the library likewise makes the readers.

If this truth is kept in view, we at once realise what a great function is that of the librarian. His duty does not end with the acquisition, classification and care taking of the volumes in his charge; in other words, multiplication and division do not constitute the main aspect of his duty; he must have a proper understanding of his books as well. If a library is too big, it becomes practically impossible for the librarian adequately to acquire such true understanding. That is why I feel that the big library can but function as a store-house, and only the small one serve as a refectory which can furnish the wherewithal for daily sustenance and enjoyment.

My idea of a small library is one that keeps books on every

subject, but only select books, not one of which is there only as an offering of worship to Number, but each one which stands on its own merits; where the librarian is a true devotee, devoid of ulterior seeking, free from pride in the mere loading of shelves, capable of discriminate rejection. A library which makes just enough provision that can be placed before its guests for their delectation, with a librarian who has the qualities of a host, not a store-keeper.

Consider, for instance, the case of a library which takes in a number of periodicals, published at home and abroad. If some one on the staff made it his duty regularly to compile a list of the specially interesting articles and hang it up in a conspicuous place, would that not immensely increase the chances of their being read? As it is, three-fourths of these remain unopened, encumbering the space and burdening the shelves as they keep on accumulating. The same is the case with new books. Very few librarians attempt to acquaint themselves, much less their constituents, with the contents. Yet, is it not obvious that the wealth they have to offer should be made known as soon as new books come to hand?

Made known to whom? In each case to a special circle of readers. Every library should have as its indispensable adjuncts such special circles of readers. These alone can give it life. The worth of a librarian I would gauge by his power of attracting and looking after such circles, of acting as the intermediary for an intimacy of relationship between reader and library. That is to say, on his is cast the burden not only of the books, but of their readers as well, and in the maintaining of both is the test of his efficiency, of the proper discharge of his trust.

And even as to the books, the librarian's duty should not be confined to those that he can gather, but he must also keep himself acquainted with all those others that are published from time to time, subject by subject. For the purposes of our school at Santiniketan, for example, we have to keep ourselves in touch with all the publications intended for children, so as to be able to make our selection. Every library should assist in work of this kind. This they could do by keeping up-to-date list of books on the different subjects, that have gained a reputation. If it became known that a particular library was endeavouring to discharge this duty, I am sure that the publishers would be glad to cooperate by furnishing it with lists of their publications, together with a resume of their contents.

In conclusion, it is my submission to the All India Library Conference that it should consider the question of preparing and circulating such quarterly, half-yearly, or at the least annual lists from which the main features of the best new books in the English language, - scientific, literary and historical, - may be gathered. If it be the object of this Conference to stimulate the founding and growth of libraries all over the country, then such object can be best promoted by thus affording a guide to the books that should be procured; incidentally also thereby assisting the libraries in what should be their main work-not the mere collecting and keeping of books, but actively acquainting their constituents with and interesting them in their contents.

2

INFORMATION AGE AND PUBLIC LIBRARIES IN INDIA

K. Sarada

We are living in an information age/society. It means that information and skills in the application of information to solve problems is the key to material activities and progress. The production and techniques of communication of information have been witnessing revolutionary changes. Information is a fundamental resource for national development and the progress of individual. Information is vital for scientific and economic progress. Both as a body of facts or ideas as well as a message endowed with response potential, information is a key input in the process of achieving behaviour modification of the individual and social development. Free access to information is a social right, and individuals and communities are entitled to have easy and free access to information. This is, what we mean by information age/society. The aim of this paper is to examine the impact of information age/society on public libraries specially in the developing world.

Public libraries are considered to be centres of enlightenment of people. At this stage of our argument, it will be useful to note the meaning of the term Public Library. The term Public (*publica*) in its Latin form as well as literal usage in European languages means, that which pertains or belongs to the whole community. Logically, we infer public library and it's services belong to the whole community, or public library contributes to the uplift and advancement of the whole community. According to the UNESCO *Public Library Manifesto*. "Public library is a practical demonstration of democracy's faith in universal education as a continuing and life long process, in the appreciation of the achievement of humanity in knowledge and culture".[1]

The revised *Public Library Manifesto* of UNESCO states "Freedom, prosperity and development of society and of individuals are fundamental human values. They will only be attained through the ability of well-informed citizens to exercise their democratic rights and to play an active role in society. Constructive participation and development of democracy depend on satisfactory education as well as on free and unlimited access to knowledge, thought, culture and information.

The public library, the local gateway to knowledge, provides a basic condition for lifelong learning, independent decision-making and cultural development of the individual and social groups. The public library is the local centre of information, making all kinds of knowledge and information readily available to its users''.[2]

Public libraries ought to be agencies of universal education as the base or foundation of democracy. Public libraries must be freely accessible for all people, or equal conditions and opportunities for the use of its services by all people be provided. Thus public libraries are agents for progress of the whole community; of democracy; and of equal use by all people. It is necessary to note that the existing structure and role of public libraries in developing countries is not conducive to operationalise the above meaning of public libraries due to a number of factors.

1. Both in the traditional cultures and the colonial periods, library is seen as a book reading and lending unit, and no more. Obviously library is confined to the literate sections of the society. Moreover library services are tailored to the needs and requirements of the elites in the society. Masses of people are left unserved by library services.

2. Libraries are essentially urban based institutions. It means vast rural population is denied the benefits of the use of libraries. In fact rural people do not appreciate its use.

3. Library profession is based on certain assumptions. Librarianship has a core of theoretical knowledge chiefly classification, cataloguing, administration, etc. Librarianship is an autonomous profession, often unmindful or unaware of its social responsibilities. The chief duty of the librarian is taken to be organisation and lending of books and other reading materials. The

> librarian is a passive agent in his relations to the reader. Apparently all these facts do not facilitate the realisation of the meaning and goals of public libraries noted above. In fact the service of public libraries is severely restricted by these facts.

We have to note some pertinent factors prevalent in developing countries. Approximately 70% of the people are illiterate, and 70% of the people live in villages. We have in the developing societies highly deversified groups of people like women, scheduled castes, scheduled tribes, backward classes, agriculturists, traders, artisans, etc; and religious groups, who are at uneven levels of development, and often with peculiar needs and requirements. There is no provision for libraries either in private homes or in the framework of social institutions. Lastly, majority of people in developing countries are hard-pressed by poverty and unemployment. Survival is their basic problem. This is the context in which libraries function in developing countries.

We notice a basic incompatability between the social, economic and cultural conditions of the people, and the principles that underlie the public library system in developing countries. Naturally libraries do not attract people. People at large are not convinced that libraries do have a meaningful role in resolving their problems. Library profession as such is in a sad mood, unable to convince itself that it is a vital link in *transforming knowledge into social power*. This requires a radical re-examination of the structure of public libraries and their relationship and responsibility to the community.

Let us identify the goals of public libraries and then proceed to examine the methods of realising these goals in the economically backward countries.

Goals

1. The foremost goal of public libraries in promotion of universal education. It means public libraries have a larger social purpose to educate the illiterate masses.

This is essential for the success of democracy. Public libraries help the advancement of the individual and also the entire community.

2. The most pressing need of the developing countries is to

foster social change and economic growth. Libraries have to function as centres for dissemination of knowledge and information to promote social and economic change. No library can afford to neglect the basic reality of its social and economic environment. In order to become a live centre of national life, libraries must be in the forefront in diffusing appropriate knowledge to resolve the urgent social and economic problems of the society. Therefore the second goal of public libraries in poor countries shall be to link the library services to the social and economic problems.

3. Due to the disruption of traditional societies and poor organisation of alternative institutions, the cultural life of the people is almost paralysed. Traditional games, festivals, music concerts and other activities of recreation and enjoyment in community have declined. Alternative arrangements or opportunities for enjoying arts and developing the creative talents of people are not forth-coming for lack of resources and organisational abilities.

This is a pathetic gap in the social life of the developing countries. Public library may become an active agent of cultural life in the community. In fact provision for the pursuit of cultural activities under the auspicious of the library, not only meets the gap in society but also becomes an asset for the library itself in attracting people and educating them. Organisation of cultural activities to enrich the community life is the third goal of public library. These are the three important goals or objectives of the public library.

Methods

Now let us examine the methods or techniques that may be employed by the libraries to realise the above listed goals. We note that the methods must be appropriate to the conditions obtaining in the developing countries. Necessarily they have to be inexpensive, and largely based upon the use of local materials and human resources. They must also be conducive to encourage participation of large number of people. We have to look at the techniques to be used by the public libraries in the context of mass illiteracy, poverty and social disintegration.

The first question we have to consider is this: should the libraries confine themselves to the educated persons only neglecting the illiterate people. If universal and continuing education is the goal of public library, naturally public libraries must address themselves to educate the illiterate people. The primary problem is how to attract the illiterate people to the library and sustain their interest in the use of library service. The library personnel are required to play imaginative roles to stimulate interest in the use of library among the illiterates. For example, the library staff may render informal verbal advise, cultivate friendly relations, meet and mix with people, read newspapers for them or exploit the venue of cultural programmes to attract people to the library. They may run night schools and adult literacy circles. They may use charts, film exhibits and other audio-visual aids to teach the illiterate people. They may give out to the various groups like the scheduled castes, backward classes, old people, women, etc., the information relating to the legislation and administrative rules and procedures of the programmes of the government for their advancement. They can utilities the educated youth to attend most of these functions on voluntary basis. The youth and other educated persons have the satisfaction of serving the local community. In other words, library services must be oriented to enlighten and educate the illiterate people. We need not have a rigid meaning for the term education, namely learning of alphabet and reading ability. In the broader sense, education means capacity of the individual to think and act intelligently and independently.

Libraries may promote the education of illiterate people in this sense of the term. Later on reading and writing will be picked up slowly by people. Librarians must understand the needs of the several groups of people in the society. Census reports, and records of several governmental agencies may be helpful in understanding these problems. All this may sound very unorthodox in the light of the entrenched image of the library service. The library staff may feel that all these functions are outside their duty. These functions enhance their workload. This is partly true, but the simple question we are examining here is how to make library services relevant to the conditions of the poor countries. The popular notions of library services however respectable and well-established they may be, have to be modified because of the social and economic reality of developing countries, and also to make library profession socially relevant. We may also note that the image of library profession is essentially a western concept and transplanted into the Afro-Asian countries. In the Western world itself the traditional image of library profession is challenged and is in the process of modification. Ironically we are clinging to the old system, blissfully unmindful of its non-relevance to our conditions and aspirations.

Libraries must perform a critical function in helping the change of opinions, attitudes and ideas of people about self and society, and work. The resistance to social change have to be weakened through the selective dissemination of information and knowledge. The use of books and materials which will create scientific approach and understanding of problems, encourage individuality and responsible conduct, promote the ideals of equality, secularism and social justice, among the readers and users of the library have to be deliberately encouraged by the library staff. They must intelligently and indirectly draw the attention of readers to those materials which will spread the above cited ideals. I had opportunity to examine the nature of book collection in four branch libraries for women in two districts. Most of the book collection comprises of short story books, novels and fiction. Also *Purnas, Mahabharata, Ramayana* and other books are available in large numbers. It is needless to add that these books do not diffuse modern ideals and scientific outlook, and do not meet the requirements and problems of either rural or urban women. On the contrary most of these books help the diffusion of traditional ideals and attitudes. The point is that the library personnel through a careful book selection policy, display of books and informal suggestions, have to help the circulation of those materials which will induce change in the attitudes and opinions of women. It has been noted that the *Zilla Grandhalaya Samsthas* do not have a book selection policy to meet the requirements of the different groups of people in the society.

The primary problem of people in developing countries is securing employment and increasing their income. Unless we can demonstrate that the use of the library is helpful to resolve their economic problems, people do not come to the library. Library services must be linked to the issues and processes of economic growth. We may conceive a host of ways to bring about this relationship. Libraries may become centres of informal advise regarding agriculture, cottage industries and other rural industries. We may explain the policies of government, give out technical knowledge, arrange group discussions of various professions for exchange of ideas and experiences, etc. Libraries may participate in programmes of functional literacy. "Literacy is functional when, as part of an overall, integrated educational process it help people to see themselves in perspective, to acquire the qualifications needed, to act on the reality of their condition through work, and to play a conscious and creative part in public life. It is also functional in so far as it is integrated with regional and national development plans and is of assistance in their implementation."[3] It is conceded that the economic growth had many components in which improvement of personal skills and human motivation is valued. Libraries may contribute a lot towards promotion of personal motivation, and improvement of competence. Libraries may collect materials on the natural resources of the different regions and stimulate people to exploit these resources. Technical knowledge of various levels may be communicated through lectures. demonstrations and books. It is appropriate to recall that one of the foundations for public libraries in mid-19th Century England was the clusters of libraries attached to machinist institutes set-up and run by social workers. These libraries were the torch-bearers of industrial revolution. These libraries were the centres of technical culture and knowledge. Technical culture was the basis for industrial revolution, which changed the face of England. It is pathetic to note that the policy makers and library personnel of public libraries in underdeveloped countries do not appreciate the linkage between the library services and economic growth. Our public libraries must become centres of scientific information and knowledge relating to agriculture, agro-industries, cottage industries, etc. We have to reorient the library services to the economic growth. This is essential to break the overwhelming indifference of the common man to libraries.

Cultural Activities

Public library may emerge as the focal point of cultural activities. Libraries may do well to tap the cultural media to perform the arduous tasks of universal education and economic growth. The people in poor countries have very weak tradition of reading habit. Their poverty and lack of facilities for regular reading at home, do not encourage them to avail the library facilities. In fact, the oral cultural media-meetings, lecturers, dramas, music concerts, *Bhajans, Harikathas, Burrakathas*, recitation of poems-is the live force of popular education. This is a means to attract people to the libraries, in the first instance, and slowly encourage them to use the library services. It is a useful device to convey rational outlook and scientific knowledge to the people. We may draw on the local talent in organising cultural programmes. This means, we involve the whole community in cultural activities and thus develop the talents of the people. We may wisely combine the traditional and modern forms of cultural media to educate the people. The form of traditional cultural organs like *Burrakatha, Harikatha*, Puppet Show, etc., may be preserved, while the message may be modernised. The modern mass media agencies, newspapers, radio, film exhibitions, T.V. may be used to educate the people. The cultural programmes have to be arranged by local people. Their expenses are kept at a minimum level. Priority is given to mass participation or appreciation of cultural programmes, instead of the appreciation by elite groups. Lastly, cultural media is an instrument to change the outlook of people.

Model of Public Library

It is observed that any profession, " as a social phenomena must interact with its environment".[4] This is the basis for the framework of a model of public libraries which is presented here. Libraries are organic parts of the society. They are social agencies to educate the public. Librarianship is not merely a technical profession or service. In a fundamental sense, it has a broad and rich meaning. It is an instrument to educate the public and promote social change and stimulate economic growth. It is a sacred call to change the way of thinking and action of people in poor countries. This mission has to be fulfilled in the context of the social and economic conditions and attitudes prevalent in a given society. Rural libraries may be established on a top priority basis, and they may function as centres of universal education, advisory agencies on matters relating to agriculture, industry, government policies, etc., and centres of social and cultural renaissance. Rural librarianship requires new approaches and techniques. It has been rightly observed, "One of the greatest mistakes is to assume that the techniques and assumptions which are accepted in an urban environment will be equally successful in a rural situation."[5] The traditional mass media is employed to enlighten the public. Library services are deliberately oriented to study, analyse and resolve the urgent social and economic problems of the community. The outstanding feature of this conception of public library is its capacity to draw out and give expression to the latent talent of the community and use the local resources available in the society. We may call it the open systems model of public libraries. Its basic aspects are: (1) Libraries are integral parts of the society. (2) Librarianship is a multifaceted activity which analyses and helps the resolution of social and economic problems. (3) The technical skills of librarianship subserve the vital goals of social and economic change. (4) Local talents and resources are used in organising library services. (5) The traditional cultural media in combination with modern methods and techniques are used in extending the frontiers of library services. This model goes hand in hand with the social and economic conditions and aspirations of the developing countries.

Implications

The adoption of this model requires radical changes at the following levels. First, policy makers must appreciate the central role of public libraries in bringing about the revolution in ideas and attitudes of people, which is a pre-condition for the social and economic growth of the nation. Large financial and other resources may be allotted to the development of public libraries. This is necessary to expand public libraries into the corners of rural areas and improve the quality of library services; and to acquire adequate print and non-print materials to meet the individual and group needs of its clientele. The government allocation have to be supplemented by the use of local resources. Secondly, library profession may have to give up the established notions of library services, professional autonomy, etc. It has to cultivate sensitive awareness of social responsibility of librarianship. New techniques and orientation in library services have to be cultivated. Librarianship is not a sheltered and narrow occupation confined to the urban centres and educated people alone. It must subordinate its claims for professional autonomy to the concept of social responsibility. Thirdly, a new programme of library education to train the personnel of public library has to be organised in the library schools. The syllabi of B. Lib. Science and M. Lib. Science courses give lot of significance to classification, cataloguing, organisation theory, and other core knowledge subjects of library science. This may be necessary for certain types of libraries. But it is not necessary to give the same degree of importance to the core knowledge subjects in training personnel for public libraries. In fact, techniques of social analysis, principles of social psychology and social change, theories of economic growth and mass communication, and rudimentary technical knowledge of operating audio-visual aids and allied subjects, which will help the librarians in directing the library services to the social and economic goals of public libraries are far more important in the training programmes for the personnel of public libraries. It is essential to have a separate library educational programme to train the personnel of public libraries. The implications of this step for library education may be examined by the library profession.

References

1. "UNESCO Public Library Manifesto", *UNESCO Bulletin For Libraries*, Vol. XXVI, No. 3 (May-June, 1972), p. 129.
2. "UNESCO Public Library Manifesto, 1994", *ALSD Newsletter*, No.s 74-75, October, 1994- March, 1995, p. 15.
3. Ursula Albertus, "The Role of Libraries in Functional Literacy Programme: Library Services For New Literates", *UNESCO Bulletin For Libraries*, Vol. XXIV, No. 4 (July-August, 1970), p. 201.
4. Gradner Hanks and C. James Schmidt, "An Alternative Model of A Profession For Libraries", *College and Research Libraries*, Vol. 36, No. 3 (May, 1975), p. 181.
5. F.A. Sharr, "Functions and Organisation of a Rural Library System", UNESCO *Bulletin For Libraries*, Vol XXVI, No. 1 (January-February, 1972), p.7.

3

COMMUNITIES IN SEARCH OF LIBRARIES AND INFORMATION SERVICES IN INDIA

L.S. Ramaiah

Introduction

India, a country endowed with rich culture and civilization from the Vedic times, spreads over today an area of 32, 87, 263 sq. km. with 26 States and 6 Union Territories with a population of 846.30 millions as per the 1991 census, inhabiting 12 big cities, 3949 towns and 5, 75, 937 villages. It is a vast country and one of the biggest democracies in the world with 26 per cent of its population living in the urban areas and 74 per cent living in the rural India.

India is a mix of many races, languages and religions. It is in a process of transformation. It has one of the largest educational systems in the world with half a million educational institutions. three million teachers and about a hundred million students. Inspite of all this, there are many sections of people without education within their reach. Nearly half of its population are illiterates. Even after eight Five Year Plans after independence in 1947, sizeable population is below poverty line with uneven development. The diversity in its unity is remarkable. Its vast manpower should be converted from mere 'citi'zens to 'neti'zens at the break of 21st Century.

Democracy and Development

India in order to reach its prestine glory and to become a super power in the offing century, two things are prerequisite. They are: (1) Removal of illiteracy and (2) Access to information. These are basic components for the socio-economic and cultural development of any country or community. A reading nation is a leading nation. However rich in physical resources a country or a community could be, devoid of access to current global information, literacy and reading habits, it becomes obsolate and static in its development. Even the UNESCO Manifesto (rev. ed. 1994) says, "Freedom, prosperity and the development of individuals are fundamental human values. They will only be attained through the ability of well-informed human citizens to exercise their democratic rights and to play an active role in society. Constructive participation and the development of democracy depend on satisfactory education as well as free and unlimited access to knowledge, thought, culture and information."

"The public library, the local gateway to knowledge, provides a basic condition for the lifelong learning, independent decision-making and cultural development of the individual and social group." Therefore, the Manifesto stresses that information should be made available to one and all regardless of age, race, sex, religion, nationality, language or social status. The provision of access to information to one and all is the bounden duty of the state.

Public Library: Indian Scenario

The public library has taken roots in the Indian soil and during the National Movement. S.R. Ranganathan was the staunch champion for the establishment of the Public Libraries under the mandate of the State. So far only 10 States out of the 26 States and 6 Union Territories have passed the library legislation. Large states like, U.P., M.P., Bihar, Rajasthan, Gujarat, Assam etc., have not yet passed library legislation. About 483.65 millions of people are outside the circle of library legislation. This accounts for more than 60% of the total population. It is estimated that there are about 60 thousand public libraries in the country. This touches only the tip of the iceberg. Besides library legislation that there are different communities in India which have scant access to education, knowledge and information. They largely live on their traditional information.

Communities without Access to Public Library Information

Scheduled Tribes and Scheduled Castes people particularly and large sections of backward, handicapped, disadvantaged and minority communities people in India don't have enough access to library and information services. There is information famine to these people. These groups are listed below in order to discuss elaborately about each group.

1. Illiterates
2. Scheduled Castes
3. Scheduled Tribes
4. Handicapped People
5. Economically Weaker Sections
6. Disadvantaged People
   - (a) Woman
   - (b) Children
   - (c) Prisoners
   - (d) Patients
7. Minorities
   - (a) Linguistic minorities
   - (b) Religious minorities

Illiterates

According to one of the surveys it is estimated that there would be 200 million illiterates in India at the break of 21st Century. Illiteracy is one of the evils with which India has been suffering. The table given below shows the magnitude of illiteracy in our country.

Illiterate persons (7+) in 1991 Census (millions)

	Total	Male	Female
Total No.	320.4	124.8	195.4
Percent	(47.8)	(35.8)	(60.8)
Rural	271.8	106.7	161.1
Percent	(55.5)	(44.2)	(69.7)
Urban	48.6	18.1	30.5
Percent	(26.9)	(19.0)	(36.1)

Illiteracy in rural India, particularly among the women is rampant. Their main stock of information is traditional which was handed over to them by their equally uneducated elders generation after generation. Illiterates are steeped in superstitions. Facilities provided by government agencies are hardly availed by these groups. They should be provided with the audio-visual information.

Scheduled Castes

S.Cs constitute 16.46% of our population. Most of these people live on the pheripheries of villages in rural India. Except 2 or 3 per cent cream layer most of the S.Cs are illiterates. The S.Cs were considered untouchables before Independence,. Though untouchability is a crime under the constitution, it is silently practiced., *The National Policy on Education-1986* laid stress on the education of scheduled castes and suggested various measures for improving their position. Due to their backwardness and unfavourable social status, the S.Cs are not in a position to use the village libraries. There are no book deposit centres and mobile libraries in their inhabitations. The S.Cs largely depend on their manual work for their livelihood. Therefore the S.Cs children also drop out from their school education due to pressures of family. They need information on labour, agriculture, health, housing, education etc. The SCs were oppressed and suppressed for many centuries. They need social justice. For that the SCs should have access to education and information. The areas where the SCs live should liberally be provided with Book Deposit Centres, Book Clubs and Mobile Libraries.

Scheduled Tribes

Scheduled Tribes live largely on the hills and in the dales of India. They are cut away from the mainstream of life. They are the most backward people with traditional customs and superstitions. They live hand to mouth with scarce facilities. Most of these people, though they have languages of their own, don't have literature and scripts to their languages. Their communication system is still oral.

S.Ts constitute about 8.08 per cent of the total population. *The National Policy on Education-1986*, says:

"The following measures will be taken urgently to bring the Scheduled Tribes on par with others:

(*i*) Priority will be accorded to opening primary schools in tribal areas. The construction of school buildings will be undertaken in these areas on a priority basis under the normal funds for education, as well as under the N.R.E.P., R.L.E.G.P., Tribal Welfare Schemes, etc.

(*ii*) The socio-cultural milieu of the S.Ts has its distinctive characteristics including, in many cases, their own spoken languages. This underlines the need to develop the curricula and devise instructional materials in tribal languages at the initial stages, with arrangements for switching over to the regional languages."

The backwardness of the S.Ts is total when compared with other communities. Some of the states in which large number of tribal people living are: North Eastern States like, Arunachal Pradesh, Tripura, Nagaland, Assam and M.P. (1, 19, 87, 031), Orissa (59, 15, 067), Bihar (58, 10, 867), Maharashtra (57, 72, 038), Gujarat (48, 48, 158), Rajasthan (41, 81, 124), A.P. (31, 76, 001) and West Bengal (30, 70, 672).

Tribal communities are characterized by a high percentage of illiteracy. They need on priority, education and mobile libraries with audio-visual materials. They need more and more 'Bare-Foot-Librarians' to take information to their door step on matters of health, education, agriculture, environment, etc. Community libraries should be established in tribal areas under special plans to bring socio-cultural changes among them.

Handicapped People

Among population there are different categories of handicapped people. Some are physically handicapped, some are blind and some more are mentally retarded.

Physically Handicapped

Among the physically handicapped, there are people stricken with polio, loss of limbs in accidents and people with deformed organs by birth like hunch backs etc. They have difficulties in walking and sitting. They are hardly find any special facilities in our public and academic libraries. Hence they hardly visit the libraries and don't have access to information.

Blind People

There are people who are blind by birth and there are others who loose their sight due to accidents and diseases. They need braille books for use. There are not many agencies in our country who can produce braille books for our blind people. There are few libraries which have braille sections. Large number of blind people in our rural areas don't have any facilities to have access to libraries and information.

Mentally Retarded

There are different types of libraries to mentally retarded in advanced countries. These people need specially prepared text-books, toys etc. Except in one or two places these people don't have any libraries in our country. They are largely left to their fate and remain crippled throughout their life.

Economically Weaker Sections

Nearly 70 percent of our population are economically backward. They have to work most of their time to earn their livelihood. They are the Industrial workers, agriculture workers, farmers, lower and middle rungs of the government employees. Most of these sections have information famine. They don't find time to go to the libraries and information centres. All our villages and most of the areas of our towns and cities don't have libraries and information centres. Libraries and information centres are situated away at distant places to them and they are also away to them.

The economic weakness of these groups of people keep them away from libraries and information. They need information on consumer problems, family matters, money matters, health problems, employment, housing, transport etc. Community information centres (CIC) are the need of the day. CICs are not established even in the rural parts of the States where library legislation was enacted. In order to put an end to the Information Famine, the Central and State Governments should declare war on both financial and information poverty.

Disadvantages People

There are some sections of people who have social and other disadvantages in having access to libraries and information services. They are (a) women, (b) children, (c) prisoners and (d) patients.

These are special groups whose informational interests are not taken care of always.

Women

Women constitute nearly half of the population. Only 39.29 per cent of females are literate. Except in Kerala, West Bengal and Delhi, illiteracy among women is rampant. There should be proper facilities and encouragement for education among women. In rural areas girls are not sent to schools for social reasons. Because of fear of elders and social ostracism girls and women folk don't come to libraries in rural areas. There are hardly any book mobiles to take books to their door step. An ancient adage says that a women is educated in family, the entire family gets educated. More and more educational and informational facilities are to be provided to this suppressed group in order to liberate them from the household work. There should be separate sections in libraries for women.

Children

Today's children are tomorrow's citizens. Books for children and children's literature should be given importance. Parents, elders and teachers should understand the tastes, interests and hobbies of children and encourage them to develop reading habits. There should be library classes in schools and the use of books should be encouraged instead of roteing textbooks. There should be children's sections in our libraries. School libraries should be developed on proper lines. If we brush aside the information needs of children today, we will be brushing away their future and progress.

Prisoners

People go to prisons due to various reasons. There can be political prisoners, criminals, juvenile offenders etc. They remain in prison for different durations. No person is a criminal by birth. They are to be reformed and made good citizens. They need educational and informational facilities to learn various professional skills to make them self-reliant when they return into society. Many of our prisons are not provided with libraries.

Patients

In undeveloped countries people become target to different diseases because of pollution, malnutrition, accidents etc. Due to critical operations and prolonged illness they remain in hospitals for long periods. As medicines are necessary to their body health, books are needed for their mental health. Books of fiction, poetry and other light reading will make patients to recover from their diseases quicker and faster. They mitigate their boredom. Our hospitals, and clinics should be provided with libraries. There should be facilities in hospitals for patients to have access to information on subjects like health, nutrition, diseases, yoga etc.

Minorities

In our country there are religions and linguistic minorities. The culture and customs of the minority groups are always at stake at the hands of majority groups.

Religious Minorities

There are different religions in our country. Adherents of some religions are very few., They come under religious minorities. Groups such as Parsees, Jews, Buddhists, Jains, Muslims and Christians in some parts of the country. They require different types of books and information concerning their religion, superstitions, customs, culture etc. Many a time their interests are lost sight of in our libraries for want of funds and the demands of the majority communities. Such people find that they are alienated from the main stream of country's life. They find that the libraries of no use to them. To ignore the informational interests of the minority groups is not healthy for the country. They should have access to information that they need.

Linguistic Minorities

There are multiple languages in our country. The country is divided into States on the linguistic basis. Besides the tribal and small nomad groups in each state, there are other linguistic minorities. Telugues in Tamil Nadu, Malayalees and Gujaratis in Maharashtra are an example. They need books in their mother tongue. They also require books and information on their language, customs, habits etc., which are different from those of the majority community. Due to linguistic chauvanism the educational and informational requirements of the smaller linguistic groups are ignored. Such communities keep distance from public libraries. Due respect and importance should be given to the informational needs of such communities.

Conclusion

Social awakening is the key mission of the public library. McKee (1987) said that 'the real business of libraries is community development, improving the quality of individual lives and encouraging the development of their communities.' According to the Public Library Manifesto of UNESCO (rev. ed. 1994) that the public libraries should be established by the mandate of Government and they should be readily accessible and their doors open for free and equal use by all members of the community. Even after 50 years of Independence in India the public libraries have yet to cover all the villages in the country. Education and information is available only to the top 35% of the people. Large potential of the vast manpower in India is wasted due to lack of access to education and information. Access to information and use of it will make people to think and work. Otherwise they will be left like Rip Van Winkles on the road side. There is urgent need to put our people into the Information Age.

Suggestions

(a) The States which have not yet enacted Library Legislation should be made to enact urgently. State Governments should give priority to establish libraries and Community Information Centres in the rural and backward areas.

(b) Both Central and State Governments should identify tribal and backward areas and develop long term plans for their educational development and access to information.

(c) Book Mobiles and Book Deposit Centres should be provided in SC., S.T. dominated inhabitations.

(d) In village libraries separate sections for children and women should be established.

(e) Information and library facilities should be available to prisoners, patients and blind people.

(f) Public libraries should not loose sight of the interests of religious and linguistic minorities.

(g) There should be interface of Public Library and Industry. Industries should come forward to invest some of their profits to establish libraries in the colonies of their workers and other areas.

(h) There should be a network of public libraries for easy access to information wherever it is available in this vast country.

(i) Both Central and State Governments should invest atleast 5% of their budgets for enhancing information and library facilities in the country.

References

1. AMBEDKAR, Babasaheb. Dr. Babasaheb Ambedkar writings and speeches compiled by Vasant Moon. Vol. 5: Untouchables or the children of India's Ghatto and other essays on Untouchables and Untouchability, Social-Political-Religious. Bombay: Government of Maharashtra, Education Department, 1989.

2. BETEILLE, Andre, Castes-old and New. New Delhi: Asia Publishing House, 1969.

3. CHALAM, K.S., Education and weaker sections. New Delhi: Inter-India Publications, 1988.

4. CHANDRASEKHARA RAO, V. Library Services for tribal community. Hyderabad: Delta Publishing House, 1996.

5. CHAUHAN, B.R. *et. al.* Scheduled Castes and education. Meerut: Anu Publications, 1975.

6. CLUGH, Eric and QUARMBY, Jacqueline. A public library service for ethnic minorities in Great Britain. London: Library Association, 1978.

7. Committee for Review of National Policy on Education, 1986. (Chairman: Acharya Ramamurthi). Towards an enlightened and humane society: Report of the committee for review of national Policy on education, 1986. New Delhi; 1990.

8. DAS, D.P. The untouchable story. New Delhi: Allied Publishers Pvt. Ltd., 1985.

9. GOYAL, Bhagat Ram. Educating Harijans. Gurgaon (Haryana). The Academic Press, 1981.

10. GHURYE, G.S., Caste and race in India, 5ed. Bombay: Popular Prakashan, 1979 (1932).

11. GURUSWAMI NAIDU, N. Library services for the disadvantaged. New Delhi: Ess Ess Publication, 1989.

12. INDIA. Ministry of Human Resource Development. National Policy on

Education-1986. New Delhi: the author, 1986.

13. INDIA. Ministry of Information and Broadcasting. India 1995: A Reference Annual. New Delhi: Publications Division, 1996.

14. JHA, M.L., Untouchability and education. Meerut: Mamita Publications, 1974.

15. KHAN, M.A. Scheduled Castes and their status in India. New Delhi: Uppal Publishing House, 1980.

16. LOHIA, Rammanohar, The caste system. Hyderabad: Rammanohar Lohia Smata Vidyalaya Vyas. 1964.

17. McKEE, Bob. Public Libraries into 1990's. New-Caste-underlyne: Association of Assistant Librarians, 1987.

18. MARTIN, William (ed.). Library Services to the Disadvantaged. London: Clive Bingley, 1975.

19. MRIDULA, Educational statistics at a glance. New Delhi: Association of Indian Universities, 1987.

20. MUKHERJEE, Prabhati, Beyond the four Varnas: The untouchables in India. Shimla: Indian Institute of Advanced Study at Delhi: Motilal Banarsidas, 1988.

21. PATEL, Jashu. Ethnic librarianship and its international development in North America. Herald of Library Science 27: 3-4 (1988), pp. 202-209.

22. PUNALEKAR, S.D. School drop-out among Harijan Children causes and cure. New Delhi: Central Institute of Research and Training in Public Corporation, 1975.

23. SRADA, K. Rural library services of India. New Delhi: Ess Ess Publications, 1986.

24. SEETHARAMU, A.S. Education in slums. New Delhi: Ashish Publishing House, 1983.

25. SHUKLA, P.D. The New education policy in India. New Delhi: Sterling Publishers Pvt. Ltd., 1988.

26. SRINIVAS, M.N. (ed.), Caste: Its Twentieth Century Avatar. New Delhi: Viking, 1996.

27. SRINIVAS, M.N. The dominant caste and other essays. Delhi: Oxford University Press, 1987.

28. UNESCO. The public library manifesto. Rev. ed. Paris: UNESCO, 1994.

29. United Kingdom. Library Association. Report of the Working Party. Community Information: What Libraries can do - a consultative document. London, LA, 1980.

30. University Grants Commission, New Delhi: Facilities to Scheduled Castes and Scheduled Tribes in Universities and Colleges (During 1978-79), New Delhi, 1985.

31. VERMA, Y.M. Problems of Tribal India. New Delhi: Classical Publications, 1986.

32. VISWANADHAM, G. and NARASIMHA REDDY, K. Scheduled Castes: A study in educational achievement. Hyderabad: Scientific Services, 1985.

4

EVOLUTION OF INFORMATION SOCIETY: IMPLICATIONS ON LICS AND L&I PROFESSIONALS

S. SUDARSHAN RAO

Introduction

We are, at present, living in a knowledge-based society; a society that demands and makes use of information in almost all kinds of human pursuits. It is because of the role played by information and its importance and also because of the involvement/ association and employment of large sections/ proportions of people in information/ information related industries in this modern society, today's society is very aptly being called as 'Information Society'.

Information and Information Society

Information–Meaning and Need

Information is the causative factor for the development of any thing and every thing in the Universe. It is both of an 'input' and 'output' of research and development in all the disciplines i.e., in Science and Technology, Social Sciences and Humanities.

Information has been viewed differently by different people. For some it is knowledge and for others it is a commodity, power and for some it is a document.

In a broader perspective 'information and transferable knowledge are one and the same thing'. Further, any transfer of knowledge is considered equivalent to transfer of information and vice-versa. This definition reveals the close affinity that exists between information and knowledge.

Georges Anderla defines information as a resource, a resource as fundamental as energy or water, which affect all human activity and an indispensable, irreplaceable link between intellectual and material activities[1]. This concept leads to a conclusion that information must be at the service of the whole community.

Ching-Chih Chen (1982) defines "Information as all knowledge, facts, data and imaginative works of mind which are communicated formally and / or informally in any format"[2]. But information is not equivalent to knowledge. Information is the raw material, the precursor of knowledge. Knowledge emerges from the distilling, shaping and integrating of the raw material into concepts and rules.

A. similar but relatively a wider definition is offered by

Mc Garry. According to him "Information is not limited to facts in documents but it covers a wide spectrum of issues, including emotions, facts, opinions, guidance and persuasions".

The need/importance of information

In the present day society, there is a great and urgent need for access and availability of information. The information need for various purposes is enumerated below as:

- Information is an aid in decision making, policy making needed for the policy makers, decision makers, managers, etc.
- Information will have a reinforcing/transforming effect on human beings on receiving it. A great deal of change can be perceived in the human minds/attitudes on obtaining the information, as it increases the ability of Personal knowledge of the recipient.
- Information generates new information. That is the existing knowledge/Information helps in generating new information, new knowledge, new theories, etc. In fact, scientists and scholars avail or use information to produce another document/ (s) like research reports, theses/ dissertations, books, journal articles, seminar papers etc.
- The users of various professions and vocations like doctors, engineers, scientists, scholars etc., acquire and apply information in order to do their jobs more effectively and efficiently. i.e., application of information for practical purposes.
- Information supports research in order to obtain effective, and fruitful results.

- Information helps in better management of (manpower, materials, production, finance, marketing, etc.)
- State-of-art kind of information of a subject helps in identifying the gaps/shortcomings in the subject field and to identify the research problems to be explored or undertaken.
- Information helps in avoiding the duplication of research.
- Information stimulates the thought process of the users, particularly the scholars.
- Information helps the scientists, engineers, scholars, etc., to get well informed with the current advancements in their subjects, and to keep them up-to-date.

The over all benefits of information can be summed up as it helps in:

1. Improved capability of a country by availing the existing knowledge and know-how achieved within and outside the country.
2. Rationalization and systematization of a country's research and development efforts, with the help of the existing information/knowledge.
3. Problem solving, based on wider knowledge base.
4. In improved effectiveness and efficiency of technical/production oriented activities.
5. In better decision making in all sectors.

Concept of Information Society

Cawkell (1987), observed that there is a three stage shift from traditional 'agricultural society' to an advanced industrial one, and then to an 'information society', where information is the central factor and where primary economic and social activities are the production, storage and distribution of information[3]. Fritz Machlup called it "knowledge Industries"-an umbrella phrase covering the educational system, media libraries, research institutions and other information intensive activities, traditionally identified as parts of the services sector. *The Information Economy* - a report of U.S.

Department of Commerce has confirmed the Machlup's thesis. The report revealed that the dominant trend in American economy involved expansion of information-related activities in the services sector. Alvin Toffler and Wainsbitt have widely publicist the concept of post industrial society - the Information society.

Manfred Kochen had identified the characteristics of information society as the society in which:

1. Information is considered to be more important than the materials that provide information.
2. At least half of its members are engaged in knowledge occupations, and such occupations are not only based on knowledge but are also knowledge generating[4].

According to Peter F. Drucker (as quoted by SM Ganguli), the real and controlling resource and the absolutely decisive factor of production to day is neither capital, nor land nor labour, but it is the knowledge. And instead of capitalists and *proletarians,* the relevant classes to the post-capitalist society are knowledge workers and service workers.... The ruling group will be knowledge workers, knowledge executives, knowledge professionals and knowledge entrepreneurs, who have the insight to allocate knowledge to productive forces[5].

The information society and its very existence has been termed in a different phrase as 'Information age' by Dizard (1989). According to him in the present times there is a convergence of rapidly changing new technologies in support of communicatin networks for information exchange. Every one on the earth will be inter-linked in order to exchange the information required by him/her[6]. Scholars like Richard Barnet calls it as 'post-petroleum society', Daniel Bell describes it as 'post-industrial society and so on. By what ever name the scholars call it the one significant issue is that of a more complex information and communication environment.

Methods of Dissemination of Information

The information society shall use the information technology to a greater extent, besides the traditional technology, in order to facilitate quick and easy access to the information and its dissemination. There shall be several information sources, namely primary sources (journals) and secondary sources (encyclopedias, dictionaries, Databases, indexing and abstracting services, etc.) available in electronic form, such as Magnetic disks, CD-ROMs. Electronic transfer of information through electronic publishing: storage, processing and delivery of information, consisting of texts, graphics, images, through electronic methods including on-line transmission of information are made use of. Thus, methods of document transmission/ dissemination shall be either through direct links or through fax cords or through modems via telephone. Most of the information shall be available either in magnetic media or optical media. The Bulletin Board Services, E-Mail, Tele-fax, Tele-text, etc. are used in transfer of information between two communicating nodes. On-line searching of distantly held databases and making use of several network resources including Internet resources are also availed[7].

Implications on LICs/L&I Professionals

In an information society, there shall be a greater demand for the information from larger sections of the society to survive in the society. Therefore, the LICs should re-orient to provide easy and quick information services, coping up with the ever increasing, enormous proportions of documents/ information and the number of users demanding information services. The people of information society shall have greater consciousness for the information and its need in their day-to-day professional, vocational and other activities. It is the responsibility of the L&I professionals to make available democratically the needed information to all sections of the society, without any barriers and bias.

To survive with the inflow of the tide of information and also to provide quick and easy access, LICs need to automate the library operations and services and also to join with the networks in order to access to the other library resources. They have to design new products/ new services that shall directly suit the information needs of the society.

Conclusions

The LICs and L&I professionals have a greater role to play in information society. The library and information professionals have to effectively and efficiently guard, store, retrieve and disseminate information/ documents using the modern information technologies. Further, in order to use the IT they should get exposed to the IT applications and also gain experience in their proper handling. The L&I professionals are expected to render consultancy services to the users and also user education and other support services to obtain information by themselves. They should be able to navigate into the other net-works including Internet in order to access to enormous amount of information held by various networks

Provision of quality services and products are going to be the essential requirements by the L&I professionals. The value added services/ products can only be marketed. And marketing becomes an important service in LICs. The information industry becomes the highly sought after business in the society. As stated by Debones, et al, there shall be a tremendous growth of information with increased applications of IT[8]. The information services can be availed not only from by the information centres but also on the home-computers and home-TVs.

The L&I professionals equipped with the LIS techniques and IT applications would find place not only in LICs but also in business, industry, hospital, newspaper, academic, research and all other kinds of establishments where there is a need for information in carrying out the activities/ operations, to fulfill the objectives of the organisations concerned. Instead of relying on one's library sources, the LICs greatly rely on other resources held by various *networks*.

Information acquisition, storage, organisation, retrieval and transmission/ dissemination, including the publishing industry, all will change to a greater extent by using the IT, in order to support easy and quick accessibility and availability of information to all the information seekers without any geographical, language and other barriers.

References

1. Anderla, Georges (1973). *Information in 1985: A forecasting study of information needs and resources*. OECD, Paris.
2. Ching-Chih Chen and Hernon, Peter (1982). *Information Seeding: Assessing and anticipating user needs*. Neel-Schuman, New York.
3. Cawkell, A.E (ed.) (1989). *Evolution of Information Society*. ASLIB,

London.

4. Kochen, Manfred. (1987). "A New Concept of Information Society", in *Evolution of an information society*, ASLIB, London.
5. Ganguli, S.M. (1994). *Towards and Information Society: Presidential Address*. IASLIC, Bombay. (XVI IASLIC National Seminar, Dec. 1994).
6. Dizard, W.P. (1989). *Coming of Information Age*. 3rd ed. Orient Longman, New York.
7. Sudarshan Rao, S. and Prufulla Chandra, T.V. (1996). "Impact of IT on document Delivery Service in LICs: An overview", *in* A.A.N. Raju, *et al.* (eds.), *Information Technology and its Impact on Library and Information Science Education and Library Management*, Delta Publishing House, Hyderabad.
8. Debons, Anthony, *et al.* (1988). *Information Sciences: An integrated view*. G.K. Hall and Co., Boston.

Section II
Classification: Some Reflections

5

LIBRARY CLASSIFICATION: AN INTERNATIONAL PERSPECTIVE

A.A.N. Raju

Introduction

The history of modern Library Classification (LC) can be traced from the epoch making year of 1876 when Melvil Dewey published his now world famous Decimal Classification. During the past twelve decades major developments and trends have taken place in the growth and development of LC giving it an International perspective when compared to other traditional branches of Library Science such as Cataloging, Indexing, and Abstracting.

S.R. Ranganathan has very lucidly presented a century of classification and recognized three distinct periods in its growth and development during the past one hundred years *i.e.* 1876-1975. These are: 1. Pre-facet period (1876-1896); 2. Transition to Facet period (1897-1932); and 3. Facet period (1933-1975)[1].

It was during the Facet and Post-Facet periods *i.e.* from 1975 onwards that LC attained international perspective, wherein various aspects of LC became topics for discussion at several International Conferences organized by Inter-governmental and non-governmental agencies like UNESCO, FID/CR, ISKO, and also other regional and national agencies interested in the growth and development of LC as a discipline and tool for organizing knowledge/ Information in Libraries and Information Centers[2].

The thrust of this paper is to present briefly the exposition and discussion of various facets of LC at several international conferences, which have greatly contributed to the attainment of LC as a discipline of International importance and significance and its role in the emerging Information Society.

International Conferences

During the past four decades i.e. to be specific from 1957 and onwards five International Conferences on Classification Research organized by FID/CR and three International Conferences by International Society for Knowledge Organisation (ISKO) have been held besides numerous national and regional conferences. The following sections briefly deal with these Conferences.

First International S. udy Conferences on Classification for Information Retrieval (1957)

The first International Study Conference on Classification for Information Retrieval was held at Dorking, England during 13-17 May 1957. About thirty six delegates representing eight countries including India participated in this first Conference. Ranganathan in his opening address dwelt upon "Library Classification as a discipline"[3]. The major recommendations of this first conference touched upon: 1. Scope of Classification, 2. Schemes of Classification, 3. Need for research, 4. Use of Classification Schemes, 5. Differences between systems, 6. Construction and application of schemes, 7. Notation for such visually scanned systems as the card catalogue, 8. Machine systems, 9. Research Projects, 10. A general scheme for classification, 11. Development of Classification Schemes and 12. Furtherance of research.

Second International Study Conference on Classification Research (1964)

After seven years of the first conference, the second International Study Conference on Classification Research was held at Elsinore, Denmark during 14-18 September, 1964. Fifty seven delegates and six observers representing fifteen countries and two international bodies attended this Conference. S.R. Ranganathan delivered the Presidential address entitled "Library Classification Through a Century"[4]. The papers presented and discussed in this Conference were grouped into five areas: 1. General theory of classification, 2. Research in mechanized classification, 3. Selected and Special Schemes, 4. Evaluation Techniques and 5. Directions for future work.[5]

Third International Study Conference on Classification Research (1975)

After eleven years of the second conference, the third International Study Conference on Classification Research was held at

Bombay during 6-11 January 1975. Fifty four delegates and sixty seven observers representing seven countries attended this conference. The recommendations of this conference were centered around: 1. General aspects of designing ordering systems for global information networks. 2. Use of empirical methods and theoretical models for designing ordering systems for global information networks, 3. Systems evaluation, 4. Inter disciplinary contacts, 5. Education and 6. Needs and problems of developing countries[6]. In this Conference I. Dahlberg presented her reflection on the meeting.

Fourth International Study Conference on Classification Research (1982)

After seven years of the third Conference, the fourth International Study Conference on Classification Research was held at Augsburg, Federal Republic of Germany during 28th June-2nd July 1982. The them of the Conference was "Universal Classification, Subject Analysis and Ordering Systems"[7].

Fifth International Study Conference on Classification Research (1991)

After nine years of the fourth Conference, the fifth International Study Conference on Classification Research was held at Toronto, Canada, during June 24-28, 1991. The Conference was attended by fifty five participants from ten countries including representatives from six classification research organizations from North America and Europe. The theme of this Conference was "Classification Research for Knowledge Representation and Organisation". The forty papers presented in this Conference fell into three broad categories: 1. General principles and policies, 2. Structure and Logic Classification and 3. Empirical Investigation.

Eric de Grolier who had the distinction of participating all the five FID/CR Study Conferences presented a Summary and Conclusion. At the end of his presentation, de Grolier proposed recommendations for determining 'Fields in need of New Studies'. He stated that research is needed into: 1. The most efficient use of new technologies, 2. The construction of practical tools serving as bridges between different systems, 3. The means of avoiding ethnocentrism, 4. The integration of classification and terminology research, 5. The relations of classification with logicomathematical models and numerical taxonomy, and 6. The study of notational systems.[8]

Sixth International Study Conference on Classific ion Research (1997)

The sixth International Study Conference on Classification Research will be at University College, London from 16-19 June 1997 on the topic "Knowledge Organisation for Information Retrieval". This is being organized by FID/CR and University College, London in association with ASLIB, the Classification Research Group (CRG) and the International Society for Knowledge Organisation (ISKO).

The themes that the sixth International Conference will explore include: 1. The role of Classification in Information Management, 2. Classification research for retrieval of information published electronically, 3. Automatic methods of Classification, 4. The Researcher and the real world, 5. Tools for classification and Classification as a tool and 6. Data modeling.[9]

International Society for Knowledge Organisation (ISKO)

The founding of International Society for knowledge Organisation (ISKO) in 1989 was a landmark for the growth and development of classificatory thought at the international level. The main purpose is to function both on a national and international levels as a connecting link between any and all institutions concerned with conceptual questions pertaining to the organisation and processing of knowledge. It wishes to intensity and accelerate exchange of experience thereby help to fill a wide spread need for classification and expansion of existing knowledge in the domain of classification.

ISKO has set before itself the following tasks: 1. Promotion of research, development and application of all methods for the organisation of knowledge in general or of particular fields by integrating especially the conceptual approaches of classification research and artificial intelligence, 2. Awaken and support an understanding for the practical and heuristic usefulness of such an organisation of knowledge, 3. Promote on a national and international level the exchange of information and experience of scientists and practitioners, 4. Observe internationally the progress made in this work, 5. Concentrate on major points of this knowledge field in special working groups and 6. Hold regular meetings in order to support these activities.[10]

In consonance with the last task, ISKO has been organizing International Conferences biennially to promote research, development and application of methods in knowledge organisation.

First International ISKO Conference (1990)

The first International ISKO Conference was held at Darmstadt, Technical University (Germany) August 15-17, 1990. The topic chosen was "Tools for knowledge organisation and Human Interface". The Conference was co-sponsored by the German ISKO Chapter and FID/CR.

There was an impressive gathering of about 200 experts representing twenty three countries. The Conference was divided into twelve plenary sessions and 12 workshops. In all about 60 papers were presented and discussed covering areas: 1. General Issues pertaining to Knowledge Organisation, 2. Algorithmic text analysis, 3. Terminology, 4. Knowledge Organisation in Universal systems, 5. Thesaurus issues, 6. Online retrieval — role of classification, 7. Knowledge organisation in special systems, 8. Retrieval from Universal systems, 9. Retrieval technologies and 10. Indexing.[11]

The deliberations were extensive and fruitful. The first Conference drew scholars of outstanding merit as well as new breed of practitioners of hardware and software, library administrators, teachers and researchers and information consultants.

Second International ISKO Conference (1992)

The second International ISKO Conference was held in Madras (India) from August 26-28, 1992. It was sponsored by the Madras Library Association, the University of Madras and the Sarada Ranganathan Endowment for Library Science. The Conference was attended by seventy one delegates from twelve countries. The theme of the Conference was "Cognitive Paradigms in Knowledge Organisation". The papers presented at this conference were grouped into the following broad categories. 1. Knowledge and knowledge organisation: The needs and modes, 2. Knowledge seeking in Libraries, 3. Knowledge seeking in Information Retrieval, 4. Knowledge seeking in problem solving, decision making and learning situations, 5. Taxonomic approach to knowledge organisation, 6. Analytico-synthetic approaches knowledge organisation, 7. Cognitive paradigms and their application to knowledge organisation and 8. Cognitive paradigms in knowledge bases.[12]

Third International ISKO Conference (1994)

The third International ISKO Conference was held at the Royal School of Librarianship Copenhagen, Denmark, June 21-24, 1994. The theme of the Conference was "Knowledge Organisation and Quality Management". Fifty six papers were presented on the following eight major topical areas: 1. Quality in knowledge organisation, 2. Theory of knowledge organisation, 3. Future prospects for Classification Schemes and Thesauri, 4. Knowledge organisation in specific domains, 5. Concept representation in Systems Design, 6. Linguistics in Knowledge Organisation, 7. Communication and Knowledge Organisation, 8. New Technologies and Knowledge Organisation.[13]

Fourth International ISKO Conference (1996)

The fourth International ISKO Conference was held in James Madison Memorial Building, Library of Congress, Washington (USA) July 15-19, 1996. The main theme of the Conference was "Knowledge Organisation and Change". The sub-themes on which experts presented papers were: 1. Library of Congress Classification, 2. Management of Change in Knowledge Organisation, 3. Knowledge Organisation in Cross-Cultural and Cross-Linguistic Settings, 4. Role of Relationships in Knowledge Organisation, 5. Knowledge Organisation in the Online Environment, 6. Impact of Technologies on Bibliographic Elements, 7. Knowledge Organisation in the Economic Environment, 8. User Focus in Knowledge Organisation, 9. Thesauri and Metathesauri, 10. Knowledge Organisation and Images, 11. Inter play of Epistemology and Knowledge Organisation, 12. Interdisciplinary approaches to knowledge organisation, 13. Natural Language Processing and 14. Dewey Decimal Classification.[14]

Conclusion

The five FID/CR International Study Conferences on Classification Research and the proposed sixth Conference in 1997 to be organized by FID/CR and the four International ISKO Conferences held so far clearly demonstrated that Library Classification/Knowledge organisation will have greater relevance, importance and role to play, in the years to come in the context of emerging Information Technology. Library Classification/Knowledge Organisation shall remain as the main focus of attention and discussion at International foras thanks to the concerted efforts made by FID/CR and ISKO in this direction. Needless to state that no other branch of Library & Information Science has reached such new heights at the international level than Library Classification/Knowledge organisation. Thanks to the vision and contributions of Ranganathan, who laid strong foundations for the growth and development of Library Classification as a discipline of par excellence in the field of Library and Information Science and now transforming into knowledge organisation and become an important theme/aspect for discussion at International Conferences, Seminars and Workshops. The proceeding sections present a perspective picture of Library Classification/Knowledge Organisation at the International level.

References

1. Ranganathan, S.R. Library Classification through a century. *Library Science*, V2, N1, 1965, pp. 1-30.
2. Raju, A.A.N. Decimal, Universal Decimal and Colon classification; a study in comparison. Delhi, Ajanta Publications, 1984. pp. 257-270.
3. Ranganathan, S.R.: Library Classification as a discipline. *In* International Conference on Classification for Information Retrieval. Proceedings. London, ASLIB, 1957.
4. Ranganathan, S.R.: Library Classification through a century. Op.cit.
5. Atherton, P. *Ed*: The Second International Study Conference on Classification Research. Proceedings. Copenhagen, Munksgaard, 1965.
6. FID/CR News. *International Classification*, V2, No. 1, May 75, pp. 37-44.
7. FID Newsletter on Education and Training Programs for Specialized Information Personnel. V4, N1, Spring 1982.
8. FID CR News 30. The ICSSR Conference. *International Classification*. V18, N4, 1991, pp. 229-232.
9. Reports and Communications. 6th International Study Conference on Clas-

sification Research. *Knowledge Organisation*. V23, N2, 1996. p. 107.

10. ISKO. *International Classification*, V16, N3/4, 1989.

11. Satija, M.P. Tools for Knowledge Organisation and Human Interface. Report of the first ISKO Conference. *International Classification*. V17, N3/4, 1990. pp. 169-176.

12. Gopinath, M.A. Cognitive Paradigms in Knowledge Organisation. Technical Report on the 2nd international ISKO Conference. *International Classification*. V19, N4, 1992. pp. 217-222.

13. Knowledge organisation and Quality Management. 3rd International ISKO Conference, Copenhagon. *Knowledge Organisation*, V21, N1, 1994. pp. 38-40.

14. ISKO Fourth International Conference. Programme. *Knowledge Organisation*, V23, N1, 1996. pp. 31-33.

6

RANGANATHAN'S CANONS OF CHARACTERISTICS: SOME REFLECTIONS

M.P.Satija

'Jevons goes on to suggest that it would hardly be too much to define logic as the theory of classification'

Brain Buchanan[1]

S.R. Ranganathan veritably described his teacher W.C.B. Sayers (1881-1960) as the first grammarian of library classification, whereas Ranganathan himself is universally acknowledged as the foremost grammarian of this field. His logically trained mind turned the work of classification from an art into an objective science. One of his important contributions is to divide the whole work of classification into three planes, namely, the Idea Plane, Verbal Plane, and the Notational Plane. The work in the idea plane, though invisible to a classifier, is the most important one. it is the planning stage of the total work of classification. In a popular parlance it is the brain work of the whole process. here, a classificationist is concerned with dividing the entities into smaller and smaller groups until every member gets uniquely individualised till no further division is possible or required and then to arrange them systematically. The work of classification does not stop until each entity is properly ranked by arranging them in arrays and chains of categories and facets. The work of division is done into chains of categories and facets. The work of division is done with the help of "characteristics", and ranking is done in arrayes and chains with the help of principles and suspecticle. The whole process falls under the purview of the Idea plane and is carried out with the help of four sets of canons[2]:

1. (Four) Canons of Characteristics
2. (Three) Canons of Succession of Characteristics
3. (Four) Canons of Array
4. (Three) Canons of Chain

The canons of characteristics are concerned with the inherent qualities of the characteristics to be used as the basis of division. A characteristic is a hammer to break a mass of knowledge into smaller pieces. In other words it is the criterion or basis of division

Definition of Characteristics

Ranganathan defines a "characteristic"as "An attribute or any attribute-complex with reference to which the likeness or unlikeness of entities can be determined and atleast two of them are unlike"[3]. Further he uses the term "Division characteristics"[4]. However, Ranganathan has interjected a new term "parameter": "In the classification of a Universe of Isolate Ideas, each of the successive characteristics used in arriving at an isolate idea are, therfore, sometimes referred to as the 'parameter' of its classification"[5]. The terms "characteristic" and "Parameter" are not really differentiated. They mean the same thing. It rather violates the canon of synonyms" in termology[6].

An entity whether physical, or conceptual may have a number of attributes, both inherent and acquired. The more complex or sophsiticated an entity, the more characteristics it will have, Therefore, the selection of characteristics to become the basis of a classification is a very judicious process. The success of classification and its intended purpose will totally depend firstly upon their skilful selection, and secondly on the order or sequence in which the various characteristics are used. These are:

1	Canons of Characteristics
1.1	Canon of Differentiation
1.2	Canon of Relevance
1.3	Canon of Ascertainability
1.4	Canon of Permanence
2	Canon of Succession of Characteristi
2.1	Canon of Concomitance
2.2	Canon of Relevant Succession
2.3	Canon of Consistent succession.

The first canon. Viz, "Canon of Differentiation" implies theta characteristic common to the whole group should not be used as the basis of its further division. It will not be able to produce any division in the group of entities. For example, being a student of library science cannot be a characteristic to divide a library science class. Similarly, we cannot divide crows on the basis of their colour as they are all black. But shades of variation in the universal characteristic can be used on the basis of differentiation. For example, though possession of two-eyes cannot be the characteristics of dividing a group of normal human beings, but the shape and colour of eyes can be.

In the light of Ranganathan's definition of the term "characteristic", this canon seems superflous. Characteristic, itself means, which differentiates in the narrow sense of classification. An attribute used as a characteristic for one group may not necessarily be a characteristic for another group though it may be present in both.

Canon of Relevance

To further divide a given group, many characteristics may satisfy the canon of differentiation. For example, a group of persons may be divided on the basis of their age, height, gender, mother tongue, religion, nationality, race, eductional qualification, and many other numerous characteristics. But for the purpose of a desired classification all of them may not be relevant. For example, height, weight, gender, race and physical strength may be a relevant characteristic for selecting a class for physical training; but for teaching mathematics, these are irrelevant.

Simply speaking the selection of characteristics should be correlated to the purpose. But this cannot be done *a priori*. There is no mechanical formula to determine the relevance of a characteristic. Ranganathan admits that it is a real problem to select the relevant characteristics amongst a large number of differentiating characteristics[7]. It requires genius, flair and experience to "reject the less helpful characteristics"[8].

Relevance of a characteristic is concomitant to the purpose of classification. Therefore, the concept of "Relevant Characteristic" itself seems vague at its best. Application of a different characteristics means a different classification. The real problem remains not to find the relevant characteristics but to find the more relevant ones to design more helpful classification. More than finding the relevant characteristics, the real difficulty lies in foreseeing the helpfulness of classification that we wish to produce for the purpose. The problem is not of means but of ends.

Canons of Ascertainability and Permanence

Both these canons address themselves to the inherent qualities of the characteristics to be applied. The canon of Ascertainability asserts that the characteristic itself should be tangible and objectively ascertainable. It should be palpable to any of the five senses. The characteristic should not be illusory, mythical or controverted. For example, one's previous birth may be a differentiating or even a relevant characteristic to divide living beings, but certainly it is not ascertainable objectively. Hence, it should not be used as the characteristic of division.

Secondly, but less rigorously, a group of teachers should not be divided on the basis of being brilliant or dull, nor authors could be classed as major or minor. Not because these qualities do not exist objectively. It is rather mostly due to the fact that these characteristics are very much subjective depending upon the obeserver. A teacher who is dull for one group of students may be a source of inspiration for some other, and vice versa. Such a characteristic also violates the Canon of Reticence of Terminology in the verbal plane[9]. Hence such controversial and subjective characteristics lead only to confusion and controversy, and not to classification.

The canon of performance states that the characteristic though relevant and differentiating should itself not be in a flux. It should be intrinsically permanent and of stable nature. For example "fame" should not be used as a criterion for classifying literary authors. Fame is not anything permanent. History of any literature clearly shows that fame or obscurity are transitory things and always changing shape like a cloud. (Shakespeare and Milton were not reported authors in their life times. On the other hand, many men famous when alive are forgotten the moment they die).

Ranganathan satirically cites the example that Indian politicians, who more often than not change party affiliations to grab power, cannot be divided permanently on the basis of their political ideology they subscribe to. If such a fluctuating characteristic is used as the basis, the members of the various groups will become inter-migratory, and as a result, we will get only a chaotic classification -a classification in a flux.

However, "permanently fluctuating" nature can itself become a characteristic. For example, some persons are more marked by their indecisiveness or their mercurial nature. If it is their permanent feature, it itself is a good basis of classification. "Migratory birds" can become a group of birds on the basis of their changing habitat. It is again emphasised the difference between the changing *nature* of entities and the changing nature of the characteristics. It is not the changing characteristic but the "changing nature of characteristic" which can be used as the basis of division. Inconstancy of the mercury level is the very basis of measuring the temperature. Individual chameleons cannot be classified on the basis of their colour; but the chameleons as a group can be identified on the basis of their ever changing skin colour.

Canons of Succession of Characteristics

To arrive at the desired grouping or for individualisation of entities, we have to apply a number of characteristics in succession. The next set of canons is concerned with the sequence in which the various characteristics (qualifying the canon of characteristic) are to be applied. These are:

(1) Canon of Concomitance
(2) Canon of Relevant Succession
(3) Cannon of Consistent Succession.

The Canon of Concomitance states that the two characteristics should not be concomitant i.e. the two characteristics applied successively should not result in the same grouping each time. Such a situation may occur if the two characteristics are synonymous. For example, a teacher may at the first instance divide a class in 1997 on the basis of the students being less or more than 20 years of age. It will result in two groups. If the next characteristic is chosen as the year of birth being after or before 1977, it will not produce any further grouping, as both the characteristics mean the same thing. Tautology should be avoided. The successive characteristics should be independent of one another.

Though this is not an analogous situation, but stalemate in further division can occur if the two characteristics are not applied in the order of their decreasing extension or increasing specificity i.e. in the order of general to specific. For example, a group of scientists may be divided on the basis of their being biologists and non-biologists. But to apply the characteristic of being scientist to the biologists will result in no classification, as all biologists are scientists first. It will also violate the canon of differentiation. Though Ranganathan has not stated explicitly, but this principle is implied in his entire theory of classification. It is a principle of logic first, on which the classification at best is based. Many other classificationists such as H.E. Bliss (1870-1955) and Sayers have stated this explicitly. Ranganathan implies it.

Canon of Relevant Succession

To divide a group minutely or rank every member uniquely we have to apply a number or characteristics. These may be all differentiating, permanent, ascertainable and respect the canon of concomitance, yet it may be a formidable problem to decide the order in which the various characteristics are to be applied one after the other. One important caution is not to apply two or more characteristics simultaneously, otherwise it will result in cross classification[6].

As the name implies the Canon of Relevant Succession of Characteristics depends upon the purpose of classification. There is nothing right or wrong in the various succession of characteristics (subject to the observing the canons of concomitance and increasing specificity). At best, two different sets in succession may be termed as helpful or unhelpful, more helpful or less helpful to the majority of the users. "There are of course", to quote Arthur Maltby, "several useful arrangements in some fields, but the object is to offer the best of these"[10].

For example, division of the class literature (useful to the majority of the readers) as discovered in the DDC and the CC is successively by language, form, period and title of the work. This is relevant as the majority of readers, being monolingual, are interested in the literature of only one language. Further, within a given language the majority is interested in one form of the literature, viz.

either in drama, or novel, or poetry. Therefore, in such cases the relevant succession of characteristics is Language, Form, Author and Work. But the order of these characteristics is not an absolute one. A special classification having a different purpose may change this order of succession of these characteristics. For example, if a library is interested in the poetry history irrespective of the language, then the relevant succession of the above four characteristics will be

(Literature): (Form); Poetry): (Period): (Language)

If some other library specialises in the literature of Nineteenth Century, it may prefer the following order of characteristics:

(Literature): (Period): (Language): (Form)

But this succession of characteristics is subject to the principle of facet sequence, viz, wall-picture principle, the cow-calf principle, and the rest of them. For example, in the case of literature to separate the work facet from period facet by an intervening facet will be a sheer absurdity. To some extent, the problem of the relevant succession is the problem of the relevant characteristic. The various characteristics are to be applied in the decreasing order of their relevance or usefulness.

The Canon of Consistent Succession

This canon is to ascertain the uniformity and consistency of classification. It purports to be a bulwork against the changing tides of fashion, to remain firmly unmoved by the whims and caprices of the person who divides. In simple words, this canon means that the order of succession of characteristics once fixed should always remain the same. *In* reality, it is an unwarranted canon full of contradictions. At best, it is superflous.

Firstly, a situation may never arise when we may have to apply the same set of characteristics to a different set of objets for dividing the latter. Either the characteristics will be different or the objects to be classified will be different. If both are the same, it will mean the same classification. If Ranganathan means that for a given set of objects the sequence of characteristics should not be changed, he negates the value of experience gained with time. It will mean that the sequence of characteristics once chosen should remain the same disregarding whether that is helpful for the majority of readers or not.

With experience and interaction with readers, one may realize a better sequence of characteristics. This canon then is contrary to Ranganathan's own's doings: he himself has been changing the sequence of characteristics in the main class E Chemistry and Z Law of his Colon Classification.

Secondly, it is also contrary to the spirit of the canon or Relevant Succession of Characteristics, as it states that the succession of characteristics should be relevant to the purpose of classification.

Ranganathan clarifies that "This canon does not say that all the characteristics chosen as the basis of classification of the subjects going with a Basic Class should be necessarily applied to all such subjects. Many subjects will take all the characteristics; one subject may take some of the characteristics; another may take some others, and so on. The demand of this canon is only that whatever characteristics are applicable to a subject of the Basic Class should be applied in a sequence which has been determined for all the characteristics applicable to one subject or another going with the Basic Class concerned"[11]. In spite of so much clarification, the Canon of Relevant Succession may be violated, as this canon as enunciated in the *Prolegomena* reads: "The succession of characteristics in the associated scheme of characteristics should be consistently adhered to, *so long as there is no change in the purpose of the* classification"[12].(emphasis added). The clause in italics satisfying the Canon of Relevance renders this canon superflous in absolute terms. *I present this small flower for the memorial garland to be offered to Professor P. Gangadhar Rao, Who always evinced considerable interest in classification.*

References

1. Buchanan, Brian. *Theory of Library Classification.* London: Clive Bingley, 1979. 10p.
2. Ranganathan, S.R.: *Prolegomena to library classification*. 3rd ed. Bombay: Asia Publishing House, 1967. Sec EAl.
3. *ibid* Sec CC2
4. *ibid* Sec CC33
5. *ibid* Sec Qa1
6. *ibid* Sec GA4

7. *ibid* Sec ED4

8. *ibid* Sec ED5

9. *ibid* Sec Chap GE

10. Maltby, Arthur: *Sayers manual of classification for librarians*. 5th ed. London: Andre Deutsch, 1975. p. 32

11. Ranganathan, S.R.: *A descriptive account of the Colon Classification*. Bombay: Asia Publishing House, 1967 Sec. G 17

12. Ranganathan, S.R.: *Prolegomena. OP. Cit.* Sec EK1

Futher Readings

1. Bavakutty, M. *Canons of Library Classification.*Trivandrum: Kerala Library Association, 1981. pp. 7-13.

2. Buchanan, Brain: *Theory of Library Classification*. London: Clive Bingley, 1979. p.52-53.

3. ·Kaula, P.N. "Canons in analytico-synthetic classification" *International Classification* 7(3) 1980: 118-125.

4. Sachdeva, M.S. *Colon Classification*. 2nd ed. New Delhi: Sterling Publishers, 1980. pp. 88-93

5. Ranganathan, S.R. *Colon Classification*, 7th ed. Revised and edited by M.A. Gopinath. Bangalore: Sarada Ranganathan Endowment for Library Science, 1987.

6. Srivastava, A.P. *Theory of knowledge classification for librarians*, 2nd ed., revised with the assistance of M.P. Satija,, *et al*. New Delhi: The Learning Laboratory 1992. 115p.

7. Bronowski, J. *The commonsense of science*. Harmondsworth: Penguin, 1960, pp. 54-55.

8. Langridge, D.W. *Subject analysis: Principles and procedure*. London: Bowker-saur, 1989. 146p.

9. Langridge, D.W. *Classification: its kinds, elements systems, and applications*. London: Bowker-sour 1992,pp.84

Section III
Academic Libraries: State-of-the-Art

7

CURRENT ISSUES IN INDIAN ACADEMIC LIBRARIES

S.D. Vyas

Libraries in colleges and universities are going to stay. However, surprisingly the development of academic libraries is still not commensurate with the needs of academics. Dr. S.R. Ranganathan was first to give impetus to the libraries by introducing library science education and training in the country. He also realized networking of public library system in the country through legal frame which would encourage the people to read and write. Since his ideas are still relevant, they should be vigorously pursued.

Indian universities were affiliating institutions in the past. The teaching was done in the colleges. University library system came into existence only when post-graduate teaching and research commenced in the university departments. While Universities were being established at a rapid rate, there was a vertical decline in colleges. Most of the colleges were taken over by the newly born local universities.

Till 1947, the library collection of the university libraries of Calcutta, Madras, Bombay, Allahabad, Banaras, Aligarh, Lucknow and Punjab did not touch even one hundred thousand books. Today of course their collections have gone up to nearly one million books. If the collection is compared with American or British university libraries, it is far below average. An average American college library has reached to one million documents. The prestigious Harvard University library has about 10 million documents.

How many books should we have for a reader? The figure will differ from one university to another, no two university libraries have the same number. Yet, an average number of books available for a reader could be calculated. According to an estimate, British University libraries make available 114 books per student.[1] In the U.S. libraries this average may be even higher because of research and more production of books.

In India, there are over two hundred universities and eight thousand colleges. But quality and quantity wise the situation is not satisfactory. College libraries face common problems like building, staff, salary, technical processing etc. No standards are set and so, neither one can measure the effectiveness of the library nor, can one know what is required. The situation in university libraries is no different. Universities and colleges have the responsibility towards the present generation of students from where doctors, engineers, businessmen etc. are born. In the personality making and knowledge gaining, the role of academic libraries is quite considerable. *University Education Report* of 1949 lays a great emphasis on a first class library system. No new university can be thought of unless a library exists. The Commission report compares library with the heart of an academic institution. Although the heart is in the hospital queue for transplant operation as pointed by Enright.[2] This is because the library budget is not commensurate with the needs of the library. Budget conditions are so severe that except books, libraries cannot buy any furniture, equipment or machines. Besides books, library needs computers, xerox machines, racks, tables and chairs, filing cabinets and many other items. It seems that academic administrators have mere lip sympathy with the heart of an institution. With no proper furniture, equipment and staff a library can turn into a fossil over the years. There are two positions. One position is that when a librarian has a control over the library affairs. He has liberty to transfer funds from one head to another to buy furniture and equipment. In another situation where a librarian has got no liberty to buy required furniture, equipment and appoint staff needed for the job. Therefore, if the librarian has more autonomy over the library affairs, he can develop library system into a living institution.

Ideally speaking, our academic libraries should be able to cater to the needs of the scholars keeping in mind their information needs. If we look at the conditions of academic libraries as given by R.N. Sharma, the picture is altogether dismal and pathetic.[3] The following are the reasons:-

1. Indian currency is lower than Dollar and Pound. Hence we cannot get the material as much as we want.
2. There is a great time lag in receiving foreign journals. Atleast it takes three months to receive them.

3. Libraries are not user oriented. Hence the use of library is not much.
4. Two of the most important functions of the academic libraries are reference service and bibliographic instruction, which are missing. Such facilities are not still very popular and developed in college library system.
5. Role of libraries in teaching is completely missing. Even without the use of the library one can pass any examination.
6. There is no co-relation between what one learns and what one does practically. There is a great disparity and difference.
7. Library standards have not been designed for academic libraries because of which no service can be systematized and measured.
8. Although there is a great interest shown in library science research, yet there is hardly any improvement in library services.
9. Libraries are not given proper funding. The funds are diverted to other activities of the academic institutions.
10. Dr. S.R. Ranganathan launched internship programme, but now it is almost disbanded. This is very important aspect and should be taken up again by the library profession. It has been observed that whenever internship programmes in academic courses were launched the programmes were not taken seriously either by academic institutions or by students or even by the libraries where they work.

About college libraries, Sharma states the following problems:

1. In academic programmes the role of libraries has not been highlighted, particularly in teaching. Educators have a dismal record of using libraries as a teaching instrument. Teachers themselves do not use the library.

2. Teachers and students both fail to consult library system properly.
3. A very high percentage of book stock remain unused.
4. Libraries have still to become an integral part of the educational institution.
5. Librarians pay for the loss of books which acts as deterrent for providing quality service to users.
6. A library has a little role in academic preparation.
7. There is a lack of co-ordination between librarian, teachers and students.
8. Librarian's academic role is not realized.
9. Students depend upon the library for the question papers and syllabus, assignment and issue and return or else they hardly feel the necessity of the library.
10. Examination system does not compel the students to use the library.
11. Many college libraries do not have separate building.
12. Librarians have been termed as mere technicians because of which they feel neglected.
13. Professors and librarians are self-centred and they hardly care for the profession.
14. According to one estimate more than 50% posts of the university librarians in the country are lying vacant.
15. There is lack of interaction among the librarians.
16. Education being a state subject, UGC cannot force the state governments to implement its recommendations.

The above problems of academic libraries could be solved provided academic librarians interact with each other and discuss problems in national, state and local seminars.

Higher Education and Research

To subscribe to secondary sources has become a costly affair. A university library would generally subscribe to the following secondary sources in area of humanities and social sciences:-

1. *Bibliographic Index*
2. *Book Review Digest*
3. *Books in Print (India)*
4. *Books in Print (USA)*
5. *Books in Print (UK)*
6. *Essays and General Literature Index*
7. *Guide to Indian Periodical Literature*
8. *Humanities Index*
9. *Index India*
10. *Indian Science Abstracts*
11. *Public Affairs Information Service*
12. *Social Sciences Index*

There can be many more secondary sources like the above. Hence the list is only a selective one. If *Chemical Abstracts and Biological Abstracts* are also subscribed, one can imagine the budget needed for it. Except a few top ranking university libraries, no library can subscribe to so many secondary sources. Recently, the author had surveyed the "*Backlog Management of Cataloguing in University Libraries of Rajasthan*" and found to his dismay that out of twelve university libraries in Rajasthan not even a single university library is subscribing to *Essays and General Literature Index*. Only two university libraries are subscribing to *Book Review Digest* and *Cumulative Book Index. American Book Publishing Record* is subscribed by three university libraries. Surprisingly, two newly born university libraries are not subscribing to the above tools which are needed for cataloguing.

Another problem that our academic library system is facing is that whether we should go for comprehensive cataloguing or selective cataloguing. If cataloguing is not a serious job then what will happen to the library collection and how can we bibliographically control it. If a library is to be research oriented then it is imperative that the library be kept bibliographically alive. A library should provide subject access to the users because usually the demands are by subject only. Subject access is to be based upon some standard subject heading list. Ranganathan's Chain Indexing has to be updated if it is to be of any use. Thus, the aim of academic library is to make students independent so that they can think on their own, and not depend on teachers for spoon feeding.

An academic library is an educational institution with teaching and research operations. Main thing is that students should learn on their own. Brian J. Enright says "the purpose of higher education is not merely to pass examinations but to develop students' ability to think for themselves and work on their own. It has been suggested that one of the main aims of a university education is to teach how to learn, to give students a means of updating their knowledge and continuing their education by independent learning for the rest of their working lives."

It is for the scholars to know what has already been discovered. Only a library can provide help to scholars in selecting research topics. The main purpose of university education is to learn how to use the resources available in a well organised library. Scholars have to be judicious in deciding what to read and retain and what to leave, as no one can read all the books. Hence a well organised library is a must for the students and teachers. A new academic fashion that has emerged is to go for M.Phil. or Ph.D. programmes, but neither universities nor libraries are well equipped. In universities and colleges no extra staff is given for guiding M.Phil. and Ph.D. students. Moreover, M.Phil and Ph.D. scholars have no background in bibliographical searching and making bibliography on their research topics.

User Education Programme

The research scholars are generally not taken round of the library and given user education training. They do not know how to make notes and how to look into the catalogue for references. Librarians should introduce user education programme despite the nonchalant attitude of the faculty and students.

It is a fact that UGC could not force the state governments to maintain standards in the academic libraries. Its suggestions and recommendations have not been taken seriously. Therefore, universities in the states are still old fashioned, and lack modern outlook. Topics like 'modernisation of the libraries' have been discussed in the national seminars a few years ago yet practically we have not achieved much. UGC inspection team at regular interval should visit the libraries and assess the situation. Ironically, the libraries within a state or region hardly discuss such issues.

A Ray of Hope

Recently National Book Trust (NBT) reported that the reading habits of people have gone up despite onslaught by TV and video. This is a good sign of our national progress. The NBT's statement is based on the sale of books. Therefore to strengthen the reading habit of people, the networking of public library system should be launched in all the states.

Higher education and research can be sustained only through universal education in which the role of public library system is immense. After all, from where will the students and teachers get their knowledge and intelligence. There is a causal relationship between higher education and research on one hand and development of public library system on the other. Only when our nation read good books, we will have higher level of education and intelligence. It will then create an academic environment in the library which is vital for our higher education and research.

8

DEVELOPMENT OF ACADEMIC LIBRARY: A STATE-OF-THE-ART

Mohammed Taher

Introduction

At the outset, let us raise some pertinent issues regarding the impact of the developments in modern education on libraries. Is the academic library faithfully following the changes that are occurring in syllabi, curricula, informal education, educational technology, etc? Is there a real cooperation and integration between the academic community and the library community. Are these two communicating well, even if the question of status and equality among the two is a debatable point? Does the student find library more resourceful than the alternatives like, personal collections? Do researchers still depend on library for their information resources or are they more interested in their own channels of information? Does the library possess core collections, or, are filled with stray resources? Does the library provide enough of resources in non-print media which are tested as better means of learning and education? Is there any collaboration, in using the educational technology, between the libraries and the class room? In the media there are many programs on education, like the EMRC and AVRC's 'information at your door steps' program are the educational libraries obtaining a copy for use in their own campuses? Does the library care for the majority who are information poor, or, is more concerned with the information rich minority? Are the academicians made aware that library is as indispensible resource on the campus as health centre, restaurant, etc.? An integrated educational system calls for a holistic approach to writing this history and to trace the influences on library growth, including influences like political, social, cultural, technological, economical, and philosophical — is there any such holistic history of academic library development? What follows is the state-of-the-art with a passing reflection on above issues. A detailed survey, which can provide answers is the need of the day which needs a team research — team of all allied fields.

The development of educational institutions and so also of libraries in any country today depends on the type of government, role of government in providing support, professional advancement and involvement in promoting the libraries, etc. It is appropriate to state that libraries have today by and large become heart of the academic library system. A word about the present status of educational institutions and their libraries is necessary to know the state-of-the-art in different countries.

It dawned at last on the management of universities that higher education cannot remain isolated from the needs of the society these are supposed to serve. A new demand on the universities world over therefore was made to reassess the present and future requirements of the society and make the education and research activities more realistic and fruitful. Today a university is additionally expected to perform the extension activities, as stated earlier. Universities started concentrating more on social and economic progress of the nation and are gradually getting integrated into the national development process.

Further globalisation of the education as a movement got in and this has made it possible for institutions in different countries to have exchange programs, interactions, and for making the education available at the door step through the distance education, informal coaching facilities, media based educational counselling, etc. International cooperation in higher education is then a modern phenomenon and is leading to advancement in the boundaries of educational limits and educational avenues.

Two or three significant factors are influencing the present day higher education system. One main factor being the political situation in respective countries, from totally regimental education to liberal and then to some what democratic patterns, is the order of the day. For instance, the education in communist countries varies drastically from military dictatorial countries, and these also vary from democratic countries like India, U.S., etc.

The second factor is the commercialisation of educational institutions, like, based on the job needs, or employment potential, the courses are started or stopped everywhere in the world. Depending on the markets, then, education is supported or dropped from the academic world. A political-economic factor is the starting or stopping of programs depending on the needs, like the growth of area-study centers relating to other countries.

Let us have a look at the educational status in the world based on *Human Development Report*, 1994. First grade intake in all 75%; primary entrants to secondary schooling is 51% and 17 percent respectively; public expenditure on education (as percentage of GNP) is 3.9% and 3.0%, respectively; on higher education the public expenditure (as percentage of all levels) is 19 and 15 respectively; where pupil-teacher ratio in secondary level is 18 and 24, respectively. A glance at the communication channels for education and information is also pertinent here. Radios (per 100 people) is 113 and 18 in industrial and developing countries respectively, similarly Televisions (per 100 people) is 54 and 6; daily newspapers (copies per 100 people) is 30 and 4; books titles published (per 100,000 people) is 74 and 5 respectively.

India

Indian educational development gained much support from the Britishers. What made real deference was the emergence of, by nineteenth century end, Indian educationists, elite, and bureaucrats. There came a clarity in the concepts and today we have not much of confusion in education. For instance, Gandhi's statement in *Towards New Education*: 'to the proper and all-round development of mind can take place only when it proceeds *pari passu* with the education of the physical and spiritual faculties of the child', and the publications of reports of committees and commissions (see Report of the University Education Commission, namely the Radhakrishnan Report 1948; Report of the Education Commission, namely Kothari Commission report, 1964-66; *National Policy of Education, 1986* of Government of India, led to much desired theoretical basis and practical support for educational foundations, which are Indian in many ways.

Further, the 42nd amendment to the Indian Constitution, 1976, made education a concurrent subject, by which the central government was given power to bring any changes in education. The Central Government, under Ministry of Human Resource Development

(Department of Education), appoints committees and commissions to assess educational status and suggest measures for development. The government has created different autonomous organizations under the Department of Education: for higher education it is University Grants Commission (UGC), which coordinates and sets standards for higher education; Central Board of Secondary Education (CBSE) for affiliating schools and conducting examinations; National Institute of Educational Planning and Administration (NIEPA), a national level resource institution, specializing in problems of educational management; etc. Similarly there are organizations for promotion of books and languages like National Book Trust, The Central Hindi Directorate, Bureau for Promotion of Urdu, etc.

Very soon India developed, in the post-independence era most of the features of modern educational system, and even gave a lead to many developed countries in establishing similar institutions. India took the British example of offering the informal system, named as open university education, to the society. Medical and engineering graduates from India, to name most important in the brain drain, received recognition even in developed countries.

The growth of higher education has been very significant, and it has evolved into a movement. Today India has over 210 universities (there were 27 in 1950-51), of which 144 are general universities, 33 are agricultural universities, 16 technical institutions, 11 medical institutions, and 6 open universities, 7,520 colleges (with 695 in 1950-51), 4.61 million students with undergraduate enrollment (from 4 lakhs in 1951-50), and 2,50,000 teachers (while only 19,000 in 1950-51). IIT's have contributed largely to the development of professional education, these five IIT's admit 2,000 students annually. The government expenditure on education today is around 200,000m, which is less then 6% of the total government spending.

Despite these recent evolutionary steps, there are many problems. To name some significant ones is pertinent. Education is still the privilege of few at all levels. More so it is neither proportionate to the job needs, nor able to fully implement the compulsory elementary education programs. Professional educational institutions are growing in number, but their quality is still not to the mark.

In addition to these the changing governments have made different kinds of impact on the education system, like opening of new universities to satisfy some groups, introduction of reservations, changing of names of universities, etc.

The growing financial crisis in the state run universities, is forcing many to devise ways to solve this problem. One such way still in the experimental stage is to collaborate with industry. More universities are allowing privatisation of education and the present decade had seen the largest number of private institutions in both technical and general education.

Libraries, of these modern educational institutions are though attached to each educational institution to secure recognition, but in fact lack the modern concept of facility and service bases. In an engineering college for example, what is acquired is books and periodicals, and whatever service that is offered is limited to lending books, with one or two professionals and a meager budget. Unplanned growth is the order of the day. The size of the user community has no match with library and its planning.

The state managed and UGC supported higher educational pattern which was a legacy of the British India, is undergoing a sea change, and the emerging scenario of lack of funds from the government and UGC is forcing universities to start self-financing schemes, fund raising programs and turn to privatisation of education. The much desired university-industry interaction has not proven to be of much benefit to the higher education and hence new avenues for fund raising are sought after for the survival of the educational institutions in the country. Privatisation seems to take off and the professional institutions have set the example in this regard, there are hundreds of colleges offering medical, engineering and law degrees in the country.

School libraries have also grown, and today there are atleast 50% of schools having library facilities, as against 94% of libraries in higher education.

U.K.

Academic institutions are now fairly better, that is they are by and large modernized. The impact of modernization is also visible in libraries' storing and retrieving information in far more effective means. A large number of libraries completed the transition from traditional storehouses to service based libraries, with automation of the entire library. Various alternative strategies for efficient storage and retrieval of information are in an ongoing process, like recent progress made in storing information in microforms, and in computerized tapes.

To change from traditional book medium to non-printmedia a combination of factors have been responsible, which include, space shortage, literature explosion, growth of new subjects, new educational technology, new teaching methods, etc. Storage, processing and retrieval in new media was more economical. The Newcastle Media Resources Organizing Committee (NEMROC) has participants from different types of institutions in the higher education, to collaborate on policies such as the standardization of equipment and interchange of programs. The concern to introduce the new media also led to development of appropriate terminology, suitable to the academic sensibilities. Like the term audio-visual focused on learning resource, rather than focusing on the teaching aids. Traditionally non-print media were used to support teaching, for instance, a talk on art used slides. But today media (non-printed sources) are being extensively used for self learning, and learning at the pace of any individual.

There are 47 universities in U.K., including the privately-funded University of Buckingham and the Open University which is directly funded by the Department of Education and Science. The Open University, the first of its kind, provides degree courses through television, radio, correspondence and summer schools. No former qualifications are required for entry to its course. Under the provisions of the Further and Higher Education Act (1992), polytechnics were given the same status as universities, with permission to use the title 'university'.

We can have a glance at the statistics of the recent past to see the level of growth of the libraries. In 1949-50 England had 63, 157 students in all its universities, with 8, 469, 400 volumes, and an expenditure of pounds 645, 328. In 1973-74 it had 189, 733 students, with 27, 160, 000 volumes, and an expenditure of pounds 16, 131, 026. This shows that the increase of students and collection is three times, in the period of over 22 years, but the real deference is in financial expenditure. For the year 1991/92 public expenditure on education was estimated at pounds 19, 920m and that on science at pounds 860m.

Like all countries, U.K. faced financial crunch and this affected all educational developments and libraries. Reductions came in when the demand for student places was on the increase and when newer universities, research and training started entering interdisciplinary areas, with a resultant increase in need for information and documentation.

This turn led to a heavy demand on British Library's Lending Division. The Lending Division also faced inflation and expenditure controls led to the increase in the charges for interlibrary lending.

Among the leading bodies are

UGC, Council for National Academic Awards, Standing Conference of National University Libraries (SCONUL: modeled on the U.S.'s Association of Research Libraries), Special Interest Group's of the Library Association like Colleges of Further and Higher Education Group, University, College and Research Section, etc.

U.S.A.

The American institutions of higher education are sensitive to the social changes and movements, for instance, effect of two great world wars of this century, effect of the great famine of 1930s, efforts to control diseases, research on the nuclear and non-nuclear controversial issues, environmental protection and safety, and similar issues. These definitely showed up in the design of curriculum, and in the programs and projects undertaken. These apart, *The Chronicle of Higher Education*, 1994, lists nine issues affecting the higher education in U.S.A.: Tax-exempt bonds for college savings, prepaid tuition plans, certification of competence in English language for teaching assistance, new policies on enrollment or tuition rates of out-of-state students attending public institutions, vandalizing of faculty members at public colleges, non-education majors for high-school teachers, assessment of students, and mid-year budget cuts.

On the whole academic institutions in U.S. are modernized, and the libraries are advancing into digital era, from paper full, to paper complete to paper less-used libraries. A variety of schemes for resource sharing are in vogue. With the advent of internet and other world wide access facilities, the academic libraries are preparing to meet the challenges of the 21st century. With the growth of multiple options for storage and retrieval libraries are trying different media and the process is still on. Full text, scanners, navigational opportunities in Internet and digital mechanisms are baffling and raising the issue of who will survive: print, computers, or librarians.

A number of educational resource centers and clearing houses emerged to provide bibliographical control and access to the phenomenal explosion of literature. Significant among these are Educational Resources Information Center (ERIC), National Council for Education Statistics (NCES), Association of College and Research Libraries (ACRL), etc.

According to the latest figures, the country has 3, 500 two-year and four-year universities and colleges, with a total enrollment of 13.7m students, 762,000 teaching staff. Federal government expenditure on educational programs administered by the US Department of Education totaled around $27, 6000m, annually, spending on education by all levels of government $280, 713m, that is, 13.8% of total public expenditure.

Australia

Education is the responsibility of the government, it is free from age 6 to 15. The governmental expenditure on education is around Australian $15, 000m (around 14% of total government spending).

There are 37 universities in Australia as of 1993, and each of these supports a library that caters to its users. The number of institutions for higher education increased due to the introduction, in 1988, of a unified national system, by the federal government, which in turn, replaced the existing two level system of universities and colleges. According to the figures in *Europa Year Book*. there are around 7,500 government schools, 2,517 non-governmental schools, with 146,477 and 52,737 teachers, and 2,193,347 and 848,310 students, respectively.

There are over 10,000 school libraries, a majority of these are managed by the government school system, through the School Library Service.

Japan

The structure of higher education has both private and national institutions. The first nine years of the elementary through high school education (till the age of 15) are mandatory. There are locally managed Grade schools, national schools and private schools. The university is called Daigaku, junior colleges are called Tanki-Diagaku, and technical institutions are called Tokushu-Kyoiku-Gakko). In 1990 there were 499 universities (which included post-graduate courses and four-year colleges), 584 junior colleges (offering 2-3 year courses), and 62 technical institutions (offering five year programs). The total student population being around 2,529,000 with equal number of male and female ratio, whereas 90% were female in junior colleges. Of all the institutions of higher education 95 national universities, 40 local colleges, 365 private universities/ colleges had main libraries, with respective branch libraries 211, 20 and 275.

In 1989 there were 39, 369 Grade schools, 168 national schools, and 2, 089 private schools. With the legislation of School Library Law, 1953, libraries were mandated as essential components for supporting the educational programs and development of personality.

Faculty status

Regarding the question of faculty status, that is often sought by the librarians, we must now decide something for ever. A lot of debate has been there on the subject matter, as to a librarian is equal to a faculty or not. The wise thing would be do forget about this matter totally, accepting that we have our own identity and we donot need a parallel from anywhere. This is an advise from a serious professional: "Librarians must cease their baseless arguments for 'faculty status', however defined. It is true that they are often inadequately compensated and true that their work requires privileges from which they are sometimes unfairly excluded. While they are not faculty members, neither they are factory workers who should live their lives by a time clock. Harvard librarians explicitly rejected faculty status and instead designed a set of proposals reflecting their unique contributions and needs." We as professionals, and as Jesse Shera often states, must simply try to maximise the use of graphic records, and that is all our job and we are simply unique in this!

Conclusion

The above review is incomplete, as the space is limited. A catalog of growth patterns is a mere indicator of the trends, and this is what is attempted here. A thorough analysis in a holistic perspective as stated earlier is overdue. NCERT, ICSSR, UGC, and AIU are probably best suited institutions who should take up full-fledged research project. The project would aim at rewriting the intellectual history of libraries; role, if any, of the book in the educational development; place of library in the integrated educational resource centers; and fix the responsibility of libraries in providing maximum resources to the information poor in a democratic society. The above named institutions can make it obligatory, if needed by suggesting a change in the constitution, for all libraries and information handling agencies to find means to integrate and act in a network, instead of functioning as independent and isolated systems.

References

1. Mary Biggs, "Sources of tension and conflict between librarians and faculty," *Journal of Higher Education*, 52:2, Mar/Apr 1981, 182-201.
2. John Cowley. Libraries in Higher Education: The user approach to service. London, Clive Bingley, 1975.
3. Bill Crowley, "Redifining the status of the librarian in higher education," *College and Research Libraries*, 57:2, March 1996, 113-121.
4. A.T. Hamlin, The university library in the U.S.: Its origins and development. Philadelphia, University Pennsylvania, 1981.
5. N.B. Inamdar and L.S. Ramaiah, eds. National policy for the effective use of educational technology. London, Routledge, 1995.
6. Mary Jo Lynch, "How wired are we? New data on library technology," *College & Research Library News*, Feb. 1996, 97-100.
7. K. Umapathy Setty. Librarianship: Change or status quo? New Delhi, Vikas, 1977.
8. Mohammed Taher and Donald G. Davis. Librarianship and library science in India: An outline of historical perspectives. New Delhi, Concept, 1994.
9. Nancy A. Van House, et al. Measuring academic library performance: A practical approach. Chicago, ALA, 1990.
10. Edwin E. Williams, Harvard's study Committee on Professional Library Personnel," *Harvard Library Bulletin*, 21, 1973, 277-319.
11. L.B. Wilson and M.F. Tauber. The university library. New York, Columbia University Press, 1956.
12. World Education Report, 1995. Paris, Unesco.

Section IV
Libraries And Distance Education

9

THE ROLE OF LIBRARIES IN NON-FORMAL EDUCATION

N.R.V. Prabhu

This article covers the role libraries play in the support of non-formal learners whether or not the learner attends a formal education programme and whether or not the library is part of an educational institution. By non-formal education is meant the learning activities non-formal students follow, after completing their full-time education, for recreation, personal development, or improvement in job skills. These learning activities occur in formal and informal education programmes but are distinguished by their emphasis on self-direction and independent learning strategies. These strategies are present, too, in conventional education with project work, reading, and research.

History

Libraries have long had connections with non-formal learners. As far back as the Middle Ages the monks pursued their studies with the help of monastic libraries which maintained proficient systems for book production and location. The Reformation and the subsequent establishment of Protestant states and cities relied partly on libraries to implement educational programmes. The town libraries in the United States (Boston and New Haven) and parish libraries, notably in Scotland under James Kirwood's ideas in the eighteenth century, were resources of variable quality for non-formal independent learners.

In more modern times, industrial societies have faced the problem of an undereducated workforce. More schooling was an obvious solution. For adults this was impracticable and in some cases libraries had to be relied upon to fill the gap. Mechanics' institutes in the United Kingdom were forerunners of public libraries providing, alongside class programmes. libraries for the self-education of the artisan. The rate - (local tax) - supported public library was established in the United Kingdom in 1850 as an educational agency in the vacuum created by parliamentary dispute over the provision of state schooling. The government's Select Committee of Inquiry was told, at that time, that reading would "add a softening and expanding influence to the great practical education and Englishman received from incessant intercourse between man and man in trade".

Public libraries were promoted as an educational force in both the United Kingdom and the United States, not by popular demand, but by the efforts of a few enlightened and philanthropic individuals who believed in the virtues "self-help" and in the value of access to carefully chosen bookstocks. In practice, their impact upon non-formal education was limited by the conservatism of their stocks and by the librarian's preoccupation with the mechanics of collection and conservation (Lee 1966, Johnson 1938).

Non-formal education through libraries was not always in the interests of the government of the time. In Russia, the non-formal education movement of the *Kul'turnitki* after the Crimean War relied upon educational centres, societies, and public libraries and was linked to the post revolutionary educational programmes of the Communist governments working through the same agencies (Raymond 1981). Non-formal education in the Eastern Block is seen as a comparative effort, which includes all libraries, working in the direct of the state's own philosophy.

Western Europe and the United States did not take such a directive approach. Non-formal education in these countries was served by libraries working with, for example, the university extra-mural movement in the United Kingdom. University Lecturers travelled to give courses of a high standard to people who had little chance of going to a university. Some universities built up large extramural libraries of their own (London, Birmingham) with specialist staff to supply students of these courses with reading matter. These libraries now provide a wider range of teaching materials for university extramural programmes. The Central Circulating Library for Students was founded in 1916 form the Worker's Educational Association's Central Library for Tutorial Classes with help from the Carnegie United Kingdom Trust to provide books for students either directly or through public libraries. It became the National

Central Library and is now part of the British Library Document Supply Centre.

After the First World War, both the United Kingdom and the United States included non-formal education in their programmes or reconstruction. The Ministry of Reconstruction's non-formal Education Committee report in the United Kingdom provided the impetus for the 1919 Public Library Act, which put public libraries under local education authorities and presented them as places for "self-development in an atmosphere of freedom" constrasted with schooling as "training in an atmosphere of restraint of discipline". In 1924 the American Library Association's Commission on Libraries and non-formal education reinforced the role of the reader's advisor in public libraries whose job it was to plan personalized reading programmes. This meant close involvement between the librarian and the library user. Historians have remarked upon the disappearance of this role after the 1930s when help for non-formal learners became much more an assumed role of the general library service. This continued until the 1960s and 1970s when a renewed concern for people, underprivileged by lack of education and information, caused librarians to develop community information services and services for non-formal independent learners.

Role of the Library

A distinction might be made between the library's support of other providers of non-formal education (for example book box supplies to evening classes) and "library learning" itself where the librarians are not usually trained as teachers and therefore more easily see themselves as supporting other educational providers. There have been more in several countries to ensure that public libraries are placed under government departments responsible for education. Though many library laws recognize the educational role of libraries, education laws commonly do not. The Norwegian Libraries Act 1971 stressed the importance of public libraries in non-formal education but the 1976 non-formal education act did not.

A study of United Kingdom public libraries (Alfred and Hay 1979) attempted to discover the extent to which they offered special services to non-formal learners. Their findings were as follows:

Libraries and Non-Formal Education

(*a*) ***The general library service.*** Access to general library stocks with special borrowing privileges in a few cases. Problems arose when materials were not available at the time required or for the length of time required. Sometimes materials would be delivered to non-formal education classes. Material includes books, audio and video tapes, film and specially prepared teaching packs, for example on local history. Non-formal classes were held in the library as a convenient and relaxed setting. In Sweden grant-aided "study circles" often met in public libraries and, as in the United Kingdom and other countries, the libraries showed films, and held concerts and exhibitions, all of which might be considered as part of non-formal learning (Griffiths 1971).

(*b*) ***The provision of educational information and advice (educational brokering).*** In the late 1970s this was a rapidly growing activity. The expansion of educational opportunities and retraining needs increased the demands for such services. In the United Kingdom these were established in colleges and as independent services (Harfield's Educational Guidance Service for Adults (EGSA), Northern Ireland's EGSA, Wagon's Contact for Learning and Educational Opportunities (CLEO)]. Libraries provided educational information themselves, but the staff were not trained to advise and counsel. Some public libraries assisted these services by sharing premises (Birmingham), by acting as a referral link (Newcastle-upon-Tyne had a direct telephone line), and by compiling indexes and information sheets (Bradford Public Library created as computerized information service). The need for an information service to support the planned Open Tech in the United Kingdom may start a new chapter in such services.

Many educational providers placed their publicity in libraries and some libraries collaborated in educational "fair" or information weeks (Leicestershire Country Council, Guildford in Surrey).

Learning exchanges (an idea of Illich and others in the United States) are an extension of educational information services where prospective learners and "tutors" (who do not need to be trained teachers) are matched to facilitate less formal, but not independent, learning. In New Zealand such an exchange became part of the services of Wellington City Library. In the United Kingdom an experimental service was started in Orton, at the Cambridgeshire County Library.

(*c*) ***Instruction in Library use.*** A most useful service provided by librarians was that of the instruction of non-formal learners in the use of the library. Competent library use is a major part of study skill and such instruction is commonplace in colleges and universities. East Sussex County Library and Norfolk County Library staff taught evening classes in public library use in connection with local history and genealogy and were surprised by their popularity.

Guides to library services in some regions were published by the Open University and other educational providers. Many public libraries had non-formal education liaison staff to maintain contacts with tutors. A well developed service was provided by Derbyshire County Library with a current awareness bulletin on the subject of non-formal education and with participation in tutor training programmes. A similar information service based on nine educational libraries but on a larger scale and computerized is operated in Austria called Das Documentation system *Erwachsenenbildung* (DOKEB) or Documentation System for Adults.

Specialist library services for professionals and others working in non-formal education exist in most countries. For example Syracuse University in the United States operates a Clearing House of Resources for Educators of Adults. In the United Kingdom the National Institute of non-formal education in Leicester maintains a library and a register of research.

Library Programmes

Developing Countries

The important Malmo Seminar (Houle 1951) had one of its three groups devoted to this subject. In countries where resources are scarce and educational systems limited, libraries provide a valuable extension of educational provision. In the 1970s, the Indian government's National Education Programme was urged to recognize the need of adults for access to books and to realize the help that public libraries can provide through discussion groups and reading aloud groups, with visual aids and drama activities. In Tanzania it is the job of the Tanzania Library Service to help people to participate in national development. Where the government has failed to emphasize the role of the library as in Zambia, the library profession has drawn attention to this.

Non-Formal Basic Education

In 1955 in Brooklyn in the United States, the public library started a reading improvement programme in collaboration with Brooklyn College, which continues to this day. Librarians are trained to teach adults at all levels. The American Library Association non-formal Services Division published its Service to non-formal Illiterates in 1964 and libraries such as *Kalamazoo*, the Free Library of Philadelphia, Enoch Pratt Free Library, and many others were soon providing non-formal reading centres and discussion groups, as well as materials. Libraries had to cooperate with other agencies and this was not always easy. A common problem was a lack of appropriate reading materials for adults.

A major project in the United States was that promoted by the Appalachian Non-Formal Education Center of Morehead (Kentucky) State University in 1972, which involved 77 libraries in 10 states by 1976. The library profession in the United States more readily accepted responsibility for non-formal illiterates than that in the United Kingdom (Lyman 1977), but the concern for illiteracy did spread to the United Kingdom where libraries, public and academic, cooperated in the Non-Formal Literacy Campaign.

Distance Learning: Broadcasting

The United Kingdom literacy programme of the 1970s was considerably reinforced by the participation of the British Broadcasting Corporation (BBC), and public libraries played a part, though a variable one. The activity brought about a much closer relationship between broadcasting and libraries. Programmes such as Yorkshire Television's Disraeli, the BBC's Road show, and Speak for Yourself drew the public library into the systematic provision ofback-up materials forthe audiences ofthese programmes.

Broadcast educational programmes have been initiated by libraries. In the 1940s, Louisville Public Library in the United States ran a radio station and later used television in its "neighborhood college", run in conjunction with the university. The Open University of the United Kingdom is an important example of a worldwide movement. Its own librarians are members of the course production teams and its course materials are stocked by many libraries. Prince Gorge's County Library in Maryland provides Open University and other material for its university's independent students. Public libraries in Quebec supported their local tele-university. In practice, students have little time to use anything other than the learning materials supplied direct to them but the adoption of project-based work by the Open University has resulted in fresh demands being made on libraries. Dependence upon libraries by non-formal learners may be more a function of the learning style than of the distance from the educational provider.

Some major developments in distance education fail to include libraries. The Norwegian Distance Education Institution set up in 1978 to coordinate television, the National Film Centre, and the University Press made no mention of the place of libraries, but the National Library Office now takes part in all planning discussions.

Open Entry to Non-formal Education

Adults should not be debarred from education because of a lack of formal entry qualifications, and provision should be easily accessible. These principles have provided another reason for "library learning".

Between 1972 and 1976 a major project was undertaken by the United States College Entrance Examination Board's (CEEB's) Office of Independent Study and Guidance Projects. Nine library based guidance and tutorial support for learners wishing to gain credits for university courses or to learn for any other reason. The work was based on the researches of Alien Tough, which demonstrated that adults undertake a great number of learning projects but often with unsatisfactory guidance and resources. The public library staff were trained, not to teach, but to make available suitable resources, to support and encourage, and to refer when necessary. Great emphasis was placed on evaluation of the outcomes for the library and for the learners (Mavor moret al. 1976, Boles and Smith 1979). Philadelphia Freet Library created a "Lifelong Learning Centre" in 1976. The Netherlands has an Open School, in which libraries cooperate in non-formal education by providing tours of the library, instruction in library use, and reading lists. Islington Public Library and the Inner London Education Authority in the United Kingdom have embarked on a research project to provide educational guidance and support services in collaboration with educational providers.

The Future

The high costs of formal education, the need for non-formal to retrain and adapt to change, and the emphasis on to retrain and adapt to change, and the emphasis on lifelong learning have resulted in alternative and more flexible learning systems. New teaching methods in secondary schools have trained people in independent study skills. All learning resources centers, often integrated with libraries, are under great pressure (de law Court 1974). College libraries are asked to allow non-formal independent learners access to their collections. Public libraries are expected to support broadcast learning. Professional training for librarians incorporates "user needs" in general and sometimes the needs of non-formal learners in particular. Their needs are for more than information; they need encouragement, clarification, motivation, and review. Special groups of learners claim the librarian's attention. In Oud-Gastel, in the Netherlands, the public library provided a course in social awareness for women, which resulted in greater use of the library's information services. The CEEB project referred to above attracted many older adults.

Research shows that it is important for librarian to concern themselves with the intentions of those who use their libraries and not simply with delivery of material. New technologies are likely to replace librarians for many of the mechanical tasks of collection and delivery. The future will tell how far libraries as resource centers for non-formal learners will be replaced by electronic resources delivered direct, and how far librarians will supply the need non-formal learners have for experienced and sympathetic guidance to the multiplicity of resources and systems available to them.

References

1. Alfred J, Hay W 1979 A Preliminary Study of the Involvement of Public Libraries with non-formal Learners, Leeds Polytechnic Public Libraries Management Research Unit, Leeds.
2. Bridge L E 1981 Serving non-formal Learners: A Public Library Tradition, American Library Association, Chicago, Illinois.
3. Boles S, Smith B.D. 1979. The learner's advisory service, *Library Trends* 28: 165-78.
4. De la Court W 1974 Openbare Biliotheck en Permanent Educatie [Public libraries and permanent education]. Tjeenk Willink. Groningen.

10

LIBRARY AS THE LIFE FORCE OF DISTANCE EDUCATION

A.P.S.V.V.S.N.L. Narasimha Raju

Libraries in Higher Education

Education is recognised as a basic pre-requisite for all our general development programmes. It is a mixture of cultural and vocational skills used to transmit the accumulated thought of the past to enable a person to have an intellectual and productive career in life. The scientific, technological and economic developments, world-wide socio-political trends, and the impact of automation in all areas have led to an enormous and increasing demand for purposive and effective education. In each country, education has gained, rapidly or a high priority in national and international programmes. Education, in whatever form it is implied, has to respond expeditiously and effectively to changing needs in a constantly moving and turbulent environment, and has to cope with both the increasing quantity as well as variety or diversity of knowledge.

How Libraries can help the distance learner

The National Policy on Education (1986) lays great stress on distance education and states that the future thrust will be on this rather than on the conventional type of education, both as a means of relieving the rush of students to universities and colleges and for enabling those who, for various reasons, were not able to pursue higher education to do so. Therefore, it can be expected that this stream of education will become increasingly popular and attract more and more students in the future.

A strong library system, with a network of well equipped and well organised libraries all over the country, is the most important element in the infrastructure to be provided for the successful implementation of distance education programmes. In developed countries where distance education systems have been introduced, large scale library facilities were already developed and available and therefore could be relied upon for their support. But in developing countries this basic pre-requisite needs to be provided before distance education is introduced.

Non-traditional students may at times need to make use of all kinds of local libraries that are willing to grant them use and/or borrowing privileges. But the libraries that will be most convenient in location and most amenable to serving the whole community are the public libraries. Studies that have been made on non-traditional students in the West point out that for most the public library is of primary importance. Yet such new students pose serious new problems for many public libraries. Their literature and service needs will be more advanced than those of the average public library patron. Non-traditional programmes are enrolling a rapidly growing segment of the adult population and a better understanding of the non-traditional degree programmes and of the adult learner's needs in general is required. Not all libraries will be able to develop special programmes of special collections for non-traditional students, but most can do something to assist them.

Non-traditional systems need liaison people to represent the college in closer co-operation with local libraries. They would keep libraries informed about new programmes, new booklists, problems students are having with libraries, the importance of library resources to the students, how essential fast delivery of materials is to the student who is working on a short-term contract, etc. Students would learn to come to the liaison people with questions or complaints about library services. They would be responsible for determining the need for training students in library use skills and for devising adequate programs of instruction. The liaison people would become thoroughly familiar with local libraries, with area co-operative library programs, and with library personalities, special needs of the students or any problems they may have can be solved through the liaison persons.

A special collection of correspondence course guides and texts, programmed learning courses, and other materials especially designed for use in independent study could be developed. Suggestions for materials and copies of any regularly used bibliographies should be solicited from the non-traditional degree colleges to aid in collection building. Perhaps such arrangements could be made between public libraries and the non-traditional colleges in order to give students convenient access to selected basic materials that will be needed by a number of students over a period of time.

The growth of this new population of 'mobile' library users is something which the library profession at large must take into account, and a new programme of partnership between the distance education systems and the different types of libraries - academic public and special within a state or a region, must be carefully evolved.

In Great Britain, the Open University system has been making use of advanced technologies for imparting instruction but the system is also such that distance students are compelled to use libraries. The main library at the headquarters caters mainly to the staff and researchers of the British Open University. However many libraries in Britain take upon themselves the responsibility of helping the independent distance education student. Some of the large public reference libraries acquire and maintain separate reference collections of study materials, meant for this type of student.

Distance Education systems in India should also develop co-operative programmes with the public or academic or special libraries., so that the non-traditional student community can have profitable access to a much larger share of information resources, which traditional or formal students can avail of. All academic (University and college) libraries must offer 'open access' to non-traditional students, so that they can utilize their resources without the constraints of nonavailability or distance. Public libraries too should have special collections of "distance materials" (reference and text books, course materials, audio and audio-visual media) so that the distance learner has more access to libraries closer to him or her than his own study centre library, and also to a wider range of materials.

Resource Sharing and Linking of Open University Library Systems

The Distance Education Systems in the country must also merge with the general pooling of library resources, and initiate steps towards automation and modernisation, the introduction of standardised formats and techniques for bibliographic service and other aspects, and the appointing of qualified staff which is an essential pre-requisite to the efficient handling of information, its processing and supply.

At the National level we have the Indira Gandhi National Open University with a Central Library at the main university headquarters in Delhi, 16 Regional Centres in major cities all over the country and 201 Study Centres located again all over the country to cater to the needs of its geographically dispersed students.

Library Support for IGNOU

Indira Gandhi National Open University aims at developing appropriate library collections in various disciplines to meet the needs of its diverse clientele, at Central, Regional and Study Centres, and to provide reading, lending, reference, and documentation services to the staff and students who comprise it: Special collections of distance education books and journals at the libraries are also to be developed, and IGNOU plans to provide comprehensive information services in areas related to distance education, to other open universities in the country.

The IGNOU Library has computerised a few housekeeping operations and provides information services on distance education from CD-ROM databases.

The Dr. B.R. Ambedkar Open University (Dr. Braou) has its headquarters and Central Library at Hyderabad and a supporting system of 87 study centres and their libraries located in the three regions of Andhra Pradesh, catering to the many urban and rural students enrolled with it. Both IGNOU and Dr. BRAOU have a number of study centres at common locations, that too in the same city or town. In Hyderabad itself IGNOU has two Regional Centres and in the state there are seven study centres. Dr. Braou has its headquarters a Central Library and also 18 study centres in Hyderabad and of the remaining study centres in the state: seven are located in the same places as the IGNOU study centres, namely Warangal, Adoni, Anantapur, Tirupathi, Vijayawada, Guntur and Visakhapatnam.

Linking of the Library support systems

The common study centres can be seen as the obvious basis for linking and sharing of resources. The resources of the libraries of these two universities, that have taken up the cause of Distance Education, can be pooled together or shared to meet this challenge effectively, and infact there are many factors that make this kind of sharing a necessity.

Wherever common, study centres of the two universities can be merged and their resources enlarged considerably, at the same time ensuring that unnecessary duplication of expensive documents such as reference tools and journals is avoided.

The vast resources of IGNOU and the Dr. BRAOU of document and nonprint media can be effectively pooled together, and with the necessary access tools — union catalogues, indexes, computerised bibliographical search and retrieval processes — the benefit to the students would be enormous and invaluable. The nearly 2 lakh student strength of IGNOU and the 65,000 student strength of Dr. BRAOU, IGNOU's 16 Regional and 201 study centres, and Dr. BRAOU's two tier central head-quarters and 87 study centres can verily be fitted into a successful network using the communication facilities available in our country, for optimal utilization of their resources, and the mutual advantage of both universities.

Existing communication facilities of NICNET, INDONET or ERNET can also be used to link up study centres with other study centres and with the Regional and Central facilities. For this, of course, automated procedures would have to be introduced and union catalogues of holding on tape or disk or computerised databases of the collections with the location of each item will have to be built up, and a lot of dynamic organisation and planning is required to workout modalities before implementation. But the success of such a programme would be far reaching and of utmost benefit to the distance learner.

In our own country, and in our state, the Dr. Braou can make a first step in this direction by coordinating its study centres and their libraries into a computer-based library network, linked to its central library as the main node or agency, which will act as the directing body, and maintain a union catalogue of all library collections.

Libraries and Resources Network

The central library can also be linked with the central libraries of other open universities in the country, thus widening the resources network, and in turn all central libraries should maintain direct two-way communication channels with the National Open University Library. Each Central Library must maintain a listing of all its holdings, study centre libraries included, and as and when the need arises provide for bibliographical or document access. The Distance Libraries can work out arrangements for pooling their resources—financial and documentary—and this will enable more documents to be purchased with each of the central libraries concentrating on certain disciplines and developing strong collections in them.

The entire open university system in the country may thus be visualised as a truly open system, linked by a communication network that is without barriers and which makes the resources of recorded knowledge open to all. Open air classrooms of the UGC are gaining in popularity, where through satellite communication and TV media, students can converse with their teachers and participate in lecture discussions.

Observations

Libraries are the life force of Distance Education, as the distance learner is dependent on them for all his study and knowledge needs. Without access to them, he becomes greatly handicapped and infact loses one of the most important basic human rights - the right to knowledge, information and education.

If all colleges could take on responsibilities of distance education and convert their class room lessons (for a selected few) to guidance courses for all who apply to them for admission, there will be a total change in campus discipline and life. Instead of regulated hours of concentrated teaching by many teachers for a few students, a pattern of general guidance courses by every teacher for stipulated periods for larger numbers of students who seek it and then study by themselves with the help of the libraries can be set up. This position would bring about a total change in the academic world. Infact it leads on to the concept of the open university with all present institutional resources of teachers, libraries and laboratories being more widely and more usefully engaged for the development and intellectual growth of the nation's youth. This indeed would prove a solution for many of the ills and indiscipline and irregularities in our academic institutions.

The library resources of all colleges now functioning, straight away can be made available for distance education students by locating their study centres in such colleges. Further, duplication of agencies and centres by different open universities and correspondence course schools of the universities would be wasteful and they must all work out a method in which they would have only one study centre at a place and not two or three in which distance education agencies would be indulging in the luxury of over-lapping functions and courses of studies. Need for stringent economy goes well with the necessity for the wide spread opportunity and operations of the distance education agencies.

Distance education flows gently like water where the levels are low towards the people in the deprived and weaker strata, bringing out a wealth of human resources from uncultivated soil and untapped sources which will give better yield, because it is almost the first - crop and these people acquiring knowledge and wisdom would prove a great economic wealth to the country.

With INFLIBNET in its first phase of implementation the network can take into the purview the open universities and their needs as well, and this will ensure the required lateral links with the traditional universities and throw open their common resources for all those who wish to move in that land where the mind is without fear. As Carlyle says: "the true university of these days is a collection of books" and nowhere is this more so than in distance education and open universities of India today.

11

ROLE OF LIBRARIES IN PROMOTING DISTANCE EDUCATION

K. Ramanaiah
M. Anjaiah

Distance Education

There was a time when a student wanted to learn had to go to the *Academy* of Plato and the *Lyceum* of Aristotle or *Ashrama* of a *Guru*. Today, the system of Distance Education and the revolutionary changes in Information Technology have made it possible to take Plato, Aristotle and *Guru* to the student. The Distance Education is meant for modern *Ekalavyas*.

The distance education has come as a boon to the people those who have discontinued their studies because of several constraints/problems either in the regular education system or in the personal life. Any how, the distance education is a highly welcome step in the direction of taking education to the door steps of students who are willing to acquire higher education. It is particularly relevant in a country like India where a larger number of students are dropping their studies at various stages on account of backwardness of the family, low educational status of parents, economic handicaps, social traditions and lack of facilities of resources.

The distance education is known variously in different parts of the world. In USA it is known as *Home study* or Independent study, in Australia it is more popular as *External study*, in Spanish speaking world it is familiar as *Education a Distancia*, in United Kingdom (U.K.) it is called as *Open Learning*. The other popular terms which are synonymously used for distance education are continuing education, extension education and self-study, etc. Most of the countries are now adopting the distance education system as a parallel to the regular education system in order to meet the educational needs of their people with different names. In India it is popularly known as distance education or open education.

Importance of Libraries

The libraries are store houses of knowledge where all the study material is procured, preserved and disseminated. They are the direct incentives to the development of educational, social and cultural activities in a nation. They transfer the knowledge and culture from one generation to other. They contribute a lot to the awakening of public in day-to-day life. In the words of Dr. S.R. Ranganathan, the father of library movement in India "Libraries are not mere store-houses, they are rich springs from which knowledge flows out to irrigate the field of education and culture". Realising the importance of libraries and the need for organising them, the late Prime Minister, Jawaharlal Nehru said "It should be our endeavour to locate atleast one library in every village in the country".

Distance Education and Libraries

Already the libraries are playing an important role in formal education system. Due to the emergence of distance education their need and importance has been further increased and they have to play a still greater role. This is because the teacher and taught are far away from each other and the instruction is given through some other media. One of the aims of distance education is to stimulate the student to do the self-study. For the self-study there is no other place than the library where he can get all that he required.

In developed countries where distance education system was introduced, the library facilities were already developed on a large scale. But in developing countries the facilities are not improved. In India, for example, we do not have a nation wide network of public libraries or academic libraries. Only a few states have so far gone for public library system based on some form of legislation. The academic library network is now at its infant stage and has its own teething troubles. The Special Libraries scattered widely and do not have much co-ordination among them. Under these circumstances, the library facilities have to be adequately planned and developed in India keeping in view the changes taking place in educational system and growing needs of people.

Already the resources available in the existing educational institutions are being utilised by the distance education system. The building and space are being used for locating their centres, the regular class rooms are converted to hold the classes for distant learners, and the regular teachers are drafted for engaging counselling and contact classes. Thus, the distance education system is growing as an alternative to the formal education system in the country. They are able to provide education to maximum people with minimum expenditure by tapping the existing resources.

In the similar way, the existing libraries can also be made useful for the distant learners with slight modifications or relaxations in their functioning. At present, more than fifty universities are conducting correspondence courses and with the establishment of National Open University, the number of user community consisting of mature distant learners has increased enormously. The distance education is an opportunity for all to pursue their studies at any time. Their requirements are diverse. Therefore, the libraries of all types namely, Academic, Public and Special should assume the newer responsibilities and focus their attention towards meeting the growing library and information needs of independent adult students.

Role of Different types of libraries

Public Libraries

Public Libraries are often called as the Universities of the people. They have an important role to play to make distance education a success. It is the public library where any citizen can get a membership to use the library. They are located at various levels, that is, state, district and local. The public libraries located at district or state level can be made as regional centres for open learning with the co-operation and assistance of distance education system. The local libraries like the municipal, panchayat and village libraries can be utilised as the local study centres of the distance education programmes.

In addition to these, the public library consists of mobile libraries which take the books to the door steps of the user community. These mobile libraries can also be utilised as home libraries of the distant learners by bringing the study material to their threshold.

Academic Libraries

The academic libraries exist at various levels that is university, college, and school levels. The university libraries possesses rich sources of document collection and well qualified staff. There libraries can be utilised as regional centres for the distance education system and the college or school libraries can be used as study centres of distance education.

Special Libraries

Though the libraries of Medical Colleges, Engineering Colleges and Agricultural Colleges are considered as Special Libraries, there are several other R&D Organisations, Industrial and Business Organisations, Training Institutions, Government Agencies which are maintaining their own special libraries to fulfil the needs of their clientele. Since they are designed for advanced studies, the working Engineers, Medical practitioners, Managers, Business personnel, Scientists, Policy makers are pursuing their continuing education through these institutions by utilising the resources available in the libraries extensively. These libraries are useful to the organisations concerned. By relaxing their functioning with slight modifications, these libraries can also be utilised for advanced learners of Distance education system to help in their particular fields of knowledge.

The professional staff available in these libraries can also be utilised as Guides to the distant learners in their day-to-day educational needs. Since they are well versed with the library sources and services, they can guide the learners properly to search and study the literature on their own.

Suggestions

The following are certain suggestions for improving the library set up to suit to the requirements of distance education system in our country.

1. ***Library Legislation:*** Since the distance education is gaining a momentum in the country, a suitable provision is to be made in the public library acts keeping in view the needs of distant learners and necessary amendments to the existing acts are to be brought. Since these libraries are available in rural areas and the most of the learners in distance education are from far off rural places they can serve better to meet the needs of learners in their self-study.

2. ***Mobile Libraries:*** The education has been brought to the door steps of the students through distance mode. In the similar way, the learning material can also be brought to the doors of the learners through mobile libraries. Therefore, the mobile library facilities are to be increased enormously and extended to the distant learners.

3. ***User Orientation and Assistance:*** Most of the distant learners are not exposed to the libraries and do not know the sources or services available in the libraries and they have to depend mostly on the libraries for their study proper user education programmes must be planned and implemented so that they can search and study independently.

Conducting of periodic user surveys will help in knowing the requirements of distant learners and suitable steps can be initiated to meet their needs.

They need help from the libraries in locating information and completing their assignments and seminars. Hence, the libraries must activate their reference sources and user assistance programmes.

4. ***Library Extension Services:*** Library extension services can be started or strengthened by conducting seminars, talks, symposia, exhibitions, etc., related to distant learners.

5. ***Information Technology:*** The libraries should be equipped with appropriate IT such as computers, videos, cassette recorders, satellite communication facility etc. to facilitate the distant learners.

6. ***Library Education:*** The incorporation of library education in the curricula of distance education programs will help in their self or independent study since most of them are not aware of the library basics.

7. ***Library Network:*** The libraries must participate in various networks available in the country and design their own LANS to share and exchange the information.

8. ***Library Co-operation:*** Co-operative acquisition, common storage and training of users, sharing of equipment and expertise can be had through proper co-operation among the libraries. This is necessary and relevant in the present days since no library is in a position to possess all that it required.

9. ***Man Power Development:*** The available staff in the libraries be given training in the field of distance education to have a proper understanding about the distance education system and the needs of the learners. They should also be provided with information about their programmes and courses so that they can plan to acquire the required material, design the services and functions to suit the needs of distance education learners.

Conclusion

The libraries can play a vital role in promotion and development of distance education since the libraries are only the centres which help the people in their self-study and at the same time the distance education is also mostly dependent on the self-study. As both the systems are working for the same goal of self-study and education of the people, the libraries can easily be converted as the educational centres for off-campus students by bringing flexibility in their functioning and extending their services and activities towards them. If suitable amendments or provisions are made to the existing laws, rules and regulations, the rich sources available in the libraries can be exploited to the maximum extent to educate the rural masses and bring awareness among them.

Section V
LIS Education: Challenges and Changes

12

LIBRARY AND INFORMATION SCIENCE EDUCATION IN INDIA FOR THE 21ST CENTURY: TRENDS AND ISSUES

P.B. Mangla

Scope

The scope of this paper is limited to formal library and information science (LIS) education programmes at the post-graduate level conducted by university departments. The LIS courren at the undergraduate level-usually conducted by library associations, libraries, teacher training institutes and even universities are excluded. Also excluded are the short-term specialised courses occurring in university departments, documentation centres, or research institutions. The term "Post-graduate" is used in the British sense, referring to courses after the bachelor's degree. Terms such as "library schools" and "departments of library and information science" are used synonymously. In this country library science courses have been designated as LIS courses since the 1970s.

Background

India, which attained independence in 1947, is the seventh largest country in the world, and ranks tenth in terms of industrialization. Primary education is free in all states and union territories and is compulsory in most of them. The overall literacy rate is 52% (according to the 1991 census) and with the implementation of the *New Education Policy* in 1986, the complete eradication of illiteracy should be achieved during the next decade or so.

The country has already developed a vast infrastructure of education and research facilities.

The Library Scene

The past history of librarianship in India (as in several

other countries in the region) is characterized by the sentiment of simply "having libraries" with little emphasis on library service in the modern sense. The recognition of the role libraries and documentation centres could play in the educational and socio-economic development of the country began to receive acceptance only as late as the 1950s.

As a result, the country now has a large infrastructure of libraries, documentation services, and information networks for use by general readers or researchers at local, state, and national levels. Further developments are envisaged during the period of the next Five Year Plan (1996-2001). Three important documents that deserve mention here are 1) a report by a working group appointed by the Planning Commission (Government of India) dealing with the modernization of library services and informatics for 1990-95, 2) the development of an information and library network (INFLIBNET), prepared by a working group of the University Grants Commission in 1988 and 3) *National Policy on Library and Information Systems: A presentation* prepared by a Committee appointed by the Govt. of India in 1986.

LIS Programmes

The need for professionally qualified personnel to manage libraries effectively and efficiently had been recognised long before independence in 1947. For example the first one-year postgraduate diploma course in library science which in several ways served as model for developing library science training programmes in the country both before and after independence was established, at the initiative of S.R. Ranganathan, at Madras University as early as 1937. Five universities offered the diploma course before 1947.

As the demand for professionally qualified personnel began to increase after independence several universities started library science course, with the result that LIS today is a well recognized discipline of post-graduate study and research in about 75 universities, including the country's three open universities.

Although created in 1946 the Department of Library and Information Science at the University of Delhi started admitting students to the post-graduate diploma course in 1947. In several respects this department had a reputation for setting trends not only in India but perhaps for the whole of the British Commonwealth. It was the first department of library science to be constituted as a teaching department. In 1948, it was the first to set up an advanced course leading to the Master of Library Science degree. In addition in the same year students were allowed to do research leading to the Ph.D. degree. Again in 1976 this department led the way in setting up the country's first one-year M. Phil. programme.

Although no new LIS department was established between 1948 and 1955, six departments came into existence between 1956 and 1959. Since the 1969s, the number of departments has increased steadily to the present figure of 75 (Table1). Several more universities plan to start LIS programmes in the near future.

In addition to the 75 Universities with LIS programmes, the Documentation Research and Training Centre (DRTC) in Bangalore and the Indian National Scientific Documentation Centre (INSDOC) in New Delhi also offer specialized courses in information science leading to an Associateship in Information Science. These were started in 1961 and 1964, respectively.

Admission Requirements and Programmes Duration

Because of recent improvements in employment opportunities for qualified personnel and increasing competitiveness for admission several library schools admit to the bachelor-level library science programmes only those who hold a valid master's degree in an academic discipline. This trend is quite encouraging because candidates with higher academic qualifications are better equipped to provide specialized library and information services.

Although admission is usually based on academic merit (Table 2) certain library schools require an admissions test or interview in addition to an appropriate degree. Some schools even ask for prior library experience as an essential requirement.

Table 1: LIS degree programmes in Indian Universities (excluding Distance Education programmes)

	B. LIb. Sc./B.L.I.Sc	M.L.I.Sc.	M. Phil.	Ph.D.
Library schools	75	55	2	30
Graduates each Year (estimated)	3000	550	10	15

Key:B.Lib Sc. or B.L.I.Sc = Bachelor's degree in library science or library and information science

M.L.I.Sc. = Master's degree in library and information science

Table 2: Degree and admission requirements for LIS programmes in India

Degree	Minimum admission requirements	Duration
B.Lib. Sc./B.L.I.Sc	Bachelor's degree	1. academic year
M.L.I.Sc (a)	B.Lib. Sc./B.L.I.Sc.	-do-
M. Phil	M.L.I.Sc	1. calendar year
Ph.D.	M.L.I.Sc or M. Phil	2-3. academic years
Associateship in Information Science (b)	B.Lib. Sc./B.L.I.Sc. or any 2nd class master's degree or bachelor's degree in engineering or medicine, etc.	2. calendar years

(a). The master's level programme at Calcutta University takes two academic years to complete. On the other hand, students at Bombay university are required to attend classes for only a few months. Thereafter they may submit their projects without attending any classes in the university.

(b). Available only at DTRC and INSDOC.

In almost all library schools, with the exception of those

offering distance education, LIS programmes are conducted on a full-time basis. For Ph.D. programmes, several universities have residency requirement of 2-3 years. It may be relevant to mention that the number of women candidates to all LIS programmes has been increasing during the past 15-20 years and they now constitute 60-70% of the total enrollment in almost all library schools.

Curricula

The curricula recommended by the Review Committee of the University Grants Commission (UGC) (with S.R. Ranganathan as its Chairman) in its 1965 report had been adopted by most library schools in the country till recently. The Review Committee recommended the following courses for this programmes: 1) Library Organisation; 2) Library Administration; 3) Physical Bibliography and Book Selection; 4) Document Bibliography and Reference Services; 5) Library Classification (Theory); 6) Library Classification (Practice); 7) Library Cataloguing (Theory); 8) Library Cataloguing (Practice); 9) Record of Practical Work.

The scheme of courses has been subject to evaluation and restructuring on the part of some library schools. For example, the University of Delhi has added courses on Library and Society, Reference and Information Courses and, Reference and Information Services. A few library schools have included topics such as documentation, history of libraries, computer applications, and audio-visual materials, as well as different types of libraries (school, public, academic), either as separate courses or as parts of courses in the above list.

At the master's degree level, the UGC Review Committee recommended the study of techniques in depth classification, documentation, and library cataloguing. It also suggested courses of the "Universe of Knowledge," and on types of library systems, as well as literature surveys in areas such as Indology, social sciences, or government documents. In addition, candidates were to undertake a project that included a documentation list and a project report on an approved topic.

These requirements have also been modified during the past 10-15 years. New areas that constitute either compulsory or optional courses include systems analysis, statistical methods, computer applications, library net-works, information storage and retrieval techniques, research methods, information science and, information systems and programmes.

The M.Phil degree programmes, in line with other subjects in the universities, consists of two parts: 1) course work in research methods, library planning and management, and one other topic area (e.g. public library systems, comparative librarianship, LIS are subject to the same regulations that apply to other university programmes at this level. Even though the first Ph. D. in library science was awarded by the University of Delhi as early as 1956, yet until 1980 very few individuals had advanced degrees in this field from India. However, during the past 10 years or so, library schools have awarded Ph.d. degrees to 50-60 more graduates. The emphasis on research in the field is increasing at present, an estimated 80 candidates are working for their Ph.D.degrees in the country.

In regard to Associateship in Information Science at DTRC and INSDOC, the syllabi for both programmes are similar and consist of required courses in information science, resources, handling, and management, as well as electives in areas such as industrial information services, systems analysis, and linguistics.

Faculty

Up to the late 1950s, the teaching faculty in library schools consisted of part-time teachers usually drawn from their respective university libraries. The University Librarian invariably functioned as head of department. In 1965, the need for full-time teachers was duly recognized by the UGC Review Committee, which noted that using university library staff as part-time teachers was not conducive to efficiency.

The trend over the past three decades has been gradually to employ full time teachers and department heads in these library schools. In addition, several library schools invite the senior staff members of libraries, documentation centres, or computer centres either to teach certain courses or to deliver specialized lectures.

There are an estimated 255 full time teachers in Indian library schools- about 20 Professors, 85 Readers, and 150 Lecturers. A Ph.D. and teaching experience of 5-8 years is usually required for Readers and Professors in Indian universities. Because LIS is a newly emerging discipline for study and research with a substantial demand for teachers, it has generally been difficult to recruit individuals with these qualifications. The situation has improved somewhat during the past decade, but a good deal remains to be done. Those Indian teachers who have studied at American or British universities have certainly helped to strengthen the teaching programmes at quite a few Indian library schools.

March towards 21st Century: Problems and Recommendation

The vast expansion in LIS education programmes and facilities has naturally raised numerous problems, which were the subject of discussion in committee reports and at conferences, seminars, and workshops over the past three decades. Some of the vital areas of concern are 1) levels of education, 2) selection of students. 3) course content, 4) accreditation, 5) research, 6) status and administrative organization, 7) employment opportunities and 8) LIS literature.

Levels of Education

As in the United States, Canada and now even to a great extent in the United Kingdom, librarianship in India is largely a post-graduate profession. One of the issues often discussed is whether the present practice of awarding bachelor's and master's degrees should be continued or changed to a two-year integrated master's degree course, similar to that in other academic programmes.

An analysis of the existing pattern indicates that it has certain advantages, especially for those who do not want to continue their studies and are more interested in getting a job after completing the bachelor's programme. At the same time a two-year master's degree programme provides the time and opportunity for a more, balanced structure of core and optional courses.

It is not advisable at present to abolish the bachelor's degree programme. However, some library schools should be encouraged to experiment with the two-year master's programme. After a period of time (5-8 years) teachers, librarians and other employers could make a comparative evaluation of the products of the two systems. The few library schools that have already started conducting two-year master's programmes should make an objective analysis of their experience, which would be useful for reorganizing the present pattern of LIS education in the coming years.

Student Selection

The majority of students entering the bachelor's degree programmes are fresh from the universities. However, although academically qualified, many of these students lack a proper aptitude for library work, s strong general background, an interest in books and readers, and a good personality, all of which are essential for being a competent professional librarian. Library schools by using methods for admitting applicants to other professional programmes such as medicine, engineering, or business administration should also screen applicants through a system of admission or aptitude tests accompanied by interviews in order to ensure that the best possible future librarians are recruited into the profession.

It must be pointed our that, for various historical and sociological reasons, top students in the natural and applied sciences generally shun librarianship as a career. Although this attitude is gradually changing, there is a great need to attract these students by offering them scholarships and fellowships, as well as informing them about the opportunities and challenges in the profession. Such steps would certainly help to develop suitable personnel for scientific and research libraries and documentation centres in the country, particularly for senior-level positions.

Course Contents

Everyone agrees that to meet the larger manpower needs in a developing country such as India the majority of students in LIS should receive the proper education in "information science" as well as in "library science". However, the information science component needs further strengthening, particularly at the master's level.

A few libraries have established computer labs in order to provide hands on experience for their students, which is a commendable development. It is hoped that similar facilities will be available to students in library schools through out the country. The need for knowledge and practical experience in handling computers and other gadgets of information technology is essential because it is envisaged that the 21th century would have more and more dependence on information, information networking and information dissemination.

In addition, as LIS is a professional subject, each student should spend at least three months as an intern in a library or documentation centre in order to obtain practical experience as a requirement for the bachelor's or master's degree. The UGC Panel has also recently emphasized the importance of supervised internships for LIS students.

Research

Up to the late 1970s, the research component in the overall system of LIS education had been rather weak. However, this situation has changed substantially during the past 10-15 years and there has been a large increase in the number of M.Phil and Ph.D. degrees awarded by library schools. The main reason for this change is the UGC requirement of a research degree for jobs in libraries and documentation centres. The increase has certainly adversely affected the quality of research work currently done and has created an urgent need for proper scrutiny and control of research undertaken in library schools around the country.

Administrative Organisation

The UGC Review Committee report and the subsequent proceeding of the Delhi University Workshop (Workshop on the Methods of Teaching and Evaluation 1973) made useful recommendations in regard to standards for the minimum number of full-time teachers at different levels, teaching qualifications, teacher-student ratios. library science collections, non-teaching staff, and physical facilities. These recommendations have been revised in the reports of the UGC Panel on Library and Information Science, as well as in the 1992 report of the UGC appointed Curriculum Development Committee on Library and Information Science. These authorities emphasize that library schools should conduct courses only at the post-graduate level, and that undergraduate courses are responsibility of library associations, women's polytechnics and central libraries, etc.

Accreditation

At present there is no system of accreditation for library schools at the national level. The UGC is responsible for ensuring and maintaining proper academic standards for higher education in the country, but until now its role has generally been limited to recommendations rather than accreditation.The need for creating a proper system of accreditation has been recognized but no suitable mechanism for this purpose has yet been devised. It is hoped that the recently established National Assessment and Accreditation Council (NAAC) would be useful in LIS education as well.

Employment Opportunities Versus New Programmes

Because there is still no system of manpower planning for the profession, the substantial annual increase in the number of LIS graduates (mainly due to larger intakes of students in open university and correspondence courses) has gradually led to a situation of unemployment or underemployment for qualified personnel. Therefore the need for more library personnel should be considered in an objective manner before starting new library schools or programmes or expanding current ones. The urgent need is certainly for the consolidation and improvement of exiting training programmes rather than expansion.

Some feel that LIS, as a professional discipline, is not amenable to study through distance education programmes. Bodies such as the UGC and the Association of Indian Universities should take early steps to ensure that quality is maintained in the operation of these programmes.

LIS Literature

As in other professional subjects, most of the LIS tests or recommended books used in teaching are published in the United States or the United Kingdom. Among the Indian publications, Ranganathan's works are the most important and widely used. In addition, during the past 15-20 years, a number of books (including text book) written by Indians have appeared. Although many of these gooks have proved quite valuable, others are based on class notes or are other wise not of high quality.

Because Hindi or regional languages are replacing English as a teaching medium. LIS books are either being translated from English or written in these South Asian languages. However, much work remains to be done in this area.

Conclusion

Librarianship as a profession has largely emerged from the adolescent stage in India and library schools have certainly made a vital contribution to this process. For the momentum of development to be properly maintained, these schools must bear a still heavier responsibility to provide high quality and relevant education. To do so, library schools would benefit from a system of regular contacts with employers and the users of library and information services. Guidance from this quarter would help library schools to design their programmes in a more logical and pragmatic manner. although some library schools do have informal contacts with employers and users. these relationships should become more formal and regular in nature.

References

1. Indo-US Conference to Library and Information Science Professionals. Seminar Papers. Delhi, 1992 (mimeographed)
2. P.B. Mangla. Workshop on the Methods of Teaching and Evaluation in Library Science: A Report. *IASLIC Bulletin*. 18 (1973) 115-138.
3. P.B. Mangla.Research in Library and Information Science and the contribution of Ranganathan. *Education for Information* 2 (1984) 267-282.
4. P.B. Mangla, ed. Library and Information Science Education in India; New Delhi, Macmillan, 1981.
5. P.B. Mangla. Library and Information Science Education in South Asia: India, Pakistan, Bangladesh, and Sri Lanka. *Education for Information*. 12(1994) 399-427.
6. University Grants Commission (India) Review Committee. Library Science in Indian Universities. New Delhi, UGC 1965.
7. World Encyclopedia of Library and Information Services, 3rd ed. Chicago, ALA, 1993.

13

LIS EDUCATION : CHANGE OR STATUS QUO ?

N.R. Satyanarayana

Introduction

Changing requirements for information by the users, radical changes in information technology together with its impact on the society have led to the recognising and rethinking for LIS education in general and LIS as a profession in particular, The LIS education has also grown extensively keeping pace with the profession. In India though the birth of LIS education dates back to 1910, the birth of full-time P.G. Courses dates back 1931 in Madras University, mainly through the efforts of Dr. S.R. Ranganathan. Since then this profession is progressing steadily. Now, after 65 years the number of educational institutions providing LIS education has grown manifold. At the moment more than seventy five Library and Information Science Departments in various universities are engaged in providing Post-graduate diploma, degrees (both BLISc and MLISc) M. Phil and doctoral programmes. Besides these, more than 25 library associations and other private institutions are offering diploma and certificate programmes in LIS. More recently IGNOU and some other state level open universities, have started BLIS and MLIS programmes through distance education for persons supposed to be having two years working experience in library / information centres. The rapid development scenario in the field of Information Technology emphasizes the importance of information and its communication. This results and necessitates for appropriate training for LIS personnel in order to duly integrating with the national development. For the last twenty years there has been an upsurge in the creation of information centres and systems in India. The invasion of computers and other related technologies and setting up of different information networking systems has widened the scope and opportunity for LIS professionals with a sufficient knowledge in computer applications. On a conservative estimate each year at least four thousand students enter the profession and get absorbed in different categories of libraries, organizations, government and private institutions for their information retrieval jobs. The LIS personnel require a better and appropriate training in order to meet the new challenges posed to the profession in the present day scenario of Information Society.

Information Society

Since independence India also embarked on industrialization and development. As a result of this industrial development several new changes have been observed in the sociological, educational, environmental, cultural, economical aspects of the Indian society. In other words, industrialization has been grafted on to a society that continuous to function to a large extent in its traditional modes. As a result many occupational roles in service sector were cropped up. But unfortunately they could not contribute much to the efficiency and productivity of the nation. The basic reason for it is the low level of information consciousness. It is much higher in the developed countries). In India only 10% of the work force constitute white collar workers and 60% are farmers. An estimated 65% of the population are still illiterate and their lack of education prevents them from the widely sharing the benefits of information. Within the population of eighty millions citizens, library and information workers in India are still a very small in percentage. They are steadily growing in numbers.

LIS Education Patterns

LIS education is a recognised professional education in India. All the university departments offering LIS courses are providing one year BLISc/BLSc. Nearly half of them are providing Master's Programmes in LIS namely MLISc/MLSc/Associateship in information services. Few universities provide M.Phil programme and offer full time doctoral programme.

Curricula

The syllabus of LIS studies taught at university level is varying. In the recent past advanced topics like computer applications, telecommunication and networking technologies, have been included in the courses. The increasing use in the number of electronic information materials, such as CD-ROMs, especially in the area of science and technology and R&D information systems necessitated for their inclusion at the post-graduate level. Some universities in Uttar Pradesh have also introduced library science as a subject in pre university pass and degree level programmes.

Quality Vs Quantity Education

There has been a gradual improvement in LIS education in the country. It is manifested more in quantity rather than in quality. Although the number of departments and professional associations and other institutes alongwith the students enrolement has steadily increased, but the quality of outgoing students leaves much to be desired. There has been a general outcry from both the students and LIS professionals, that the university level education should concentrate more on development of professional skill among the pradictioners. The current course content of LIS programmes show no relevance of the subject to our present day informational demands of the society. Keeping in view the veracity of the curricula, few years back UGC has constituted a committee, Curriculum Development Committee in LIS education, which has partially focussed on the steps to be taken to bring out necessary improvements in curriculum standards.

Need for a National Plan

In order to develop over all plans for meeting the library and informational needs of the nation in general and the library and information manpower requirement in particular, and to cope with the new developments in library and information services, a suitable strategy for manpower development is necessary. A uniform pattern and standard of library training and education should be followed in all parts of the country.

Emphasis on Regional Languages

Another major fault in our system of LIS education is the language used for teaching. Almost all university departments and institutes provide their courses in English, which is an indicator of the feeling that subject is well favoured only for the elite society. Reformative measures in shifting the emphasis from English to the vernacular languages oriented programme through comprehensive measures is highly desirable. It is unfortunate that neither the universities nor the UGC has paid any attention to this aspect in their guidelines.

Part-Time Vs Full-Time Faculty

Another common problem in a majority of LIS schools is the absence of full time faculty. Part-time teachers are still there for specific periods. A part-time teacher may be good in their field in practical aspect but many a times it is found that they lack teaching skills. This lacuna damages the interest of the students in the subjects, as they are not exposed to the subject in the appropriate way. Some times, even a high ranking full-time teachers also lack practical experience. Of late another phenomena seen in India is that of a competent LIS personnel preferring to serve the industry rather than joining the faculty mainly because they are good pay masters. There is thus an urgent need for good, competent, inspired, full-time faculty having both theoretical and practical knowledge.

Lack of Emphasis on Training

As a tradition LIS schools in India aim at producing students who could later be absorbed mostly in educational establishments and in other public and private sector undertakings. The job requirements in these establishments require the entrants to have some practical experience. Barring a few schools, most of the LIS schools in India do not have proper facilities for training the students. The BLIS degree holders with almost no practical training from LIS schools invite criticism from various quarters. Majority of LIS schools in universities find it difficult to possess a laboratory of its own.

Inadequate Infrastructure Facilities

The near absence of departmental library facilities having sufficient numbers of classification schedules, catalogue codes and other reference materials due to insufficient financial support from the university, deprives the department, and the students from having access to their valuable tools which are essential. Old and obsolete books are inappropriate for present curriculum. This also results in loss of enthusiasm of the students.

Curricula Redefined

Our curricula in most of the schools patterned on the model suggested by Ranganathan half a century ago in which classification and cataloguing share almost half. There is a strong need for a new curriculum giving emphasis to information and communication technologies clubbed with sufficient practical training. The LIS courses should be aimed at creating consciousness within the professional circles. Development of skills and value oriented syllabi and alternative teaching material should be given high priority in the LIS courses.

Career Opportunities in LIS

In almost all its diversified fields of human activity LIS education has a wide scope career opportunities in our country. Most of the students are absorbed in libraries attached to Institutions of education R & D organizations. Very few of them go to public library systems. This is due to lack of opportunities in public libraries in our country as majority of the states still yet to have public library system. Though, the course content contains general topics with certain options. But these options mostly remain on paper because of lack of interest on the part of teachers, which adversely affects the enthusiasm of the students. As a result of this many students after completion of their studies in their LIS programme switch over to other fields of employment.

Apprenticeship Training

There is strong need for inclusion of apprenticeship training in the curricula to ensure relevance of the programme to the students in acquiring adequate levels of professional skills, with increased emphasis on social, political and technological aspects. This calls for a change in the education methods in cooperation with the practicing librarians. This will help in focussing attention on purpose of value oriented LIS education. Also, there is need to follow the course structure as recommended by the University Grants Commission (UGC) by all universities in LIS departments. Research oriented subjects should be introduced in the course patterns with subject specialisation like academic libraries, special libraries, public libraries. It is also desired to introduce specialised subjects on conservation of documents, computer applications, research methodology, communication skills in the specialisation curricula. The LIS departments should take advantage of the UGC projects in various fields and appoint researchers. This may in one way raise the employment opportunities and on the other help students acquire relevant practical knowledge. The faculty members should also take special interest in the fields of research and publication of the research results. All this can help explore ways by which an effective and efficient library and information service could be provided to the society.

Suggestions

1. The present course patterns of LIS should be made more interesting by providing sufficient exposure to the advanced technological innovations like computers, satellite, laser, informatics and electronic delivery systems, so that the students may acquaint themselves with the nature of work in ever changing modern information industry.
2. The internship training programmes of about two months be introduced in present curricula. In order to gain practical knowledge in developing skills of a minimum standards.
3. Keeping in view of the importance of library services especially in a developing country like India relevance of library service and the role of librarian as a social communicator in the society should be given high priority.
4. There should be a national plan for LIS education, keeping in view about the annual demand and the annual national output of LIS personnel. Over production of LIS personnel results in more frustation and under - employment among the young trainees. Thus, the training goes waste and yield no fruitful benefit to the society.
5. The process of offering LIS through distance education must be reviewed fourthwith, as the majority of the intake of students are freshers disguising them-

selves as working.

6. UGC guidelines with regard to the recruitment of teachers in LIS should be reviewed. A minimum of atleast, two years working and research oriented work should be included as educational qualification.
7. The old patterned curriculum which gives greater emphasis to two white elephants in the library curriculum - classification and cataloguing - should be discouraged. The LIS teachers, information personnel, communication planners should prepare guidelines for LIS education. The UGC should support these efforts by preparing a common syllabi for all the LIS departments.
8. Efforts should be made for developing library literature in Indian languages. Proper guidelines, incentives and encouragement should be accorded to library science teachers and other professional for taking the writing work in regional languages seriously.
9. The insufficient infrastructure in LIS departments effects the efficiency and standard of the students. There should be a minimum basic infrastructure for providing effective training leading to the development of skill before introducing the programme. The UGC should also encourage the departments who have taken initiative son their own without getting any assistance from either government or UGC.
10. M.Phil, and doctoral programmes in LIS should be initiated to provide the students an opportunity for higher studies. This will help in the development of his field through R & D.
11. The LIS departments must subscribe to practical aspects by involving library professionals, information personnel and communication technologists. The department should install requisite number of computers systems and encourage the students to prepare their own programmes. Good knowledge in handling these instruments is highly desirable. The university and

UGC should provide requisite equipment to all the LIS departments.

12. Library facilities are generally poor in all university LIS departments. To overcome this problem, UGC and university should grant more financial assistance for library development on priority basis.
13. Besides providing the usual education practice the university and UGC should conduct short term correspondence and refresher courses for LIS persons and teachers to enable them to improve their ability in correlating the learning and its application in the work place.
14. To meet emerging challenges in LIS education, UGC should take immediate steps to fill up the posts lying vacant for many years.
15. Special attention should be given by the LIS departments to creating employment opportunities for their products, as various management department do. In this regard, the department should keep constant, live contact with information organisations and other libraries. Appropriate information regarding the scope and future prospects in various areas would enable to students choose their lines as appropriately suited to them.

Conclusion

Of course these are general deficiencies in our system of LIS education. The information organisation has an important role to play in minimising these deficiencies. This requires a planned study, action and inter-change of ideas among education system and professional organisations. As change is essentially a process at all levels, certain specific task oriented proposals, agenda and finally action frame works be planned in a broad network to meet the challenges for the present and the future. If the planned frame work does not meet the objectives and need of the purpose, there is a chance of degradation of LIS education. This ultimately will have an adverse affect in the quality of the information industry. To achieve social goals, both the role of communication media and our system of LIS education are equally important.

References

1. Ashok Basu and J.K. Sarkal : *UGC Report on Curriculam Development in LIS, 1993; an assessment*. XVI IASLIC National Seminar; 1994.

2. *IASLIC Newsletter*. July - August, 1994.

3. P.B. Mangla : *Library and Information Science Education in South Asia : India, Pakistan, Bangladesh and Sri Lanka*. (*Education for Information*. v. 12; 1994).

4. *RRRLF* : Documents on National Policy on Library and Information System. 1985.

5. *UGC. Report of the Curriculum Development Committee in Library and Information Science*. 1993.

6. *World Encyclopedia of Library and Information Services*. 3rd ed., 1993.

14

CONTINUOUS QUALITY IMPROVEMENT IN LIBRARY AND INFORMATION SCIENCE TEACHING THROUGH DISTANCE EDUCATION IN INDIA APPROACHES AND EXPERIENCES

Harish Chandra

Introduction

Presently, education is considered as a basic need of the mankind and every one rural or urban, poor or rich, young or old practically realise that education alone can help them to upgrade and enhance the level of understanding and the way of working. Accordingly, after independence the Government of India along with State Governments is actively engaged to provide equal educational opportunities to the people. However, it is not reaching all irrespective of caste, creed and religion due to various reasons including lack of infrestructural facilities and high cost involved. In view of this fact, our government has promoted the concept of Distance Education (DE) which currently, is considered as a good alternative to the traditional system of education. With this fact and aim, various universities under DE environment are conducting various courses including science and vocational courses. Table-II indicates the spatial distribution of the enrollment in higher education in India and Table-III depicts the course wise distribution of distance education students in our society. This establishes that DE is progressively getting sound footing even in professional courses.

The area of Library and Information Science is also influenced DE environment. It is a known fact that Library and Information Science education in India has achieved a very strong and sound base, mainly due to the devoted and dedicated efforts of Dr. S.R. Ranganathan. With the passage of time, library and Information Science education has emerged as a well established and recognised area of study. There are number of universities in the country offering various types of programmes of study in Librarianship leading to certificate, diploma, degree, M. Phil, Ph. D. and even D. Lit. Various factors and facets have motivated Indian educational administrators to give a serious thought to work out a via-media for providing equal eductional avenues and opportunities to the drop-outs, housewives, working people and people living in rural and remote areas through the nontraditional system of teaching. Library and Information teaching is not an exception to this fact. Currently, there are number of universities which are offering the courses like C.L. and I. Sc. (Certificate of Library and Information Science), D.Lib. Sc. (Diploma in library Science), B.L. and I.Sc. (Bachelor of Library and Information Science) and M.L. and I.Sc. (Master of Library and Information Science) through DE. Table-I indicates the popularity of Library and Information Science programmes conducted at various universities in India wherein a large number of men and women are participating and taking the advantage of DE.

Library and Information Science teaching under DE environment is progressively increasing. On the one hand, it has been observed that there are universities which are utilising the faculty and other staff of the traditional stream and on the other hand, there are other universities which are having independent faculty and staff for Library and Information Science teaching through DE. This factor of variation motivates us to re-orient the entire efforts and to introduce continuous quality improvement process in the teaching of Library and Information Science through DE.

Objectives of Distance Education

DE in the area of Library and Information Science has the following major objectives:

1. To provide opportunities to earn qualification in the area of Library and Information Science to the persons who could not join formal stream due to various factors.

2. To upgrade and enhance the professional level of knowledge and understanding of the working librarians who are not having formal qualification.

3. To supplement and enrich the formal qualifications of

the library professionals who need higher qualifications for their career development.

4. To equalise the professional educational opportunities among the people who are in dire need.

5. To provide self supported and less expensive professional education to the working professionals living in rural and remote places.

QIP is one of the most important and vital techniques of TQM (Total Quality Management). It has great potential to revitalise and revolutionise the teaching of Library and Information Science through DE. The basic aim of the QIP is to upgrade and enhance the expertise and capabilities of the faculty and the staff involved through extending an opportunity for understanding the latest trends and developments in the area of Library and Information Science extensively.

Areas of Concern for Quality

We have seen that DE has made considerable progress and contribution to the teaching and learning of Library and Information Science in India. However, there is need to overcome the practical difficulties which will ensure quality based teaching of Library and Information Science under DE environment. The following are the main areas for improving and introducing the quality concepts advocated by Quality stalwarts.

1. Training programme
2. Delivery system
3. Evaluation process
4. Assignments
5. Personal contact programme
6. Support services
7. Academic counselling
8. Study centre
9. Course material

There is an urgent need to introduce continuous Quality improvement process in the area of Library and Information Science. JAL Stark (1) identifies the following essentials of a quality improvement process which can certainly be useful to us while introducing the improvements in the quality teaching and learning process in the area of Library and Information Science.

* Visible commitment from the Top
* Permanent Culture and Attitude Change
* Draw out Middle Management Cynicism, Fear, Insecurity
* Understand That All Work is a Process And the Performance Standard is Zero Defects
* Measurement and Prevention Philosophy
* Quality Communications and leadership
* Involve Everyone and Recognise Success
* Continuous Improvement -Build into Business Plan
* Customer Driven
* It's hard work - Plan and Support

The steps as suggested above may generate desired results if implemented in the following major areas which will ensure the continuous quality improvement in the teaching of Library and Information Science.

1. Training programme
2. Delivery system
3. Standardisation of evaluation
4. Change of attitude
5. Multimedia application

Training Programme

The work and requirements of the teachers under DE are totally different from the teachers working under traditional system of education. Here, the teachers are not having formal class environment and their students are sitting at different places in the country or the region where teacher can not teach physically. They depend upon the fast and effective communication, good printed material, audio-visual system, computers etc. As teachers need proper training in the usage and application of the gazettes of New Information Technology and Educational Technology for deriving maximum benefits for the students or these courses. Training pertaining to teletext, video text and tele-conferencing will certainly give maximum satisfactory results of the DE environment in the area of Library and Information Science.

Delivery System

The future and value of DE is totally based on the delivery system. The students under this system are scattered and sitting in the rural and remote areas. The study material prepared are required to be sent to them in time and complete. But it is usually seen that students always remain unsatisfied because study materials reach them incomplete and late which hardly serve the basic purpose of joining the course. There is an urgent need to revamp the delivery system with the help of postal and railway authorities which will come to help the students. The quality improvement in delivery system will certainly generate excellence.

Evaluation Process

The evaluation process is the backbone of the traditional and non-traditional system of education which requires extensive objectivity. Under DE the evaluation may be based on the experiences of the teachers who are actually involved in the DE teaching as the level of students under DE environment is different from the students who are in traditional system of education. There is strong need to asses and evaluate in view or the real level of working and performance of the participants. The evaluation may generate good results for making the entire DE system more realistic and qualitative in the area of Library and Information Science.

Change of Attitude

With the passage of time DE has attained the marked progress in bridging the gaps by awarding certificates, diplomas and degrees for those who due to various reasons could not get under traditional system of education. However, there is feeling that the output under DE is still comparatively not good due to various reasons i.e. non-availability of good library facilities, lack of continuous contact among students and teachers, non-availability of extension lectures by distinguished librarians and teachers etc. To overcome it, there is need to give full opportunities to the students for extension lectures on new emerging areas which libraries are in dire need.

There is need to have a well defined quality policy to deliver top quality students in service of the society and also to adopt a climate responsive to the change.

Multimedia Applications

The problems and processes of DE are totally different when we compare it with traditional system of education. Under DE system, teachers, students and the instructional materials are not at one place, all are available at different and remote places. This requires integration so that the desired output could be equally good. Multimedia application has great potential to make DE more realistic and qualitative. It has the capability to present the information to the end users efficiently and effectively. The expression and exposure of the problems of the target audience is highly encouraging and appreciable in all the areas due to the following factors;

1. Ease of use
2. On screen visibility
3. Learning more easily
4. Self sufficient learning
5. Video, graphics, animation makes the learning process more realistic and interesting.

There is no doubt that the application of multimedia technology will certainly generate good results through making Library and Information Science teaching/learning process more alive and qualitative.

Developing Relevant and Flexible Course Structure.

There is an urgent need to develop more relevant courses suiting to the new libraries and information centres environment and requirements. The age old concepts need to be dropped and the new emerging areas like New Information Technology, Marketing of Information Products and Services. Library Networking. Digital Libraries. Multimedia Application. Patents Information System. Media Resources. Internet. Electronic Publishing etc. needed to be incorporated in the course and to be taught so that the products could not find difficulty in getting placement easily and also can enhance the level of knowledge and skill of the working librarians who have joined the course so that they can contribute to their respective areas effectively. The arrangement will help the universities to bring a quality in library and information teaching/learning process in real terms.

Involvement of Working Professionals

The quality process can easily be introduced and maintained if the working librarians and information scientists are also involved in the course design, evaluation, teaching, counselling. This is essential and inevitable in view of the practical exposure of the problems and the future user's aspirations are well known to them. Their rich experiences can also be utilised in the form of their involvement in delivering special or extension lectures during personal contact programmes or on study centres from time to time. The composite experience of working librarians and Information scientists along with teachers of library and information science will definitely bring a drastic qualitative change among the students of library and information science under DE.

Conclusion

It is an accepted fact that DE has made a considerable progress in the area of library and information science. However, there is still need to make it more qualitative and practical. The introduction of New Information Technology, application of Educational Technology, involvement of working professionals, proper co-ordination and revitalised delivery and support services will certainly make library and information science teaching/ learning process more qualitative. There is an urgent need to introduce and countinue the process of quality improvement in the teaching/ learning of library and information science under DE environment on continuous basis. The ground realities of the present higher education system indicate that quality improvement is essential and unavoidable not only for the survival of DE system but also for facing the major changes and challenges of today and tomorrow in the field of library and information science teaching under DE environment.

References

1 Jal Stark, TQM at BP chemicals in Total Quality Management Proceedings, 3rd International Conference on 1990 Springer Verlag, Oakland, p. 132.

2. UGC, Annual Report, 1989-90, New Delhi.

3. proceedings of Conference of Vice-Chancellors, Oct. 10,1990, Ahmadabad, UGC 1991.

Table 1: Spatial Distribution of enrolment in Higher Education in India

	College Univer-sity Deptts.	Distance Education	Total	Share of Distance Education in Total
SOUTHERN REGION				
1. ANDHRA PRADESH	2,99,913	76,075	3,75,988	20.2
2. KARNATAKA	2,74,103	17,615	2,91,718	6.0
3. KERALA	1,53,753	10194,	1,63,947	6.2
SUB-TOTAL	10,11,623	3,02,168	13,13,791	23.0
NORTHERN REGION				
5. DELHI	1,10,921	55,839	1,66,760	33.5
6. HARYANA	82,588	2,959	85,547	3.5
7. HIMACHAL PRADESH	22,437	19,257	41,694	46.2
8. JAMMU & KASHMIR	31,256	1,939	33,195	5.8
9. PUNJAB	1,46,574	16,303	1,62,877	10.0
10 RAJASTHAN	1,92990	22,546	2,15,536	10.5
11. UTTAR PRADESH	5,48,791	4,769	5,53,560	0.9
SUB-TOTAL	11,35,557	1,23,612	12,59,169	9.8
CENTRAL AND WESTERN REGION				
12. MADHYA PRADESH	2,87,240	303	2,87,543	0.1
13. MAHARASHTRA	5,14,809	20,423	5,35,232	3.8
14. GUJARAT	2,32,602	152	2,32,754	0.1
SUB-TOTAL	10,34,651	20,878	10,55,529	2.0
EASTERN REGION				
15. ASSAM	87,235	-	87,235	---
16. BIHAR	2,73,303	3,262	2,76,565	1.2

College	Distance University Deptts.	Total Education	Share of	Distance Education in Total
17. MANIPUR	11,941	—	11,941	—
18. MEGHALAYA				
19 NAGALAND	10,103	—	10,103	—
20. ORISSA	78,771	4,323	83,094	5.2
21. WEST BENGAL				
22. TRIPURA/SIKKIM	3,04,738	—	3,04738	—
SUB-TOTAL	7,66,091	7,585	7,73,676	10.3
ALL INDIA TOTAL	**39,47,922**	**4,54,243**	**44,02,165**	**1.0**

Source: Proceedings of Conference of Vice-Chancellors, October 10,1990, Ahmedabad

Table II: Coursewise Distribution of DE Students in India

		1988-89	% OFTOTAL
UNDERGRADUATE			
1.	Pre-degree/foundation/Inter	9,423	2.1
2.	B.A.	1,84,964	40.7
3.	B.A. (Hons)	571	0.1
4.	B.Com. & B.Com (Hons)	65,000	14.3
5.	B.Sc.	11,489	2.5
	Sub-Total	2,71,447	59.8
POST-GRADUATE COURSES			
1.	M.A.	67.604	14.9
2.	M.Com.	21.7674.8	
3.	LL.B. BGL	2,815	0.6
4.	B.Tech.	460	0.1
5.	Bachelor of Library and Information Science	767	0.2
6.	Bachelor of Journalism		

		1988-89	% OFTOTAL
	and Mass Communication	997	0.2
7.	MBA	134	0.0
8.	M.Phil.	73	0.0
9.	M.Lib & Information Science	353	0.1
	Sub-Total	51,633	11.4
DIPLOMA AND CERTIFICATE COURSES			
P.G. Diploma courses		9,913	2.2
Diploma courses		19,762	4.3
Certificate Courses		7,237	1.6
TOTAL		**4,54,243**	**100.00**

Source: Proceedings of Conference of Vice-Chancellors, October 10,1990, Ahmedabad

Table-III: Universities having facilities for correspondence Course in Library and Information Science during 1989-90

	University	Title of courses	Enrollment men	women	total
1.	Andhra Pradesh Open Univ.	B.Lib. & Info. Science	401	175	576
2.	IGNOU	B. L. & I. Sc.	NA	NA	1522
3.	Kakatiya University	B. Lib. & Info. Science	41	27	68
	Cert. in Lib. & Info. Science		62	38	100
3.	Kashmir Univ.	Cert. in Lib. Science	494	109	603
5.	Kota Univ.	Dip. in Lib. Science	2298	1202	3500
6	Madras Univ.	B.L. & I. Sc.	682	397	1079
	M. L. & I. Sc.		380	131	511
	Cert. in Lib. Info. Sc.		646	178	824

University		Title of courses	Enrollment		
			men	women	total
7.	M.K. Univ. Info.Science	Cert. in Lib.	270	101	371
8.	Punjabi Univ. Info. Science	Dip in Lib. &	156	300	456

Source: U.G.C. Annual Report 1989-90

15

CURRICULUM IN ON-CAMPUS AND OFF-CAMPUS LI S EDUCATION PROGRAMMES IN INDIA - A COMPARATIVE STUDY

K. Sugatri Devi

There is a growing demand for information by an even wider range of users, researchers, planners, managers and the citizens at large. People are increasingly conscious of the implications of the 'information explosion', particularly the need for developing information system and service to channel the mass of information for effective use in national development. In the light of this rapid development in the information scenario in India, it is imperative to incorporate a significant change in the structure and content of the present programme, so as to make it relevant and meaningful to the scientific, social, political and economic environment of the country.

There is also a consequential need for human expertise to provide the interface between the user and information either by traditional or by mechanised means. Hence the L & Is schools are striving to develop manpower suitable for the needs of present day Information Society.

Need for Manpower with high Competence

The Information age is not exclusively an age of electronics. As Horton (1984) points out, "it is also an age in which highly skilled human resources will be in great demand. The real pay off is going to come in training and grooming new kinds of Information Age human resources". So it needs reciprocal changes in the development of information handling competence among professionals. It is the knowledge and skill of personnel who handle the modern information technologies which determines the rate at which information resources will be utilised.

Under these circumstances Lib & Inf. Science schools shall have to produce personnel with necessary additional knowledge about new technologies being introduced in libraries.

Role of LIS Education Programmes

The field of Lib & Inf. Science is a dynamic and interdisciplinary area of study, involving many subjects such as management studies, communication studies, psychology and statistics. Lib & Inf. education is a professional education and it is a specialized area of human training. Accordingly it has a concrete content and objectives in the same way as the training taken by teachers, lawyers, doctors and engineers. Further, as Lancaster (1983) says "we must shift the focus of our professional concern away from the library as an institution and towards the skilled professionals, who will become a professional practitioner on par with medical and legal practitioners".

Preparation for library & information work requires a mastery of the knowledge and techniques utilised in library & Inf. operations and services which constitute the discipline 'Lib & Information Science'. This involves an understanding of the historic and current functions of the library to collect, organise, preserve and transmit for both immediate and continuing use of the records of civilization, the ability to apply information techniques, understanding and appreciation to planning and executing an effective programme of Lib. & Inf. Science for a given channel at a given time in a given situation.

The primary aim of education for lib & inf. science should be to train the intellect in matters pertaining to human knowledge and information for the benefit of mankind.

LIS Education Programmes in India

LIS Education in India has its tracings to 1911 when the first training course was started in Baroda by W.A. Borden, Asa Don Dickenson, the librarian of Punjab University also organised a library science training course of three months duration in 1915. The growth and development of LIS schools became quite steady in the post independence period as it synchronised with the growth of the institutions of higher learning, libraries, documentation and information centres and similar other information systems attached to other organisations.

Modes of LIS Education Programmes

In addition to the regular on-campus LIS education programmes, some distant Education Institutions and Open Universities are offering LIS education programmes through distant mode. Distance Education has great potential to serve multitudes of eager learners. Being flexible in nature, it can be adopted by individuals who are place bound and have employment or house commitments. The Institute of Correspondence Education (I.C.E.) University of Madras was the first one to start one year MLIS course through correspondence. According to the then Co-ordinator Late Prof. P. Gangadhara Rao "There were number of representations from the working librarians to introduce MLIS through DE". Thus the seed planted by Late Prof. P. Gangadhara Rao has spread its roots widely, and motivated other universities like Annamali and IGNOU to start MLIS through DE.

Objectives of the Present Study

The aim of the present study is:

(a) to trace out the foundations of LIS curriculum & its characteristics.

(b) to compare and contrast the curricular programmes offered through on-campus and off-campus LIS education programmes, taking into consideration, the factors such as the syllabi, methods of teaching, hours of teaching, practicals component and attendence etc.

(c) to identify the limitations in the existing curricular programmes and to propose suggestions for its improvement.

The scope of the present study has been confined to the curricular programmes of degree level which includes B.LISc & MLISc Programmes. The study of research programmes may form a further area of study.

Restructuring of LIS Curriculum Programmes

Lib. & Inf. Science education is largely a 20th century phenomena. It is a professional education which brings efficiency, competency, confidence and leadership of personnel. Hence the education offered in the library schools has to be in relation with the realities of library work.

We are now moving to a relatively new concept namely 'Information Society'. Infact we live in what Alvin Toffler calls Infrosphere in which all information, past and present produced anywhere and everywhere in the world constitutes a vital resource as matter, energy and the like. Hence, to develop personnel adoptable to this new environment, the LIS schools have to develop suitable curriculum content. Further, the future development and growth of the discipline will be largely affected by the initial planning of the curriculum. Therefore, the curriculum planners have to ascertain what new learning experience could be offered to learners to make education more meaningful to meet the challenges for modern times. The new role expectations of library personnel demand newer concepts in LIS education.

The LIS educators have responded to the situation positively and rėvised, restructured the curriculum from time to time, accommodating the newer demands of information society.

Restructuring of library & inf. science curriculum is a major issue of concern to-day with the advent of new technologies, the situation in libraries & information centres is changing. These technologies facilitate better means of monitoring information use and the ability to make use of it for the management of information.

Thanks to UGC, it has taken curriculum development for LIS as thrust area and appointed a committee for the purpose. It has been taken up of late partly because the rate of change makes it difficult for LIS schools to keep pace with developments with in their normal views on process. The need to provide stability to students passing through the system is also essential. The curriculum followed so far was basically designed in 1960's and was based upon seemingly immutable trinity of library administration, bibliographic control and information retrieval methods. This still remains, although this common core is increasingly under challenge. Another important factor is the link between education and employment opportunities and more particularly what the employer experts from LIS education.

Comparison Between On-Campus & Off-Campus LIS Education Programmes

BLISc: All most all universities offer the same course for B.L.I.Sc except one or two who offers computer applications as one of the subjects in on-campus LIS education Programmes.

In off-campus B.LIS programmes, the courses are similar to those offered in on-campus except in one or two universities.

In most of the universities the duration for MLIS is one year but NEHU, Shillong, University of Madras, University of Mysore and Andhra University (from the academic year 1994) are offering two year composite course (while Calcutta University is offering two year part-time course and Srikrishna Devaraya University, Anantapur is offering two summers MLIS course).

From the study of syllabi in both on-campus and off-campus LIS education programmes it can be inferred that there is no variation in the course contents. However the of-campus programmes are a step in advance, in the introduction of courses like Bibliometrics, Computer Application, Research Methodology etc.

Methods of Teaching

In traditional on-campus LIS Education Programmes teaching is mainly imparted through regular class lectures, study tours and practical work. The students can clear their doubts immediately as the lecturers are always available. The regular student can benefit by the direct association with the teacher and peer group discussions. The class room teaching is supplemented by expert lectures, seminars, study tours etc.

On the other hand in off-campus LIS programmes, the students are always at a distance from the teacher. There will not be any direct communication between the teacher and the learner. However, to avoid these limitations, the Open Universities and Correspondence Institutions are conducting counselling and contact classes as a regular feature at selected study centres. Both theory and practical subjects will be explained to the students in these classes. Further, teaching in distant mode has been established through assignment evaluation. The teacher evaluates the assignments and through his comments imparts learning techniques to the students. The other modes of teaching in off-campus LIS programmes are through audio-video methods. However, the study material supplied is the main source for the off-campus learner.

Traditionally education has been directed towards giving to the student, facts of knowledge and training his mind. However, distant mode of education also follows the usual methods of teaching with special emphasis on self-study. Imparting self-education skills is necessary for the distant learners as the learner is in isolation, away from his peer group and the target. The emerging trends in information technologies and telecommunications have helped a lot for distant learners. For eg IGNOU is using television to broadcast its course in the morning transmission.

There is vivid variation in the methods of teaching through on-campus and off-campus programmes. Both the systems have their own advantages and limitations. The traditional methods of teaching are better accepted than the later. Being of recent origin, the off-campus teaching methods have to find their roots for their general acceptance.

Teaching hours

The U.G.C. Review Committee (1965) mentioned that the time-table of the BLIS course should provide for atleast 400 working hours during a session comprising lectures, tutorials and class practicals. About one half to class practicals and tutorials. The time-table of the M.L.I.Sc course should provide for 300-325 hours of lectures tutorials and seminars. The time needed for guiding the M.Lib.Sc students in their project work or for practicals should be in addition to the provision suggested above. But unfortunately none of the schools to-day are in a position to stick to these norms due to various impediments, chief among them are shortage of staff, large number of holidays, loss of working days due to strikes, pressure of examination schedule and many others.

On the other hand in off-campus LIS programmes, the Open Universities/Correspondence Institutions are organizing contact and counselling classes which provide face to face relationship between the students and teachers and provides the student to clarify his doubts in the subjects. It is observed that the number of days for such classes are varying from course to course and from university to university. For example BRAOU is conducting contact classes on every second saturday and two sundays in the month. Besides it has a schedule of compulsory contact programmes for 10-15 days having 8 hours duration for a day. Madras University is conducting one month contact & counselling classes during summer vacation i.e. May & June, Annamali University also organizing contact classes of 45 days duration.

As distance education is student oriented and depends mainly on study material, the hours of teaching are not comparable with on-campus programmes. The on-campus students are benefited by the seminars, study tours and direct contact with the teachers.

Practical Component

In on-campus programmes, the students do their practical work i.e. classification and cataloguing regularly under the guidance of the teachers. The concerned schedules are always at hand for the regular student to clear his doubts immediately by consulting the lecturer.

On the otherhand in off-campus programmes, the distant student is always at a loss in practical work. He has to depend on study materials and work hard to acquire better knowledge of practical experience. the schedules are not available to him. However, inservice candidates have fair chances with practical work.

'Computer application in Information Storage and Retrieval' is included in the curriculum of both on-campus & off-campus LIS programmes. The main limitation is although many universities are offering computer course in their curricula, the practical knowledge is not imparted and hands on practice is not available as the departments are not provided with computer systems. This is the situation prevailing in on-campus & off-campus programmes. Hence the knowledge acquired by both students is the same.

Attendance

Attendance is not compulsory for off-campus students. They are allowed to write the exams without attending the contact classes and counselling programmes. In on-campus programmes also in some universities attendance is not strictly followed. There are occasions when students are allowed to give examinations without full attendance. However, in some universities 10% of attendance is made compulsory and in some off-campus programmes also for eg. BRAOU attendance to contact programmes is compulsory for appearing the examinations.

Conclusion

To conclude, all areas of LIS need to be enriched through new knowledge and new methods of teaching and training. The curriculum can never be static and must always change as the frontiers of knowledge expand with time. Keeping in view, the basic considerations and the developments that are taking shape under the direction of U.G.C. the curriculum planners should always aim at training the LIS students with sound innovative vigour and approach.

The off-campus LIS education programmes are new to India, However these programmes provide an excellent opportunity for the interested students who are unable to attend the campus programmes because of their personal reasons.

The comparative study reveals that there is not much variation between on-campus and off-campus library and information science education programmes regarding curriculum. However, the off-campus programmes are much advanced by the inclusion of computer applications as one of the subjects.

The method of teaching is different in off-campus programmes as it is mainly student oriented and the study material supplied is the only source for the distant learner.

The on-campus students are more benefited in hours of teaching as they spend more time for practical work like classification and cateloguing under the guidance of teachers.

In the computer operations both on-campus and off-campus students are in the same position due to the absence of computer systems.

Regarding attendance, both on-campus and off-campus programmes are making it compulsory to give the examinations.

Suggestions

The comparative study of curriculum and other factors in on-campus and off-campus library and information science education programmes indicates need for modification in the curriculum. The following few suggestions may be considered to improve the existing situation.

1. To establish an accreditation body for library and information science education programmes to achieve

standardization. *Otherwise, there are one year B.L.I.Sc. one year M.L.I.Sc., two year M.L.I.Sc programmes, some under science faculty and some under Arts Faculty.*

2. U.G.C. has to insist on all institutions that impart LIS education to follow the recommendations of UGC : CDC report to achieve uniformity.
3. To make one year apprenticeship compulsory after M.L.ISc. to overcome the variations in course contents and methods of teaching etc. This solves the problems of insufficient practical knowledge.
4. Introduction of new courses, like Information Economics, Marketing of Information services has to be made both in on-campus and off-campus LIS programmes.
5. As the distant-learner depends mainly on study material supplied, the course contents should be revised atleast once in every five years.
6. The electronic media available should be used in addition to the personal contact programmes to teach the off-campus students.

Reference

1. Barron, Daniel D: "Distance education and the closing of American library school. *The Library quarterly* 61(3), July 1991.
2. Good *C.V. ed.*, Dictionary of Education, New York 1959.
3. Hayes, R.M. "Core curriculum for library and Information Science Education" in 'Library Education Programmes in developing countries with special reference to Asia" ed by Russell Bowden. The Library Association, London 1982.
4. Horton: As quoted in Lancter F.W's : Implications for library and information science Education. *Library Trends (winter). 1984.*
5. Lancaster. F.W. "Further Librarianship preparing for an unconventional career" *Wilson Library Bulletin. May. 1982.*
6. Wiggins. Robert: Distributed information processing. travels and implications. *ASLIB Proceedings* 37(2) 1985, 74.

16

CONTINUING EDUCATION FOR LIBRARY PROFESSIONALS AND TEACHERS IN LIBRARY AND INFORMATION SCIENCE : A STUDY OF PROGRAMMES CONDUCTED BY ACADEMIC STAFF COLLEGES

N.B. Pangannaya
V.G. Talawar

Introduction

Education and training are life long processes. The acquisition of a professional qualification is not the end in itself. Infact, it serves as a means to acquire more competence and confidence in the person. Basic theory and practical techniques are inseperable entities of Library and Information Science (LIS) education. Professional competence need to be sharpened through persuing professional journals; attending conferences; discussing with the colleagues and by constant practical experience. Most of the academic libraries, particularly college libraries are hardly exposed to the above situations. On the other hand, ever increasing new knowledge, new tools of information technology, multimedia and non-print materials, and the winds of change witnessed in the information seeking behaviour and information gathering habits of the user community, all demanding more skills and sophisticated approaches in information handling and dissemination.

Establishment and Academic staff Colleges

The National Education Policy 1986 formulated by the Government of India has emphasized among many other things, the need for upkeeping knowledge and teaching skills in the teachers by providing short term refresher courses, orientation programmes, workshops etc. This resulted in establishing 45 Academic Staff Colleges at various universities in India. The host universities are required to provide basic infrastructural facilities like building for office, class rooms, accomodation for participants etc. Where as UGC, provides 100% financial assistance to organise refresher courses and orientation programmes and to meet expenses towards staff salary, equipment and library books. Each college has an Advisory Committee under the Chairmanship of Vice-chancellor of respective university. The Director of the Academic Staff College normally be the Ex-Officio Member and Convener of the committee. Other members ranging between 9 to 11 consist of Deans of different faculties of the host university and the other universities coming under the catchment area, Director's of College Development Council and other experts in education field. The colleges organise programmes throughout the year for lecturers in degree colleges and in universities.

Programmes for LIS Professionals in Mysore University Academic Staff College

The Mysore University Academic Staff College established in 1988 has organised succesfully 95 Refresher Courses and 25 Orientation Programmes for lecturers / library professionals in degrees colleges and universities. It has also organised one workshop for Degree College Principals, three Computer Awareness Training Programmes for principals, teachers, administrators. In all the college has organised 125 programmes covering 3861 teachers, librarians, administrators etc till December 1995.

Of the 94 subject refresher courses that the college has conducted hitherto, 5 are Refresher Courses in LIS. Out of total 3029 participants undergone these subject course, 226 are LIS teachers and practicing library professionals. In addition, 26 librarians have benefitted by orientation programmes. Of the total 226 LIS professionals who have undergone refresher courses 181 were men and 45 were women and they were drawn from 9 different states.

The state wise distribution of librarians and teachers in LIS who have undergone the programmes is detailed in Table 1 given at next page.

Table 1: Statewise distribution of LIS professionals who have undergone Refresher Courses

Sl. No.	State / University		No. of Librarians / LIS professionals undergone RC
1.	Karnataka		176
	University of Mysore	41	
	Bangalore University	29	
	Mangalore University	28	
	Kuvempu University	29	
	Karnataka University	27	
	Gulbarga University	22	
		176	
2.	Andhra Pradesh		16
3.	Kerala		16
4.	Tamil Nadu		10
5.	Maharastra		3
6.	Pondichery		2
7.	Orissa		1
8.	Haryana		1
9.	Meghalaya		1
		Total:	226

Objectives of Refresher Courses in LIS

The following are the broad objectives of the Refresher courses organised for librarians and LIS professionals:

(1) Update the knowledge of working librarians and teachers in LIS in various branches in the field;

(2) Equip them with latest information in different areas of LIS;

(3) Discuss the various problems that the LIS teachers and practicing library professionals encounter in class-room teaching and library organisation management respectively and find suitable solutions to them;

(4) Discuss the contents of core syllabus of LIS courses

of various Universities and suggest necessary modifications if required;

(5) Equip teachers and librarians with needed skills so as to make teachers to impart better education to their students and to prepare librarians to serve their users better.

Course Structure and Duration

The duration of Refresher Courses is four weeks consisting of 96 sessions of one and half hours bringing the total hours in each programme to 144. Of these 96 sessions, nearly 80% are devoted for upgradation of the subject and 20% sessions are meant for general topics. The methods adopted for imparting include lecture-cum-discussions, demonstrations, participant seminars, group discussions, filed work etc. The break up of duration for each method is given below in Table 2.

Table 2

Sl. No.	Method Adopted	Average % of sessions devoted in each programme.
1.	Lecture - cum - discussions	54%
2.	Demonstrations / practicals	16%
3.	Participant seminars and group discussions	18%
4.	Field work / Education tour	6%
5.	Panel Discussion	6%
		100%

More emphasis on the use of newer technologies like overhead projectors, slide projectors and computers was given to expose and acquaint the participants with them. Also, interaction by participants with resource persons and as well from among themselves was encouraged through participant seminars, group discussions etc. to make the programme more lively, practible and participative.

Resource Persons

The resource persons for delivering lectures and to lead

demonstrations etc. are the experienced and scholarly persons invited from different universities research institutions, industries and such other organisations. The resource persons are teachers as well as practitioners not only in LIS but also in education, educational administration, management and computer science. The number of resource persons invited in each programme varied between 30 & 45, and the sessions each resource person handled vary between 2 & 4.

Reading Material

In each programme the teacher - librarian participants are provided with reading material in a bound book form consisting of texts / synopsis of topics dealt by each resource person, copies of relevant articles published in journals, papers presented in seminar by participants etc.

Facilities for Participants

The outstation participants are provided with accomodation and food facilities apart from travelling allowance to attend to the programme, where as local participants are provided with working lunch and tea/coffee in between sessions in the morning and evening. They are also provided with local conveyance allowance of Rs. 10/ - per day on working days. The participants apart from having Academic Staff College library for their reference and borrowing, an access to the resources of university main library has also been provided. Each participant is provided with 2 borrowers tickets to enable them to borrow needed documents from the main library. This facilitated participants to find useful materials for preparing for seminars and for discussions. The resident participants are also provided with T.V. facility to spend their leisure time.

Subject Themes Covered in Refresher Courses

The course co-ordinator appointed for organising the course are given full freedom to consult colleagues in the department and other professionals in the field and also working librarians in colleges and universities and design course contents and also select suitable resource persons keeping in view the norms provided by the UGC. Thus, opinion of the Faculty members in the Department of LIS, peer group from outside formed the basis for selection of themes for the course. Further, opinion sought by the participants librarians at the end of each programme were also considered in designing contents for the future programmes. The areas thus, covered broadly include the following:

Table 3: Areas covered in 5 Refresher Courses

Sl. No.	Areas covered in Refresher Courses
1.	Role of Academic Library in learning and development.
2.	Ethical and social responsibilities of librarians.
3.	User needs, user behaviour, user studies and user education.
4.	Information resource development : Quality vs quantity.
5.	Problems of collection development.
6.	Effective use of library resources and services.
7.	Auditing for effective library management.
8.	Trends in information retrieval systems and information storage media.
9.	Communication and Interpersonal relations in libraries.
10.	Public relations in libraries.
11.	Role of Library Associations in professionals development.
12.	National Information policies and strategies.
13.	Library Networks and Networking.
14.	Budget preparation and financial management.
15.	Research methods and quantitative techniques in LIS and areas and Research in Library and Information Science.
16.	Planning, designing and preparation of various information products and services.
17.	Information technology and impact on libraries, selection & procure ment.
18.	Computer applications to libraries.
19.	Library software packages; features, selection, procurement and use.
20.	CDS / ISIS and its application to libraries.
21.	Multimedia : current trends.
22.	National and international bibliographic databases : features and their use.
23.	Economics and marketing of information, information products and services.
24.	Conservation and preservation of library materials.
25.	Human resource development and Personnel Management in LIS.

In addition to above themes, many areas like effective use of space, problems of stock verification and weeding out, problems of library professionals and professional excellence etc. are also covered.

Evaluation of the courses

At the end of each programme oral opinion as well as written feedback relating to programme and facilities are sought from each participant. Further assessment of each resource person, relevance and coverage of the topic dealt etc. is also sought. A summary of the assessment of 5 refresher courses:

Table 4: Over all Assessment of the Courses on the Basis of Participants Feed back at the end of each Programme.

Sl. No.	Description	Opinion Expressed by 226 participants of 5 RC in LIS (in %)
1.	Extent of participation	
	(i) Everybody participated enthusiastically	76.35
	(ii) Participation was satisfactory	23.12
	(iii) Participation not satisfactory	0.53
2.	Resource Persons	
	(i) Very competent	69.90
	(ii) Competent	30.10
	(iii) Not so competent	0.00
3.	Reading Materials	
	(i) Sufficient	67.5
	(ii) Not sufficient	27.5
	(iii) Not at all sufficient	3.75
	(iv) No opinion	1.25
4.	Library Facilities	
	(i) Good	69.85
	(ii) Satisfactory	27.47
	(iii) Not so satisfactory	2.15
	(iv) No opinion	0.53

Sl. No.	Description	Opinion Expressed by 226 participants of 5 RC in LIS (in %)
5.	Hostel facilities	
	(i) Good	68.29
	(ii) Satisfactory	19.35
	(iii) Not so satisfactory	1.61
	(iv) No opinion	10.75
6.	Duration	
	(i) Too long	27.43
	(ii) Just all right	63.44
	(iii) Not at all	3.22
	(iv) No opinion	5.91
7.	Impact of the programme Broadening the approach	
	(i) To a great extent	76.36
	(ii) To some extent	22.04
	(iii) Not at all	0.53
	(iv) No opinion	1.07
8.	Inspiring	
	(i) To agreat extent	76.35
	(ii) To some extent	23.65
	(iii) Not at all	0.00
	(iv) No opinion	0.00
9.	Skill Development	
	(i) Adequate	83.33
	(ii) Not so adequate	16.13
	(iii) Not at all adequate	0.54
10.	Possibilities of Implementation	
	(i) To a great extent	48.92
	(ii) To some extent	50.00
	(iii) Not at all possible	1.08
	(iv) No opinion	

A look at the data in the table gives an impression that the courses conducted have largely enhanced the knowledge and skill of the librarians and LIS teachers. However, the possibilities of application of knowledge and skills acquired through these programmes seem to be not much encouraging. It is therefore, felt essential to review the programmes thoroughly and findout the weakness in the organisation of present programmes and design the future programmes to make them more and more need based.

Limitations

Some of the limitations observed in the present programmes are:

1. Inadequate infrastructural facilities and teaching aids like computers, CD-ROM and E-mail workstations etc.
2. Lack of skilled personnel to impart practical training to participants.
3. Lack of motivation among participant LIS professionals.
4. Poor facilities and apathy of management in respective colleges from where the participant librarians are deputed.
5. There exists no fitting model for systematic evaluation of the programmes and participants undergoing the programme.

Suggestions for Improvement of the Programmes

Following are some of the suggestions to improve the present LIS training programmes in ASC's.

Study of areas of training

It is necessary to study the training need and the areas in which the trainee needs to be updated his/her skill and knowledge before the course design and implementation of the course. If the training is designed on the basis of established needs, better implementation is possible and also the need motivates the trainee to take the programme seriously and be more participative and attentive.

Theme oriented programmes

It is better to organise the Refresher Courses on specific themes such as computer application to libraries, information technology, planning, designing and marketing of information products and services etc. This facilitates to delimit the scope of the area and give indepth training to the participants.

Short term programmes

There could be short term courses of 5 days to 10 days duration on specific topics such as hands on training on CDS / ISIS, design of specific information products etc. This will help in reducing cost, it also makes the programme more meaningful and directly useful. Further more trainees could be covered within limited time span.

Emphasis on practice

Courses need be more practice oriented rather than theory. Lecturing should be minimised and participants be made to work and learn different techniques, methods, procedures etc. For this purpose the training institute has to develop certain models on specific themes.

Limited Number of Participants

It is appropriate to have between 20 and 25 participants in each programme. This facilitates economy and at the same time helps to maintain quality as individual attention in imparting training is possible.

Orientation for College Principal and Management

There is a dire need that the Management and the Principals of colleges realise the importance of libraries. As such an orientation for them is required. This will help to create conducive environment for librarians to implement the knowledge and skill acquired during training.

Conclusion

Of late, our country has realised the importance of training for the job of librarians. Indeed, good many opportunities are open today for working librarians and LIS teachers to uptodate their knowledge and skill. the UGC has done commendable job by providing an avenue to working librarians and LIS teachers in colleges and universities to undergo Refresher Courses and Orientation Programmes through Academic Staff Colleges. This has opened indeed a new chapter in the history of academic libraries and librarianship. Though, the present training programmes conducted by ASC's have certain limitations let us hope, that this beginning will help to transform the library system in our country and lead libraries towards modernisation.

Section VI
LIS Profession and Professionalism

17

TRADITIONAL LIBRARIES TO AUTOMATED MEGASYSTEM: NEEDED ATTITUDINAL CHANGES

Anand P. Srivastava

Social and technological developments have always made our institutions to change adopting new developments. The 'library' is one such institution. How far the modern technological developments have changed the 'library' in last 30 years? This question has to be asked by all concerned, particularly by the librarians and the library authorities of the nation. In the library world, three major revolutions have taken place so far

1. *During post war era (1945 to 1960s):* movement of library consortia started, e.g. BLCMP, CRL of USA (1949).

2. *During 1970s:* the advent of computing networks, and

3. *During 1980s:* development of on-line knowledge for use by library clientele.

These three revolutions demand numerous attitudinal changes in transforming traditional libraries into an automated system. The impact of these revolutions has been on all organisational sectors of library and information, viz. the library authority, the library materials, library clientele and the library staff, as the following visual shows

Some of the important attitudinal changes needed are

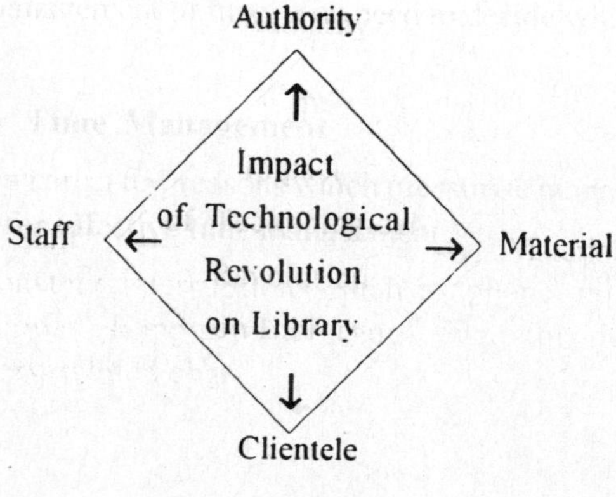

1. The library has to move from the state of being merely a passive consumer of knowledge to the level of becoming a platform for generation, exchange and utilisation of knowledge (KGEU).
2. The attitude should move from sole acquisition to collaborative access by interfacing with computer technology.
3. So far the organisation and retrieval of knowledge in libraries has been on traditional lines. Now, the new technology has brought in a quantum change, wherein retrieval is done from on-line catalogues and texts or through searching bibliographical databases.
4. From searching through a traditional library classification scheme or through a particular traditional type of catalogue, we have to move to the details of searching behaviour of users and natural language interfacing, with linguistic interpretation in a syndetic manner.
5. Earlier, users used to identify their materials themselves from an organised library. Now, the librarian has become *de facto* intermediary between the user and the knowledge sought. Hence, the librarian shall have to analyse and synthesis "user environment" and "knowledge environment". For this kind of task, the librarian shall have to
   (i) use methods from communication theory, psychology, knowledge classification and sociology, and
   (ii) develop theoretical bases of information / knowledge needs of various types of users, by going beyond "mission-oriented" and "documented-centred" approaches so that necessary postulates are developed fro predicting knowledge needs of various sectors.
6. So far the librarian was the sole agent for organising and retrieving knowledge. Now this traditional role is being gradually replaced by that of assisting users to perform on-line searching. This new role requires the librarian to impart instructions to users, through formal and informal methods, until they achieve independence.

7. The greatest need for attitudinal changes is for the "bosses" of parental organisations of libraries with regard to fund granting, network development and on-line utility of knowledge. For example, with a non-recurring grant of about Rs. 150,000,000/- (Rs. Fifteen crores only) for on-line connection of about 300 libraries all over India and about the same amount as annual recurring expenses, the journals, which already are on on-line in the whole world, can be made available to users in the whole of India. But it is difficult to find people in power who could support this kind of planning. All are busy in applying merely a shot-gun approach in scattering funds and grants in primitive styles.
8. Our governments and educational administrators should identify the following
   (i) What models of information provision can provide access for all through commercial enterprises?
   (ii) What should be the role of nationwide libraries within the universe of information delivery to all?
   (iii) How to make the nation's major libraries as one, well knit, megasystem by liberating them from individual sovereign owners? Is individual and exclusive ownership of a library any more feasible?
   (iv) Is there any justification for categorising libraries into various types - academic, public and special?
   (v) Can we not form a corporation of all libraries in each city and connect them statewise and regionwise to make one national grid?

   All these factors are important in the modern technological information society.

9. The Sixth Law - Common Corporate Authority for Libraries. The theory of evolution works not only in the case of biological life but also in the case of institutions. The library movement started with the types of libraries - academic, public and special libraries-with their vertical structure and government.

Now, the cost factor, modern technology, and new communication devices have forced the conversion or metamorphosis of vertical structure and government of libraries into a horizontal structure and government of libraries and resources. Now the law is, libraries at one geographical place should be under one common corporate authority for rendering services to all through hook-up. You can take it as the sixth law of library science or the extension of the fifth law, as you please. But the fact is that the sovereignty of the parent institution over its library stands diluted. For example, the University of Delhi can no more have its library system as its exclusive possession. The modern librarianship is largely beyond the walls of the concerned library. Call DELNET, BONET, CALIBNET, or any net and hook-up of local, regional, national or international nature. It is under these vertical and horizontal dimensions that the modern librarianship shall be required to live and grow. Historically speaking, such a metamorphosis is neither strange nor unnatural. Remember that three hundred years ago we had our individual wells for water supply and individual lanterns for light supply. Today, we have a joint water supply corporation and a common electricity undertaking. Similarly, if we today have a separate Library System of Delhi University, Patel Chest Institute Library, CSIR Library, DESIDOC, INMAS Library, Solid State Physics Library, etc., all within one mile radius, nothing shall stop it tomorrow to develop into one library authority or at least a consortium. Similarly, day after tomorrow nothing shall be able to stop the emergence of Library Authority covering Delhi University, Jawaharlal Nehru University, National Physical Laboratory and other libraries in Delhi. The modern man run multinational companies and other super organisations. Why can a Board not run information services for a city? I see no hurdles except the lack of conceptual innovation on out part. So, let us hope that our successors shall able to run mega units of library services in the country in near future.

10. The libraries in our country had for a long time been "more or less a useless conventional accessory." In the information age, the libraries are the first essential requirement for progress prosperity and happiness. Such a complete break away from the traditional notion about libraries and their services must transform the attitudes of people in power in all sectors of the Indian Society.

The passport for living in the world of XXI century is the ability for "independent learning" and the visa for entry into it is acquaintance with "information technology." It is a global question today on all campuses - from Harvard to Delhi - as to which section of a university should have specific responsibility for cultivating abilities of "learning skills" and literacy of "information technology" in the youth. It is a university graduate who becomes a school teacher or goes to various other key-role positions. If she or he is equipped with learning skills (LS) and information technology (IT) during college life one can take the mission to schools and other places in society. Various subjects under the faculties of sciences, humanities and social sciences have clearly found "learning skills" (LS) and "information technology" (IT) exogenous to their disciplines and have, therefore, allocated these species to the genus of library and media centres in educational institutions. This allocation has been through unanimous resolution because there is no other claimant of these roles in educational institutions. The result is that for developing independent learning skills and for cultivating literacy in information technology the library and librarians have moved into the centre in schools and colleges.

Once the library obtained such a favourable biological mutation, the human factor (in the librarian) responsible in moving the library for such important roles is bound to obtain ratiocinative value. But, we must know how we should really work. The real attitude prevailing in our educational culture appears to be "Library is important. But the Librarian (as the prime mover of library) may not be really important. At least, she or he does not appear to be able to command that importance." We somehow forget that the librarian can help people in the following areas.

(i) there is very wide range of learning resources which should be used in schools and colleges, for different ages and abilities,

(ii) teachers and students need assistance and guidance from the librarian for using these resources effectively, and

(iii) there should be a sequential programme for developing learning skills from primary to post-secondary stages, for which resources may be available for use within the institution concerned or outside the institution.

A qualified librarian, possessing the same academic credentials as teachers and others do, can contribute in proper environment, in cultivating learning skills. The librarian can work constructively on learning skills curriculum, which contains the following:

(i) ability to locate and select resources,

(ii) ability to integrate and interpret the contents in resources,

(iii) ability to communicate the acquired knowledge and understanding through general patterns. These vital attitudinal changes have to take place in our educational system in favour of the librarians.

A great deal of attitudinal changes have to take place concerning the form of materials. The hard bound printed form of materials. The hard bound printed from of documents has ruled the world for many centuries. Due to various factors, knowledge containers have obtained micro forms. The clientele of libraries shall have to develop a habit of using the modern micro forms for knowledge utilization. The miles and miles of stacking is no more possible. Millions of books can be accommodated on hard "disks". These innovations cannot be avoided for long. We all have to develop suitable notions for using micro forms of knowledge in our daily life.

These are some of the attitudinal changes that we have to bring about in ourselves in the present information age. It is necessary that the people associated with information field develop an awareness for these details.

18

CHANGING TRENDS IN LIBRARY PROFESSION

S. Gopalakrishanan

Introduction

It is an "age of unreason" where the changes being marked by "discontinuous", cannot be predicted, often do not follow a pattern or linear direction.[1] New Technology has led to a created environment where quick response to changing circumstances is often more advantageous than careful planning.[2]

Information will be continually assembled in new and unpredictable way. due to this implication of information all the professions are undergoing a sea-change. Turnarounds, Mergers and acquisitions, diversifications, strategic alliances and other aspects take place in vast scale. All these are pursued with the goal of achieving the cutting-edge of competence to face the emerging competition with fortitude.

No doubt, development of high technology witnessed a changing emphasis in the role of information and its management. This changing emphasis necessities the information professionals to be exposed to the new technologies and modernise their infrastructure to the future needs of the users.

Increasing rate of innovation and rapid development in higher technology induce remarkable change in job qualification and substantial transformation of library structure. In this regard Barbara Quint also succinctly pinpointed that Information professionals must accept the necessity and take on the task of restructuring their services.[3]

Over the years there have been dire predictions that computerization would spell the total end of library and information work. What has in fact happened is that the boundaries between the roles of libraries, information scientist and computer specialist have become more fluid and less distinct. The career opportunities have widened, not diminished and the information technology has an increasingly valuable contribution to make to the work of the organization.

Current trend

Basically, the role of Librarian, retrieving information and providing the same for the right person at the right time, has not changed through the decades. Over the decades only this objective has been pursued but the technique of retrieving information and providing the same that was used have changed. Outstanding characteristics of the professionals through the centuries have been a willingness to provide the information and an intellectual curiosity about its utility. "Why?"," What?" and "How?" have all served to stimulate an effort to find required answers to many types of queries. Another characteristic associated is the ability to access the views of the users. The library services are to be organized and properly operated, taking advantage of the technological developments. Until recently it was enough to acquire the ability to manage complex queries and to provide information.

To-day libraries face an era of turbulent change, the sources of which are varied. The libraries and information centers are no longer a physical location but instead a conduit for information. It is no longer a place, but instead a function. With some effort, librarians learnt to cope with the problems that flowed along a reasonable predicable course. The greater challenge by far, is to cope with high speed change subject to frequent in directions. An accelerated pace is the only thing that will keep from being overrun by every one else on the move. Unless librarians learn to manage dramatic change it will not be possible to survive in to-day's conceptional business.

Acceptance and Integrating

The concept of providing universal, ubiquitous access to information is alluring, the real challenge to-day is to provide only the best information to answer a particular question at a very specific point in time, and at a reasonable cost. It takes too long and that in the long run it is a waste of human potential; and the utility of information for the right purpose might be delayed. In other words specific technology that develops a "function culture" with respect to complex system. Librarians must know how to manage and interact with complex information system consisting of computer networks.

Profession like ours which has constantly to interact with society and technological environment, it is essential to review periodically its performance, status and to foresee the environmental changes so that those changes can be appropriately responded to.

It is necessary to know how to think in broad outline that systematically incorporate a variety of information and knowledge. The human resources that are being invested in making new knowledge readily accessible are disproportionately small compared to those invested in generating it. The net result is that new knowledge is not being asborbed into the culture as readily as it is being generated, and some of the value of that knowledge is lost by it not being readily accessible to the people who need it. The essential task is distilling new knowledge from the literature and restructuring it for efficient dissemination. The emerging need necessitates that something must be done. The old attitude has had to change from a sort of benevolence given in terms of liberty. The first evolution and obsolescence of newer technologies, necessitate to have a basic substantial grounding for professionals, to which specialized knowledge could be added during the professions careers. It is clear without up-to-date technological knowledge it is impossible to deal with information explosion.

Hallmark of a profession is a commitment to valuable service and has two facts: one is the satisfaction of the serving society and the other is a professional's pride. All the professions, to state the obvious, include a range and abilities from low to high.

Need for New Breed

In the present era of economic imbalance and escalating competition the professional winners will be those who seize and exploit technology as a strategic weapon. Now what is required is the emerging wisdom, thus indicates not mere librarian. The new paragon is an executive who can envision a future and inspire colleagues to join in building the library for the future, perhaps the most noticeable departure from conventional practice. Inevitably, many of us view technology with suspicion and fear. At present the librarians do not changes, but instead think how to adopt it. The problem poised before us are:

- How to position among fertile technologist?
- `How to steer it away from those that are played out?
- Hot to seize and exploit technology as a strategic weapon?

Since the future is hidden from us, till it arrives, we have to look to the past for light on it. This is the period of structural crisis and a time of confusion about the direction of improvement, because *intrusion* of technology aimed at this end has offered little response. How shortsighted, after all, in the process of investing funds to this new technology from "Library Profession: Save from Ruin".

Now-a-days the chief competition for the library professionals are the professionals from management and computers. To-day computer professionals found *intrusive* into library profession Technology advances in recent years have not only eliminated time and other barriers, but also change the way of many professionals in their operations.

Emergency of New Breed

"What will the information profession look like in future years and will there be one?" The doubt gets further strengthened by the successful transmission in management from scientific management era to system and structure era. It is not yet possible to blue print the managerial style of the future. But it is possible to analyze some of the forces that will shape it. Management of the future is a combination of functionally related computerized sub-system and skilled people who will perform the functions. In a complex, unpredictable and rapidly changing world the organization that recognize, utilize and appreciate the poineering spirit of the information age. No longer the conventional leadership will help to manage the present organizational setups. Intelligence and innovations are both, the products and process of information age which values the managers what they know now and what they can learn in the future.

In the new age, the new management personnel, is the person of the mind, not the body. Brain or brawn will keep any organization competitive. Management practices that evolved during the industrial age are inadvertently undermining the value of the brain power. It is brain power, not physical labour that will play the central role of the economic success in the near future. These type of professionals will be engaged in the complex problem solving not bureaucratic, drudgery or mechanical routine, they are imaginative and original, not docile and obedient. Their work is challenging, not repetitions and their results are rarely predictable or quantifiable.

The new leadership style termed as THINKOVATION (THINKing + innOVATION)[4] one of the most significant advancement expected in the next decade. If these new breed of worker finds intrusion in the library profession then the statement "Library profession: will there be one" will become true.

Curricular Implications

One of the functions of any professional education is to impart the attitudes and values of the profession to its students. "The present system of library education does not seem to provide information professionals with the necessary intellectual abilities and inter personal skills. Looking at the prevailing system, attempts are being made by some schools to include modern methods of information technology, managerial skills and so on in the curricula." Hence information professionals could

- ensure that the information needs of the users are met and valued added and not merely menu-selected services provided.
- Move out of the library and find out how information is used and what types of information are needed.
- keep track of new developments in information technology and the newer media of communication.
- observe newly emerging information needs and target the appropriate information to users.
- practice co-operative problem-solving as a precursor to the work place environment.

It is also important to have attitudinal flexibility to nurture interpersonal relationships to accept the culture and ethics of the new environment/ Ability to take along with pressure of competition will be essential ingredients to succeed in the present dynamic work environment. Any tendency to stay at the surface without having insight to probe deep into intricacies would lead to formation of an idea of lack of maturity in the profession. Development of an executive skills is an arduous but achievable task spread over a period of time that requires a constant vigilance against dynamics of change which has not become more turbulent. Such a preparation will facilitate a quick absorption in the changed work environment.

Conclusion

The traditional paradigm of professionalism encourages a static condition which is incompatible with the dynamism inherent in a truly client-centered professional orientation in the present world. It is important to perceive the changes that may come about in the nature and scope of service provided to users. It is also essential to gear up ourselves to meet those changes and challenges.

The pace of change is so fast that unless we keep our sight, on to-morrow, it is possible to keep *in touch* with to-day. Therefore it is necessary to resolve to make concerted and dedicated efforts to prepare ourselves for the future. It is needless to say that the profession itself would be the biggest beneficiary in maintaining professional excellence. On the other hand, a failure on this front may threaten the survival of the profession in the long run. It is necessary to put in our best endeavors in discharging our responsibilities to justify the confidence that reposed instead of selling the profession to others.

References

1. Handy, C.: The Age of Unreason, Harvard Business School press, Boston, 1989.
2. Senge, P.M.: The Fifth Discipline, Double day, New York, 1990.
3. Quint, B.:"High risk on-line", *Searcher*, Jan 1995, pp 6-8.
4. Gopalakrishanan's. : "THINKOVATION: A new direction in management in the year 2000 and present direction of librarianship" Lecture Notes in ISTE Summer school on Recent trends in library management held at SJCE, Mysore during July 17-24, 1991.
5. Suseela Kumar: "How much good does the library do", *MALA News letter*, Vol. 8, No. 4, Oct. 1995

19

MEMBERSHIP OF COLLEGE AND UNIVERSITY LIBRARIANS IN PROFESSIONAL ASSOCIATIONS : A SURVEY

V. Pulla Reddy

Introduction

It is necessary for the members of any profession to involve in different activities of professional development such as keeping abreast of the latest developments in the profession by reading professional literature, holding of membership in different professional organisations, participating in conferences, seminars, workshops and refresher courses, and contributing to professional knowledge in the form of books and articles in order to become successful practitioner and there by raising the status of the profession in the society. The extent of involvement of the members in the above said activities of professional development also reveal their professional zeal and interest in the profession. It is essential to conduct the surveys on the involvement of the members of the profession in those activities in order to take steps, if necessary, for making them to involve in those activities. The present survey makes an effort to study one of the activities of professional development namely membership of practitioners of librarianship in different professional associations. However, due to limitations of time and cost, it is restricted to study the membership of college and university librarians working in Delhi.

Objectives

The following are the specific objectives of the present study:

1. To know the extent of holding membership in different professional associations,
2. To know the differences if any in holding the membership between college and university librarians and junior and senior librarians; and

3. To know the type of membership they were holding in national and regional associations and the period from which they were holding ordinary membership.

Methodology

The term 'librarian' in this study means any professionally qualified employee, who is working in a professional capacity at any level in a library. Persons, who are working as a College Librarians or Assistant Librarians in universities or those working in equivalent cadres and above are treated as Senior Librarians. Persons who are working below the above mentioned cadres are treated as Junior Librarians.

Selection of the sample

The population in this study consists of professional staff of the college and university libraries of Delhi. The libraries attached to the institutions, which have the status of a university are also considered as university libraries. Due to the constraints of time and cost a random sample of 150 members has been drawn from the population. However, the investigator received complete responses only from 104 members.

Collection of data

The data were collected with the help of a questionnaire. The respondents were asked to write down the associations in which they were holding membership, type of membership, period from which they were holding membership, their scale of pay and type of the library in which they were working. The questionnaires were distributed and were collected from the respondents personally.

Analysis and results

Analysis of data reveals the following findings:

Membership in Associations

The distribution of professional staff according to the holding of membership in professional associations, type of the library and managerial level is shown in Table 1.

Table 1: Distribution of Professional staff according to the holding of membership, type of the library and managerial level

Membership	Library		Managerial Level		Total
	College	University	Junior	Senior	
Membership non-holders	16.7	25.7	34.6	11.5	23.1
Membership holders					
In 1 association	40.0	40.5	44.2	36.5	40.4
In 2 associations	33.3	23.0	15.4	36.5	26.0
In 3 and more than 3 associations	10.0	10.8	5.8	15.4	10.6
Sub-total	83.3	74.3	65.4	88.4	77.0
Grand Total	100.0 (n=30)	100.0 (n=74)	100.0 (n=52)	100.0 (n=52)	100.0 (n=104)

CHi square = 1.68 Chi square = 8.22

Degrees of freedom (d.f.) = 3 d.f. = 3

Not significant at .05 level Significant at .05 level.

It is evident from Table 1 that most of the professional staff (77%) are holding membership in one or more of the associations. It is also evident from it that 23.1% of them are not members of any association, 40.4% of them are members in one association, 26% of them are members in two associations and the remaining 10.6% of them are members in three or more than three associations.

It is also clear from it that there is no significant difference between college and university librarians in holding the membership in different professional associations. This is evidenced by Chisquare value, which is not significant at .05 level. However, there is significant difference in holding of membership in different associations between junior and senior librarians as evidenced by Chisquare test and the value is significant at .05 level with three degrees of freedom. That means senior librarians are holding memberships more in number campared to junior librarians.

Names of associations

If a person holds membership in more than one association, he is counted more than once while determining the number of members of each association. The names of associations in which professional staff are members and the number of members of each association are shown in Table 2.

Table 2: Names of Associations and Number of Members in each association

Name of association	No.	%	Rank
Delhi Library Association (DLA)	39	37.5	1
Indian Association of Academic Librarians (INDAAL)	38	36.5	2
Indian Library Association (ILA)	31	29.8	3
Indian Association of Special Libraries and Information Centres (IASLIC)	8	7.64	4
Association of Library and Information Services (ALIS)	4	3.85	5
Delhi University Professional Assistants Association	3	2.9	6
Staff Association of College Libraries (Delhi)	3	2.9	6
Association of Agricultural Librarians and Documentalists (India)	2	1.9	7
Rajasthan Library Association	2	1.9	7

Table 2 gives a list of associations in which professional staff are members. It is evident from it that most of the staff (37.5%) are members of DLA. It may be due to its being a local library association. Hence, DLA is getting first rank for having more number of professional staff as its members compared to other professional associations.

INDAAL is getting second rank for having more number of members. It may be due to its appropriateness in solving the problems of academic librarianship.

ILA and IASLIC are getting 3rd and 4th ranks respectively. It is also evident from it that only a few librarians are members in the remaining associations.

Membership in Delhi Library Association

The distribution of professional staff according to the type of membership in DLA, type of the library and managerial level is shown in Table 3.

Table 3: Distribution of Professional Staff according to the type of membership, type of the library and managerial level

Type of Membership	Library		Managerial level		Total
	College	University	Junior	Senior	
Life membership	16.7	14.8	15.4	15.4	15.4
Ordinary membership					
1-9 years	25.0	22.2	23.1	23.1	23.1
10 and above	25.0	18.5	15.4	23.1	20.5
Unanswered	33.3	44.4	46.2	38.5	41.0
Total 100.0	100.0 (n=27)	100.0 (n=12)	100.0 (n=26)	100.0 (n=13)	(n=39)
Percent	69.2	30.8	66.7	33.3	100

It is evident from Table 3 that most of the professional staff (84.6%) are holding ordinary membership and the remaining (15.4%) of them are life members. It is also clear from it that 23.1% of the professional staff are holding ordinary membership from 9 years, 20.5% of them are holding from 10 years or above 10 years and 41% of them have not answered.

It is evident from it that there is no considerable difference between college and university librarians and junior and senior librarians in holding the type of membership in DLA.

In the group of professional staff, who are members in DLA, most of them (69.2%) are from college libraries and the remaining (30.8%) are from university libraries. If managerial level of staff is considered, most of them (66.7%) are from junior level cadre and the remaining (33.3%) of them are from senior level cadre.

Membership in Indian Association of Academic Librarians

The distribution of professional staff according to the type of membership in INDAAL, type of the library and managerial level is shown Table 4.

Table 4: Distribution of Professional Staff according to type of membership, type of library and managerial level

Type of Membership	Library		Managerial level		Total
	College	University	Junior	Senior	
Life membership	00.0	00.0	00.0	00.0	00.0
Ordinary membership					
1 year	00.0	12.9	18.8	4.6	10.5
More than one year	71.4	71.0	56.2	81.8	71.1
Unanswered	28.6	16.1	25.0	13.6	18.4
Total	100.0 (n=7)	100.0 (n=31)	100.0 (n=16)	100.0 (n=22)	100.0 (n=38)
Percent	18.4	81.6	42.0	58.0	100.0

It is evident from Table 4 that all the professional staff are holding ordinary membership. It is clear from it that 10.5% of Professional staff are holding membership from one year, 71.1% of them are holding membership from more than one year and 18.4% of them have not answered.

In the group of professional staff, who are members of INDAAL, most of them (81.6%) are from university libraries and the remaining (18.4%) are from college libraries. If managerial level of staff is considered, most of them (58%) are from senior level cadre and the remaining (42%) are from junior level cadre.

Membership in Indian Library Association

The distribution of professional staff according to the type of membership in ILA, type of library and managerial level is shown in Table 5.

Table 5: Distribution of professional staff according to type of Membership, type of library and managerial level

Type of Membership	Library		Managerial level		Total
	College	University	Junior	Senior	
Life membership	6.3	20.0	16.7	12.0	12.9
Ordinary membership					

Type of Membership	Library		Managerial level		Total
	College	University	Junior	Senior	
1-4 years	25.0	46.7	83.3	24.0	35.5
5 and above	37.5	6.7	00.0	28.0	22.6
unanswered	31.3	26.7	00.0	36.0	29.0
Total	100.0	100.0	100.0	100.0	100.0
	(n=16)	(n=15)	(n=6)	(n=25)	(n=31)
Percent	51.6	48.4	19.4	80.6	100.0

It is evident from Table 5 that most of the professional staff (87.1%) are holding ordinary membership and the remaining of them (12.9%) are life members. It is also clear from it that 35% of professional staff are holding membership from 1-4 years, 22.6% of them are holding from 5 years or more than 5 years and 29% of them have not answered.

It is also evident from it that there is no considerable difference between college and university librarians and junior and senior librarians in holding the type of membership in ILA.

In the group of professional staff, who are members of ILA, nearly half of them (51.6%) are from college libraries and the remaining half (48.4%) are from university libraries. If managerial level of staff is considered most of them (80.6%) are from senior level cadre and the remaining (19.4%) are from junior level cadre.

Conclusions and Suggestions

Conclusions

The major findings of the present study are summarised below:

(i) Most of the professional staff (77%) are holding membership in any one or more of the professional associations.

(ii) There is no significant difference between college and university librarians in holding the membership in different professional associations.

(iii) Senior librarians are holding memberships in professional associations more in number compared to junior librarians.

(iv) Delhi Library Association gets first rank for having more number of professional staff working in college and university libraries of Delhi as its members compared to other associations. INDAAL, ILA and IASLIC get 2nd, 3rd and 4th ranks respectively in this regard.

(v) Most of professional staff are holding ordinary membership in DLA, INDAAL and ILA.

(vi) There is no considerable difference between college and university librarians and junior and senior librarians in holding the type of membership in DLA, INDAAL and ILA.

(vii) Among the group of professional staff, who are the members in DLA and ILA, most of them (69.2%) and 51.6%) respectively are from college libraries. However, in the case of professional staff, who are members in INDAAL, most of them (81.6%) are from university libraries.

(viii) Among the group of professional staff, who are the members in DLA, most of them (66.7%) are junior librarians. However, in the case of professional staff, who are members in INDAAL and ILA, most of them (58% and 80.6% respectively) are senior librarians.

Suggestions

1. About 23% of professional staff are not members in any professional association. Hence efforts are to be made to make them become members of professional associations.

2. Schools of Library and Information Science should motivate the students to become members of professional associations.

3. Research is to be carried out to find out the reasons for not becoming the members of any professional association.

The studies of this kind are to be carried out on professional staff working in college and university libraries in different regions of the country to confirm the above findings.

20

IMPACT OF INFORMATION TECHNOLOGY ON LIBRARY SCIENCE PROFESSION - NEED FOR REDEFINING OF ROLE & FUNCTIONS

Md. Gouse Riajuddin

Information Technology - Introduction

Information Technology is a term that has become part of our daily parlance. The ramifications of information technology has generated a variety of information products. It is all pervasive in that it has application at all stages of information work viz. the generation, organisation, storage, retrieval and dissemination of information. These products have mobility to move straight from the author to the targeted audience. Its role was most predominant at the stage of generation of information. Technologically the movement of information from person to person may not need intermediaries. But, there is need due to psychological, educational, economic and social needs. Technology in essence, has brought in a wide scope for facile capture, presentation and dissemination of information.

We are living in an information society: A society in the throes of an information revolution which has gathered momentum as a result of the convergence of computing and telecommunication and corresponding emergence of information technology.

The new technology has been described in various ways in the literature. The UNESCO definition of IT will be adopted, since it offers a particularly broad view of this rapidly evolving discipline. The people who witnessed this change would have been as amazed and thrilled as we are today, watching the revolutionary developments that are now taking place in information technology.

Impact of Information on Libraries

It has become common parlance that we are entering the "Information Age" we should like to take the reader with us on an exploratory voyage to the edge of some current information-age computer technology that may transform the library. A precondition for joining this expedition is an understanding of the "new world" which we hope to discover and build. It is a societal state in which the library has become one of the anchors of what we call "The Network Nation" an era in which the amalgamation of computers and communications will reduce the time and cost needed to span distances between people and information, and among people communicating, to practically zero.

In the process of changing the environment by way of search and research man has created a number of things for his comforts and to meet the social needs. The invention of computers for data analysis and information handlings is unique in this country and it has become and indispensable tool for every organisation to improve the efficiency. Libraries too come under the influence of computers from 1960 onwards and as a result electronic media in the form of tapes and disks is replacing the printed documents, as the most convenient channel of information communication.

Information Sources

The sources contain information of relevance to various types of uses and the task of the library is to access to the source either by getting copies of the sources or linking access to centres containing the information.

However, the availability of information resources on print, electronic and audiovisual media has made the situation more complex. It has been estimated that by 2001, publication in print-on-paper forms is the exception rather than the rule. While a few high-circulation journals have been able to retain their printed form, most of the research literature (whether in the science, social science or humanities) exists only in electronic versions. Some journals are issued on electronic media for use with domestic television receivers or home computers: these journals can also be accessed through the network of on-line service centres. Most journals, together with files of technical reports, patents, standards and specifications can still be obtained in paper or microform, but most of the use is now on-line. Technical reports are available in microform but rarely in paper from: again most of the use is through on-line access. Majority of secondary data bases (including some national bibliographies) exists only in machine-readable form, accessible through on-line terminals.

For popular magazines, fictions, other works of imagination and recreational materials in general, print on paper has been replaced much less extensively. While attempts have been made to publish such literature in electronic form, no significant market has yet developed. The great cost of publication on paper, however, including the escalating costs of distribution through "Conventional" mail service, has caused a very drastic reduction in the number of magazines available and most of them are now published on multimedia. It is just not economically feasible to sustain a print-on-paper publication unless an extremely large market can be reasonably assured.

Optical storage technology is removing the constraint previously exercised by the high storage cost of image information and encouraging the development of multi-media information files. Information systems are likely to exploit this multi-media potential to greater advantage in future by storing more full text graphical and image information. This is a digital optical disc like a music disc which can be produced inexpensively in large quantities. The size varies from 12" to 4.72" and in market the smaller ones are preferred on micro computers. They can hold 5,400 digital page images. CD-ROM are becoming the most important form of optical storage device for data base distribution. By juke box mechanism information can be retrieved from as many as 100 disks by random search through computer links.

The main reason given for reduced on-line use is that CD-ROM, are cheaper and are always available for searching and infact would be searched without any accompanying telecommunication difficulties. The following advantages of CD-ROMS have made them effective media for information storage.

(i) They can store as much as 6.4 Gigabite on a single double sided disc, produce full text products regardless of critical quantities of copies.

(ii) Complete individual full text compilations depending on the special needs of each library.

(iii) Expand the total storage capacity upto 13 terabyte

equivalent to more than 200 millions of pages. At present we witness the advent of erasable optical disks based on Magneto-optic technology providing 650 Megabyte on removable double side 5.25 inch disc.

Organisation and Storage of Information

The information acquired by a library or an information centre in different packages should be organised and stored. Here again conventional manual methods are fast giving way to the modern sophisticated methods made possible by information technology. The predominant practice in the storage of information is the computer according to pre-conceived systems suited for the purpose of their convenient and quick retrieval.

A point to be noted here is that there is a trend already evident of many libraries adopting technology for all or some of the operations in the library. Libraries and information centres are institutions concerned with the collection of the packaged information and its organisation, storage and dissemination. The acquisition, processing, storage, retrieval and dissemination were being done solely by the manual method until some years ago. In India, many of the special libraries, especially those functioning under the CSIR, and those attached to the IITs, IIMs etc. have gone in for this technology.

Today, on account of its vast volume of the literature produced in each field, its organisation has become very complex. The information required by a scholar may lie scattered in a variety of sources. But with the use of suitable designed computer software, it will be possible for the required information to be retrived in an expeditions manner.

Information Services

Services have been introduced in the libraries to bridge the gap between the source of information and the user. Various services have been introduced from time to time to overcome the barriers such as information, proliferation, language barrier, time barrier, cost etc. Starting with reference service, various services such as documentation, bibliographies, CAS, SDI, referral and supportive services like translation and reprography have been developed. The ultimate aim of these services is to reach out to the user and achieve user satisfaction. The advent of Information Technologies has facilitated to attain this objective with more accuracy, relevance and speed.

A precursor to the on-line information industry of today is the use of the computer for the generation of printed subject indexes, one of the earliest examples being the productions in 1961 of chemical titles - a KWIC index of journal title-derived keywords-by the chemical abstracts service.

Information investigate automated methods for handling the explosion of scientific and technical material. Most widely-used reference sources have been made available in machine-readable form. Many databases offer in excess of a million references, with growth rates measured in hundreds of thousands of entries per annum.

The document delivery is one of most importance services that a library or information centre could offer. The traditional method of document delivery is through providing the user with the actual document or a duplicate of it. However, the advent of I.T. has changed the situation. The present trend is to provide access to information available anywhere in the world, rather than the physical unit of a document.

Technology and marketing pressures are likely to promote increased automation in document delivery to specialised audiences, the library world being one of the audiences that could benefit most from electronic document delivery, it has been suggested.

OCLC has developed a compact disc based system for the storage, distribution and retrival of electronic documents, the goal being to print on demand any article that has been typeset and stored electronically. Experimental though, this system may does serve to highlight developments in electronic publishing which further challenge the future role of the library.

During the past few decades it has become obvious that libraries can no longer afford to take the Universe of knowledge. It is simply not reasonable either economically or physically to expect any one library to collect informational resources without serious consideration of available finances and local needs. Thankfully, during the same time frame when libraries are coming to grips with economic reality, international and national bibliographic databases and organisation such as OCLC, RLIN, URAS and WLN have developed which provide libraries with excellent access to information on other libraries holdings. This information has been used to good advantage by coordinating collection development programs and in making more effective resource sharing arrangements.

There should be networking of libraries where by it will be possible for each library to know about the resources of others and have access to them. For such networking information technology is essential. Here, apart from the computer which stores information, telecommunication technology also comes into the picture. There has to be an effective communication system between the libraries so that information about the availability of resources can be conveyed from one library to another effectively and expeditiously.

Today data bases are maintained in each discipline or a group of related disciplines. Massive information is collected and stored in these databases. They may be bibliographical databases, that is, databases which maintain information about the primary sources of information as well as databases, which store information per se, that is information in the original and not packaged form. The MEDLARS is one such database relating to Medical Science maintained by the National Library of Medicine, USA. It should be possible for the information stored there to be accessed by aspect of medical science, can have access to this database.

Major element in resource sharing and one which must work hand-in-hand with any cooperative collection development effort, is under library load, which is itself a venerable institution within the library community. Interlibrary loan can take many forms from the casual, occasional borrowing and/or lending which virtually all libraries have participated in, to more formal reciprocal borrowing arrangements.

Library House Keeping

The automated library, devoting one in which house keeping functions are executed with the aid of a computer, is a well-understood concept and a number of proprietary products are available in the software market.

Library circulation control may be linked to a standard stock control application, an impact - output system in which acquisitions to, and withdrawls from stock must be recorded in the inventory (catalogue).

As in the stock control situation computer assisted methods of data captures have had an important impact on the recording of inputs to and outputs from the system. In the library situation, given a clean environment and the need to employ a portable, non-intrusive identifier for both users and loanable materials the bar code has assumed a position of dominance. Libraries are looking towards in-house on-line ordering and cataloging systems. In order to avoid the tedium of keying in bibliographic data at the time when an order is placed, compact discs may, in future, offer opportunities for the downloading of such data so that the appropriate records relating to items selected for purchase may be transferred easily into the library's catalogue file.

In addition to acquisition, circulation and catalogue computers play a vital role in serial control system. The inventory maintenance of current subscription, missing issues, non-supplies etc. are being managed by computers with extreme accuracy.

Office management is yet another area where in computers are being opted for financial management, regular correspondence, maintenance of various records etc.

Changing Role of Library Information Centre in the Development of the Nation

The Library Information Centres have responded positively to this changed information environment. They have redefined their role and restructured their functions so as to contribute their might for the development of the nation. Indeed, the role of the Library in Education, Scientific and Technology Development, R & D, decision making industrial and business growth has been a well established fact. However, with the impact of technologies the library information centres are able to serve better the nation with accurate, reliable and relevant information in any field. The following services are evident to show the significant role of libraries, equipped with information technologies, towards dissemination of knowledge for the development of the nation.

Government as well as autonomous bodies have sponsored networks to facilitate access to remote databases and thus facilitate sharving of data through communication links. The Government sponsored networks include (a) National Information Centre Network (NIC NET) sponsored by NIC, Planning Commission and Government of India, to provide computing and communication infrastructure to and planning and monitoring of schemes and decision making activities of the Government (b) INDONET, developed by CMC, (c) I-Net, developed by DoT for Business Information Communication. The development of NISSAT (DSIR), NIC-MEDLARS, INFLIBNET (UGC) etc. have a significant role in the dissemination of scientific information.

The launching of VSNL, by Government of India has paved way for the development of Integrated Services Digital Network (ISDN) which offers most sophisticated services such as Telex, videotext, view data, Tele facsimile, Tele conferencing, moving pictures, E-mail etc.

On-line searching has become an increasingly common place of activity. The on-line encompasses a variety of services such as videotex, CD-ROM, in-house system and OPACs. The range of information, now available on on-line is tremendous and the predominant feature of it is Global access. In India the Government as well as commercial organisations are now providing the online services to Bibliographic or primary data bases in almost all fields of universe of knowledge.

All the advanced services offered by academic and special libraries contributes in the dissemination of information. The vital role played by the information in the development of our native land is a well established fact. The Government and the people are deeply aware and have a good insight about the immense benefits which would result from effective and fast communication of information, so that major economic changes could be brought about, at much faster rate than happening at present.

Thus, with the impact of I.T., the libraries have redefined roles as follows:

- Access to information not to document
- Access to information at global level instead local level.
- Priority for resource sharing through networking than work for self sufficiency.
- Processing of information as a cooperative venture instead work in isolation but not the users of individual library.
- Users community includes the global users.

With such redefined functions, the library information centres, by utilizing the advantages of I.T. are playing a vital role in the Nation's Development by offering timely and relevant Scientific, Technological, Academic, Managerial, Business, Industrial, Medical and Health Information to the door steps of the citizens.

References

1. *Christapher. Cynkin* Machine Translation and the documentation process. *ASLIB Proceedings* Volume 44 (March) 1992, 121-125.
2. *Enser, P.G.B.* Information Technology and the Librarian: Meeting the challenge. *ASLIB Proceedings* (September) 1991, 73-93.
3. *ISSAC, K.A.* Information Technology: Scope and Impact in online Information Retrieval Ed. by Devarajan. G, Ess-Ess Pub. New Delhi, 1996. 1-4.
4. *Lancaster, F. Wilfred.* The Role of the Library in our Electronic Society.
5. *Nagi Reddy, Y.* Impact of Information Technology on Libraries. *University News* September 1992. 11-14.
6. *Perryman, Wayne R.* The Impact of Technological Advances upon the Acquisition and Dissemination of International Resources. 1988, 1-11.
7. *Varalakshmi, R.S.R.* On-line Information Retrieval: Techniques and Services. In Online Retrieval, Ess-Ess Pub. New Delhi, 1996. 188-196.

Section VII
LIS Management

21

TIME MANAGEMENT : STRATEGIES TO AVOID THE TWIN PERILS OF APATHETIC LETHARGY AND STRESSFUL HYPERACTIVITY

Jagtar Singh

Introduction

Each individual has only twenty four hours a day at his disposal. During these twenty four hours he is to play different roles. He is required to honour his personal, family, institutional, professional and social commitments during these twenty four hours only. Another problem is that we can increase all other resources, but it is not possible to stretch this valuable resource (time) even for a second. The only way is to work out how to make productive and optimum use of this precious resource. This perhaps can be done by organising our routine systematically and thus relieving this valuable resource for more pressing work. If it is not done, then the result will be stressful hyperactivity. Stress can be motivating and distressing as well. It manifests itself in its good, bad and ugly forms.

Job Stress

"Stress can be defined as an environmental force, either real or imagined, that interacts with an individual's tolerance and which has a motivational or stimulatory affect. If the stress's force exceeds the individual's stress tolerance level it will have a derogatory effect upon the individual. Stress is the response that the human system makes in adjusting to demands or activating life events."[1]

If a person is lethargic by nature and apathetic to his job, he will be a continuous source of stress for everyone, including himself. The work will go on piling up on his desk. the end result will be strained relations and chaos. "Many people manage their time poorly. The things they have to accomplish in a given day or week are not necessasily beyond completion if they manage their time properly.

The well organized employee, like well-organized student, can often accomplish twice as much as the person who is poorly organized."[2] If a person is suffering from a vaulting ambition and unable to fix his priorities, his behaviour will result in stressful hyperactivity. Therefore, it is necessary that the concept of time management is internalized and chaos eliminated.

The Challenge

With the emergence of information society, library and information managers are working under great pressure. Sometimes there is information overload, and sometimes information drought is around. Shrinking resources and growing universe of knowledge and information are the real challenges. The roles in all the situations are deinstitutionalized. As such, the library and information managers are under pressure to compete with other players of the information industry for their survival and status. They are required to satisfy their customers, peers, bosses, and subordinates by cost-effective methods of delivering the goods. One such route to increased productivity is effective time management.

We should always keep in mind that "it's not that some people have more time than others; it's that they know how to manage their time better through efficient management practices."[3] The most important thing is to identify the time wasters' and the 'methods of effective time management.'

The first stage in managing time is self-analysis. This can take two forms. The first is to analyse how your time is spent, and in the second, analysis will concentrate upon the sort of person you are. This means, what is your management style. This style will certainly affect your management of time. You need to decide what your role should be.

Reasons for Time Management

Following are a few reasons which pressurise managers develop strategies for effective time management :

a. Constant interruptions, such as phone calls, or colleagues dropping into your office for personal or work-related chat.

b. Numerous petty, routine jobs.

c. Thick-skinned visitors and hyper-sensitive managers.

d. Non-availability of timely information.

e. Little time for planning because of a lot of problems and crises.

f. Inability to finish the task by a set deadline.

g. Considering routine memos as unique papers.

h. Too many unproductive meetings.

i. Lethargic attitude.

This is only a small check list. There can be many more activities which result in the wastage of time, indeed, a rare resource.

Useful Strategies

To cope with the above mentioned interruptions, conscious time management habit should be developed and the following strategies may also be used:

a. A list of things to be done during a specified period must be drawn.

b. Don't stagnate in routine activities. Try to initiate change and create new things. This approach releases extra energy.

c. Don't waste time on moaning or listening to others' moans.

d. Develop communication skills and organize your telephone calls in a better way. Learn to get rid of undesirable people.

e. Reduce time spend on meetings. Try to manage negative people in meetings who have nothing to offer but are always full of complaints.

f. Try to find you bio-rythem, when you are at the peak of your energies and concentration.

g. Make creative use of this time. Fix visitors time during busy hours only.

h. Move to other room to finish important tasks.

i. Keep on standing if you don't want the visitor to waste your time.

j. Keep your desk uncluttered.

k. Learn to say no.

l. Learn to delegate and trust your subordinates.

m. Relax for some time and do something you enjoy each day to compensate for unpleasant, activities.

n. Keep the information needed repeatedly readily available. In fact, a daily list of tasks to be completed is a strong recommendation in all the time management literature.

Seiwert recommends LEADS :[4]

List activities

Estimate time needed

Allow time for unscheduled tasks

Decide on priorities.

Scan Scheduled tasks at end of each day.

Basic strategies for effective time management are as under:-

a. Objectives and Priorities

b. Planning

c. Organization

d. Assertiveness

e. Relaxation

f. Standards.

Time management is pervasive of every other kind of management, whether of finances, staff, stock or services "Effective time managers therefore should learn to delegate, and to persuade their supervisors to delegate to them. Delegation,however is not just about trusting staff to carry out jobs satisfactorily. It is about motivating and supporting them with resources that enable them to do the job properly. In this context motivating means getting on agreement with your staff, or agreeing with, your supervisor, precisely what is expected from a project, in terms of outcomes and time limits."[5]

Research has shown that, "Library managers ranked attempting too much at once and estimating time unrealistically as number one, followed by a cluttered desk and personal disorganization, and third, meetings."[6] The consensus in the professional literature is that the meetings wasted most of the valuable time. The above said problems can be solved with the help of new ways of decision making and workflow; delegation of authority, and utilizing time management techniques.

Setting up of priorities is a very useful strategy in time management. "Supervisors and their staff should discuss and agree on priorities so that the team or work group is clear about the relative importance of different tasks and projects. This is where time management needs to start if staff are to be effective (achieving the essential goals of their work) as well as efficient (doing their work with the greatest possible care on a continuous basis. A few other associations in business management field have also given special attention to it. Certainly, there is need for continuous research in this area.

Conclusion

It must be realized that time is an intangible commodity made equally available to each individual by nature. But sometimes, there are constraints of time on formal occasions, and we are required to assert and obtain our missions within the specified time limits. At home and at work, we must learn to put premium on time and spend it in a judicious way. This is a precious resource, which can not be increased, but it can be relieved by various time management techniques and strategies, such as by fixing one's priorities or delegating the routine jobs to subordinates. To ensure success, always move ahead of time. One thing we must always remember that if we don't learn to manage time, then time will manage us ultimately.

References

1. Jo Bryson, Effective Library and Information Centre Management. Bombay:

Jaico, 1996, p. 303.

2. Stephen P. Robbins. Organizational Behaviour : Concepts, Controversies, and Applications, 6th. ed. New Delhi : Prentice - Hall of India, 1995, p. 647.
3. Helan M. Gothbern and Donald E. Riggs. Time Management in Academic Libraries, *College and Research Libraries*, March 1988, p. 131.
4. Lothar J. Seiwert. Managing Your Time. London : Kogen pages 1989, p. 10.
5. Noragh Jones and Peter Jorden. Case Studies in Library Management. London : Clive Bingley, 1988, p. 46.
6. Helen M. Gothberg and Donald E. Riggs, *Op.Cit.*, p. 137.
7. Noragh Jones and Peter Jordan, *Op. Cit.*, p. 47.

Select Bibliography

1. Blake, Robert R. and Mouton, Jane Srygley. How to Improve Your Management : Style and How the Management Grid can Help. New York : Amacom, 1979.
2. Blake, Robert R. and Mouton, Jane Srygley. The New Managerial Grid. Houston : Gult Pub., 1978.
3. Blanchard, Kenneth and Johnson, Spencer. The One Minute Manager, Escodido, Calif: Blanchard-Johnson, 1981.
4. Douglass, Merrili and Donna, Manage Your Time, Manage Your Work, Manage Yourself. New York : Amacom, 1980.
5. Gothberg, Helen M., Time Management in Academic Libraries, *College and Research Libraries*, 49(2) March 1988, p. 13-14.
6. Gothberg, Helen M., Time Management in Special Libraries, *Special Libraries*, Spring 1991, p. 119-130.
7. Gothberg, Helen M., Time Management in State Libraries, *Special Libraries*, Fall 1991, p. 257-266.
8. Hall, Jay., Decision. *Psychology Today*, 1971, p. 51-54, 85-88.
9. Haynes, M.E. Practical Time Management : How to make the Most of Yours Perishable Resource. Tulse,

OK: Penn Well Books, 1985.

10. Jordan, Peter, Staff Management in Library and Information Work, Bombay: Jaico, 1996.

11. Jones, Noragh and Jordan, Peter, Case Studies in Library Management. London: Clive Bingley, 1988.

12. Kozumplik, William, Time and Motion Study of Library Operators, *Special Libraries*, 60, Oct. 1969, p. 585-88.

13. Lakein, Alan. How to Get Control of Your Time and Your Life. New York : Wyden, 1973.

14. LeBoeut, Michael, Managing Time Means Managing Yourself, *Business Horizons*, 23, Feb. 1980, p. 41-46.

15. Logsdon, Richard H., Time and Motion Studies in Library Libraries, *Library Trends*, 3, Jan. 1954, p. 401-9.

16. Machenizie, Alec R. The Time Trap. New York: Amacom, 1972.

17. Martin, Thomas, Malice in Blunder land. New York: Knopf, 1984, p. 33.

18. McGregor, Douglas. The Human side of Enterprise, New York: McGraw-Hill. 1960.

19. Naisbitt, John. Megatrends. New York: Warner, 1984.

20. Peters, Thomas J. and Waterman. Robert N. In Search of Excellence; Lessons from America's Best-Run Companies. New York : Warner, 1982.

21. Robbins, Stephen P. Organizational Behaviour : Concepts, Controveries and Applications. New Delhi: Prentice Hall of India, 1995.

22. Samuelson, Howard, Increasing Public Library Productivity *Library Journal*, 106, Feb. 1, 1981.

23. Seiwert, Lothar J. Managing Your Time. London:

Kogan Page, 1989.

24. Toffler, Alvin. The Third Wave. New York: Bantam, 1981.

25. Turla, P. and Hawkings, K. Time Management Made Easy. London : Pather Books, 1985.

26. Whigenhunt, D.W. Administrative Time Management. Washington, D.C.: University Press of America, 1987.

27. Williams, Graham L. Getting Results with Time Management. Sheffield: Library and Learning Resources Sheffield City Polytechnic, 1988.

22

DATA BASE MANAGEMENT : A TOOL IN AGRICULTURAL MARKETING DEVELOPMENT IN INDIA

Bipul Kumar Chakrabarty

Introduction

An efficient system of marketing is an essential pre-requisite for agricultural development. The phenomenal increase in agricultural production in the wake of new strategy for agricultural development in India in the mid-sixties further underlines the need for a well organised management system in the field of agricultural marketing. It was realised that to sustain the tempo of growth in agricultural production, it was essential not only to correct imperfections and distortions in the existing system but also to expand it further to enable it to absorb the increasing volume of turnover.

Keeping in view the above fact, the pace of modernization of agricultural marketing or the creation of databases with the evolution of Information Technology (=IT) has a tremendous impact as far as the 'productivity' for economic development is concerned.

In this paper, therefore, the need arises to reevaluate agricultural marketing in a global perspective to understand the impact of "information" in the form of "Data" not only to survive but succeed in today's highly competitive global market.

Present Status of Agricultural Marketing in India

The application of marketing management techniques coupled with Govt. policies and programmes in the agricultural sector have increased the production of several commodities and the resultant marketable surplus has touched new heights, transforming Indian Agriculture from a subsistence to a near commercial enterprise. This also resulted in a significant increase in the agricultural produce markets in the country. In this context, agricultural marketing management system is fast changing with the new concept of

Information Technology arising from the globalisation of Indian economy.

Agricultural Marketing Management

Agricultural marketing deals with the management of produce from the point of harvest to its ultimate consumption. Storage, transportation, assembling, grading, packing, processing, transfer of ownership from sellers to buyers, system of sale, price determination, market information, extension, etc. are all different components having their role in the marketing system. The marketing system, in effect, is a mechanism co-ordinating production with distribution and consumption activities. An integrated approach to agricultural marketing information leads to effectiveness in cost, time and space. So, in order to develop effective marketing system, need for the creation of databases in the area of agricultural marketing in the global scenario is necessary.

System Approach to Marketing Management

A system approach desires comprehensive and coherent analysis of organisational activities. It covers the objective of the organisation, its organs and their functional role for the attainment of those objectives and designing of alternatives for effective development. With the expanded domain of goals, the organisational, the organisational structure also grows with a galaxy of its systems and sub-systems' knitted in the decision making network and inter dependent roles. (Fig. 1).

Market Organisational System

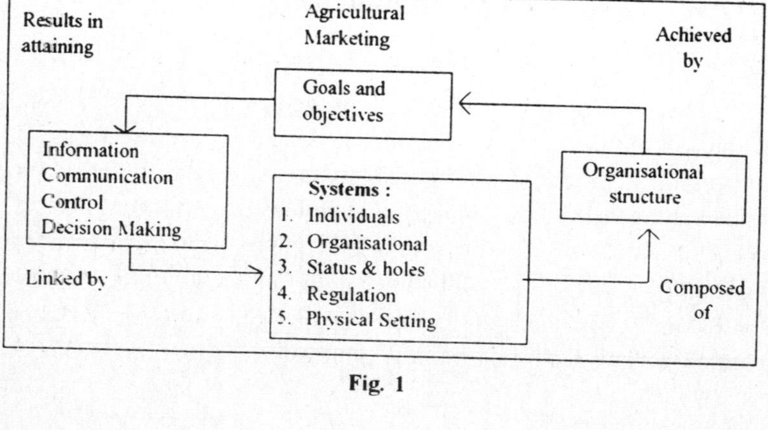

Fig. 1

The accelerated movement of traffic, goods, personals and communication puts pressed on decision makers and for them, the systematic approach to handle the large volume of information becomes an indispensable necessity.

The general process of agricultural marketing management emerges out of interaction of managerial functions like planning, directing, organising, controlling and feed-back in the management of the market, these functions interplay with distinct characteristics.

Role of Information Technology in Agricultural Marketing in India

The role and need of Information Technology (IT) in the field of agricultural marketing in India is not so much encouraging as compared with the global industry of the advanced countries. In this regard, it may be stated that a design framework for IT-based Agricultural Marketing Network (AGRIM-NET) was proposed by Mandavia, U.K., in "Design, Development and Implementation of AGRIM-NET", October, 1992. Accordingly, Gujarat, Maharashtra, Rajasthan and Karnataka states are projecting an encouraging scenario in India.

In addition, computer installations at the State Agricultural Marketing Boards are being utilised for creating state level databases of the domestic trade, enhancing these databases with trade information from other states and nations, on-going research and publications and routine administrative procedures which are automated to a great extent now. The National Informatics Centre has been the focal organisation for creating a national level database through its District Computer Centres and the national network, NICNET. Professional inputs and assistance over being incorporated appropriately as part of the whole process of implementation Information regarding the local trading is being disseminated to the producers and trades of agricultural marketing through the mass media, such as television, radio and newspapers.

Information Technology for International Trade in Agricultural Marketing

Planning and conceiving the international trade logistics, though require to be in conformity with the domestic trade practices and procedures, involve much more broader outlook and the level of complexity of information gathering and analysis compared to that required for planning the domestic trade. Over and above, the traditional and conventional uses of the IT under any organisational framework, the following are more distinctive and specific in nature for the global competitive trade:

- International Market Research through global Computerised Database
- Planning, Analysis and Policy making
- Exports Order Entry and Processing]
- Trade Documentation
- Electronic Data Interchange

International Market Research through Global Computerised Databases (GCDB)

There exists a pool of collective knowledge of export/import trade in some of the global databases to which a tiny machine can be plugged to fetch a small but required piece of information and make a giant contribution towards the global trade. Large commercial databases, located in the U.S.A. and Europe, can be accessed for retrieving necessary data on a time-sharing basis by authorised users from any corner of the world. It is possible to know from these databases that how much castor oilseeds were imported by the United States from which agencies belonging to which countries during the last season? Or what was the total production, consumption and import of sugar in the U.S. during the last fifteen years ? Answers to those querries can be had directly through the GCDB system.

It is now possible to access such databases from India through Public Switched Telephone Networks (PSTNS) or limited number of Data Networks (PSDNs). Videsh Sanchar Nigam Ltd., a modal Govt. of India organisation, provides a gateway to international networks as shown in Fig. - 2. Any organisation, exporter or farmers' co-operative interested in knowing exports market information can easily tap these information sources by registering themselves with VSNL with a nominal charge for each connection. Annex-I provides the details of Computerised Databases and monetary considerations, one-time & recurring in nature, for establishing on-time connections to the global databases through VSNL.

In addition, ANNEX-II lists some of the prominent global sources of computerised databases, which can be accessed through PSTNs or satellites depending upon the technical feasibility, authorisations provided by the host databases administrators & regulations of the Govt. of India.

Planning Analysis & Policy-Making

Availability of comprehensive database in the field of agricultural marketing is a pre-requisite for any meaningful analysis. The use of IT in evaluating the demand of Indian agriculture commodities for a specific target market can be demonstrated with the

- ——— Forecasting & other quantitative techniques
- ——— Simulation Modelling & Decision Support systems
- ——— Comprehensive database of trade-specific information

Order Processing

This is an another potential area in which the contribution of DBMS can be of tremendous use. The large export houses state owned export corporations may browse through their databases of potential suppliers & ask for their rates. If qualified suppliers are found to be available, the system can generate a proforma invoice which may be mailed to the foreign buyer for order confirmation. The foreign buyer, if satisfied with the rates, delivery schedule, terms & conditions, etc., can issue the Purchase Order & the letter of credit in the name of the co-ordinating body or the trader in India. A computerised system can typically assist in this whole process of order processing by storing information on potential suppliers, comparing their rates, selecting a few who satisfy required qualification, etc. & thereby increase the efficiency of the procedure.

Trade Documentation

Preparation of documentation according to the prescribed guidelines given by the Govt. during the course of exports order processing is quite demanding & time-consuming. Efficient software systems can reduce the number of hours spent in the routine work & thereby, increase the efficiency of export operations.

A careful analysis of the lengthy documentation requirement shows that a limited amount of information is required to be processed & printed separately. A computerised system can be of tremendous use in this case because it is possible to store the information & generate repetitive statements with minor modifications every time.

Electronic Data Interchange

Electronic Data Interchange or EDI is one of the most popular areas of application of Information Technology Advanced countries like U.S.A., U.K., etc. have successfully developed & implemented vertically integrated Electronic Data Interchange services involving tiers of suppliers, large manufactures, stores & warehouses dealers & retailer chains for effective information management & communications.

In India, the state owned Export Corporation assist the exports of agricultural commodities, spices, etc. By providing the Electronic Data Interchange, the same information between the nodal organisation & the supplier, the efficiency of the whole process can be increased by several fold. (Fig. 3).

In order to fulfil the above objectives of information technology in Agricultural Marketing in India, impact on Agricultural Marketing needs to be re-evaluated considering the impact of globalisation of economy.

Impact of Agricultural Marketing Research

The National Commission on Agriculture (NCA) has classified the subject of Agricultural Marketing Research into two broad categories :

(a) those relating to physical marketing functions which include assembly, storage, grading, processing and transportation of the produce and

(b) other intangible functions stemming from the transfer of ownership that includes pricing, risk bearing and financing.

Promotion of Agricultural Marketing Organisations in India

The first ever step that was taken by the government was to set up a central marketing organisation in January 1935 on the recommendations of the Royal Commission on Agriculture (1928), to promote and implement the marketing policies and programmes as the Government agency in India. This central marketing organisation which is now known as the Directorate of Marketing & Inspection (DMI), Faridabad.

Similar organisations (Govt., Public and Co-operative Sector) were created over a period of time to delegate specific functions in this enlarged sphere. During the third and fourth five year plans, the Govt. of India also created a number of national level organisations like, Agricultural Prices Commission (APC) - now known as the Commission for Agricultural Costs & Prices (CACP), Food Corporation of India (FCI), National Co-operative Development Corporation (NCDC), National Agricultural Co-operative Marketing Federation of India Ltd. (NAFED), National Consumers and Co-operative Federation (NCCF), Cotton Corporation of India (CCI), Indian Grain Storage Research Institute (IGSRI), National Institute of Rural Development (NIRD), Institute of Rural Management (IRM), Agricultural & Food Products Export Development Authority (APEDA), ICAR and Its institutes like, IARI, Indian Agricultural Statistical Research Institute (IASRI), Agricultural Universities and some other autonomous/private organisations like, Indian Institute of Foreign Trade (IIFT), Indian Institute of Packaging (IIP), Central Warehousing Corporation (CWC), Modern Food Industries Ltd. (MFIL), National Institute of Agricultural Marketing (NIAM), National Council of Applied Economic Research (NCAER), Indian Society of Agricultural Economics, Indian Institute of Management (IIM), Gokhale Institute of Politics & Economics, Rural Credit Institutions, etc. which act as modal organisations in the country and they are initiating a new way of thinking and approaching a long term formulations for a vibrant agricultural trade globally.

Formulation of DBMS on Agricultural Marketing

Before adopting the DBMS for Agricultural Marketing, it is essential to define different objectives/fields and roles of the markets followed by its functions so that utility of DBMS in market management can be visualised. the agricultural marketing is a multi-dimensional activity performed in a vast area. Like any other marketing field, it enables the transfer of produce from producers to consumers. But, unlike manufactured produce, the producers in agricultural marketing form the unorganised group of millions of farmers spread over the length and breadth of the country releasing their marketable surplus of various commodities at different seasonal periods for the consumption of equally large number of consumers.

In order to attain the objectives of rendering market services like maintenance of market yard, provision of market facilities, curb on market malpractices leading to exploitation of farmers, contribution to civic amenities, market intelligence to users and other marketing developmental measures, the broad outline of the functions of market management are as follows:

——— Operation and maintenance of market facilities and infrastructure.

——— Licensing of market functionaries.

——— Enforcement of rules & bylaws.

——— Regulation of inflow & outflow of commodities, persons and transport.

——— Assessment and collection of fee & charges.

——— Information Dissemination.

——— Personnel and Financial Management.

——— New Developments and Planning.

Out of the above functions of market information, the most vital issue is the dissemination of relevant information from various sources of raw data. Thus, the utility for DBMS is this context, can be seen on the following counts:

———The large volume of data gets generated during the market operations on varied aspects like arrival and prices, trades and functionaries, commodity details which are required to be stored.

———The data is frequently used for several information details. The daily price and arrival is to be disseminated properly not only as market bulletins but also for assessment of market fee.

———The Market data needs to be updated frequently and on regular basis.

——— The data of different kind have their utility, span, transport flow, etc., may not have use in their daily details after a year but may be stored in aggregate form of periodic documents. The redundant data required to be eliminated.

———There are more than one use of data at a time. The prices and arrivals are needed for marketing system as well as for assessment and collection of fees. The stored data like list of licenced traders, details of suspended and cancelled licenses, the premise allocation, etc. are frequently called by different functions leading to duplication and delays. The demand of multiple users of data of different reference period is a necessity in market functions.

———Since the data in the market operations is the prime sources of control, its safe custody is to be assured and data network is necessary for this purpose.

Conclusion

Agricultural Marketing in India and its various facets, in the present context, needs to be re-evaluated considering the explicit and under currents of globalisation of economy. Such re-evaluation exercise can rightly be undertaken under the framework of re-evaluation of several important facets of Agricultural Marketing, such as, credit, institutional support, exports, etc. Thus, the role of Information Technology (IT) can provide some of the most innovative and exceptional tools, usages in the field of Agricultural Marketing in general and exports trade in particular. An attempt to enumerate various possibilities of Information Technology (IT) usage in agricultural exports, in conformation with the domestic trade policies and international technological sophistication has been highlighted in this paper.

Information Technology (IT) can also be effectively utilised for planning, analysis and policy-making with the help of DBMS is the area of agricultural marketing, forecasting, modelling and other quantitative techniiques. Information Technology (IT) can also be utilised by the trade organisations or trade supporting organisations for order processing, Export-Import Documentation and Electronic

Data Interchange with private or co-operative entities located at the grass-roots level.

An appropriate institutional framework involving existing and new organisational entities at national, state and grass-roots level, with explicit application of DBMS in Agricultural Marketing, is recommended for the effective implementation of technology.

References

(1) Agricultural Marketing, V. 33 (2), pub. by Directorate of Marketing & Inspection, Govt. of India, New Delhi; July - Sept.' 1990.

(2) Indian Agriculture in brief, 22nd Edition, pub. by Directorate of Economic & Statistics, Govt. of India New Delhi; 1988.

(3) Infotech Consultants : "Consultancy Report on a State-wide Communications Network for Agricultural Marketing", submitted to Gujrat State Agricultural Marketing Board, Gandhinagar, Ahmedabad; 1992.

(4) Mandavia (UK) : Design, Development & Implementation of Agricultural Marketing Network (AGRIM-NET), Workshop on "Information Systems for Agricultural Marketing: Present Role & Future Challenges", Jaipur; October, 1992.

(5) National Conference on Agricultural Marketing pub. by Directorate of Marketing & Inspection, Govt. of India, New Delhi; November 15-16, 1988.

(6) Regional Seminar on Rapid Appraisal Techniques for Agricultural Marketing Systems in Asia and the Pacific and the Fifth General Assembly of AFMA, Jakarta, Indonesia; 20-24 August, 1991.

(7) Report of the Working group on Agricultural Marketing for the VIII Five Year Plan (1990-95), pub. by Directorate of Marketing & Inspection, Govt. of India, New Delhi.

(8) (The) State of the Art for Agricultural Marketing Research Methods in India: Country Paper, by FAO/AFMA/AMIS/BULOG : Regional Seminar on Rapid Appraisal Techniques for Agricultural Marketing Systems in Asia & the Pacific and the 5th General Assembly of AFMA, Jakarta; 20-24 August, 1991.

Annex-1

Details of Access to Global Databases Through V.S.N.L.

Database	**:**	**EasyNet**
Subjects	:	Agricultural Commodities Export/Import
	:	U.S. Census Information
	:	Market Research & Marketing Reports

	:	Demographics	
	:	News and World Affairs	
Other Accesss	:	BRS-IT	
	:	Data-Star	
	:	Dialog	
	:	NewsNet	
	:	Orbit	
	:	Telescan	
	:	VU/TEXT ISI	
Pricing	:	Subscription Fee..	Rs. 3000 per year
	:	Connect Time	Rs. 4 per minute
	:	Data comm. Charges.	Rs.2 per 640 bytes
	:	Search Aids...	Rs. 10,000-50,000
	:	Training	Rs. 5,000-20,000
Contact	:	General Manager	
	:	Videsh Sanchar Nigam Limited	
	:	M.G. Road, Fort	
		Bombay- 400 001	
		Phone : 022-262-4020	
		Fax : 022-262-4003	

Annex-II

List of Prominent Global Databases

Global Database	Subscription Fee	Online Access Charges	Printing Charges
Infomaster	$ 25 per year	$ 9 per hour	———
Dialcom	$ 10 per month	$ 17 per hour	———
Orbit	———	$ 35- $ 300 per hour	$ 1.25 per hour
Brkthru	$ 75 one-time	$45-$125 per hour	———

Global Database	**Subscription Fee**	**Online Access Charges**	**Printing Charges**
Compuserve	$ 10 per month	$ 15 per hour	———
NewsNet	$ 15 per month	$ 48 per hour	———
Dialog	———	$ 15-$ 300 per hour	$ 100perhour

Section VIII
Information Resources: Caring and Sharing

23

INFORMATION NEEDS AND USES OF FINANCIAL AND INDUSTRIAL INFORMATION: PROBLEMS AND PROSPECTS

J. Abraham

Introduction

Decision making and planning are the daily routine of the management of any organisation. Irrespective of the nature of business and philosophy, either profit orientation or non-profit as the case may be, decision has to be arrived everyday. Keeping systematic record of financial transactions for decision-making is indeed the key to successful business operations. In modern business, finance is the control point of all business activities. Most crucial decisions of the firm are related to finance. The financial management is the managerial activity which is concerned with planning and controlling of the financial resources.

Financial Management

According to Joseph and Massie "Financial management is the operational activity of a business that is responsible for obtaining and effectively utilising the funds necessary for efficient operations".

The financial management not only covers the acquisition of funds from various resources but also their effective utilisation. Therefore it includes financial planning, financial administration and financial control.

Financial Information

Information is broadly defined as "knowledge concerning some particular fact, subject or event in any communicable form". It is fundamental to communication process. Although there is no hard and fast classification of the kinds of information available for Trade and Industry, Cyert classifies as

1. Information about the environment relevant to the firm

2. Information about the firm for internal use,
3. Information about the firm for external use.

The success of a business firm largely depends on financial information and policies regarding budgeting, general accounts, cost accounts, internal audit etc. The financial decision making is the most important specialist activity which affects the efficiency of all other functions. The financial decision making covers a wide range of factors like demand, cost, price, profit and capital budgeting. The basis of financial planning and decision making is the financial information. Accounting system is the main internal source of financial information. The accounting system helps to accumulate, measure and communicate the financial information to various users such as owners, creditors, managers, employees, customers, suppliers and government for making economic decisions. The internal sources of information enable the management to take right decision in a competitive environment.

Management Information System

The optimum use of available financial resources of the firm is greatly facilitated by providing relevant financial information system that helps monitor actual performance in comparison with planned performance. Therefore for the effective management of finance function, the scope of Management Information System (MIS) has to be widened to include the financial operations of the firm for reaching sound business decisions.

Management Information System provides a continuous, formalised and structured collection of information both internal and external and plays an important role in the development of corporate strategy. The Management Information system can help management to make strategic financial decision and measure performance against organisational and departmental objectives.

In most companies the most current external data and other relevant informations are analysed for making financing as well as investment decisions.

Sources of Financial Information

In a globalised economy more reliance of internal sources alone will not help arriving at right decisions. They need to use many other sources of financial information, for they have to compete with their business rivals in an effective manner.

There are two types of sources of financial information namely

1. internal sources and
2. external sources

Internal sources of Information

Company information is generated internally and externally. Internal sources provide information about the condition of the organisation on financial, business and other aspects, whereas the external sources provide information about trade and industry to which the business concern belongs. Thus the external sources provide a macro information to the concern. The principal sources of internal information about a company are its financial statements consisting of the balance sheet, profit and loss account and statement of changes in financial position. These statements of information on the basis of which conclusions can be drawn regarding the operations of the firm.

External Sources of Information

Many popular and widely circulated sources of information about companies emanate from outside are external sources. These sources supplement the company generated information and other information not found in the materials made available by companies themselves. The financial decisions should be based on some reliable information and most current information. There is a great variety of sources of financial information about the money, stock and commodity markets, industries and individual companies.

Financial Information management

The process of management involves planning, organising, staffing, implementing and controlling. The managerial activities involve a flow of information through formal and informal channels of communication and through various sources of information. Since the organisation interacts with its internal and external environment while taking an appropriate decision a new dimension added to has been the financial information management and has correspondingly attained vast proportion and complexity. The financial planning and decision making processes depend heavily upon information needs of the organisation which can be classified into three broad types: (1) Environmental, (2) Competitive and (3) Internal

1. Environmental information needs can be classified as political and governmental considerations, demographic and social trends, economic trends, technological environment and factors of production.
2. Competitive information is the information concerning factors that affect the operation of the firm within an industry and include date concerning industry and firm demand as well as data on the competitors.
3. I. .ernal premises that affect the planning decisions of the organisation in some respects are more important than the external environment.

The business environment and premises are no doubt very important for decision making in a firm mainly by top management, but internal planning premises are vital for subsidiary planning at all levels in the organisation. The internal data are aimed at the identification of the organisation's strengths and weaknesses, whereas external information are vital decision making premises that help managers shape future plans.

Published sources of financial information

Financial information is available from different published sources. This may relate to a verity of subjects of economic, commercial and industrial interest. There may be information about different industries and organised markets including commodity exchanges, stock exchanges and bullion markets, individual companies and so on.

The purpose for which financial information is required determines the source of information. In fact there is a wide variety of extensive information compressed in different published sources, so much so that one would be totally confused unless one is able to get at the exact source of Information and knows what he is looking for. It would not be possible here to exhaust the varied sources of published information, for this is a task by itself and no effort to list them accurately is ever likely to succeed.

Books generally do not play a vital part in the financial information. The demand for current information is partially met by substantial periodical, serial and newspaper holdings. On the other hand reference books in particular those with statistics, corporate files and indexes that are usually alphabetically arranged are more often used of current business news can also be obtained from the leading banks, many of which publish news letters often obtainable free of charge.

The purpose of this paper is not to detail out the important published sources of financial information but to convey an idea of select references on financial information. This financial information may possibly be available in some technical jargon with which the user will have to be familiar. These are economic and financial dailies, journals, periodicals and magazines-local, national as well as international which are published by industrial houses, professional bodies, financial institutions, the government, the private agencies, individuals and soon. These financial information is useful to make economic investment and financing decision making.

Use of the sources of Financial Information

Until recently financial information of any type was most difficult to obtain, if indeed it was obtainable. However the real beginning of corporate information might be traced to the securities Act of 1933 and 1934 (USA) and to the publications of Investment and Financial Services by Moody's Investor's Service, Inc and Standard & Poor's Corporation (USA). both these services offer basic information on company histories, income statements, description of outstanding securities, acquisition, dividend payments etc. These services are kept current by means of frequent looseleaf supplements. They also publish periodic reports on firm's operation and recent developments, informations on pertiment share price data as well as other financial data on stock and bond markets.

Problems in the use of financial information

Non-availability discourages the use of information and some times becomes a big loss to the enterprise as well as the industry. Those who are responsible for making policies and plans need to have a variety of information for well informed judgement. The information need for trade and industry in particular have so far received hardly any systematic attention in terms of size and in most countries of the world. Therefore a controlling organisation and mechanism, have to be set up to regulate and co-ordinate these financial information, as the corporate sector has correspondingly attained vast proportions and complexity. For the effective management, acquisition and supply of information for decision making, National Information System must be built up in order to

1. to help worth while financial decision making at the gross root level and
2. to help research and development at the industry level.

However in our country the effort to find new alternatives and approaches to the solution of the financial information planning and management for Trade and Industry has been strengthened with the establishment of National Centre for Trade Information (NCTI), New Delhi.

National centre for Trade Information

The National Centre for Trade Information (NCTI), a joint venture of Indian Trade Promotion Organisation (ITPO) and National Informatics centre was recently setup at New Delhi. NCTI will provide the latest trade, business and economic information to help Indian as well foreign enterprises in promoting trade to and from India. The centre will act as a promotional and operational agency synerginsing the efforts of different organisations presently engaged in the collection, processing, analysis, and dissemination of trade and commerce information. It would develop value added information using the raw data available in different data bases of different organisation; and establish linkages and maintain a liaison with trade and access to direct global information via the highspeed NICNET national info highway.

Conclusion

Finance is the life blood for all type of economic activities whether profit oriented business activities or non profit social service activities. Financial management basically involves two types of decision making -financing decisions and investment decisions. The financial controller or manager may go through the relevant publications containing the required information before taking any decision considering the company's financial position and the expected developments in the general economy into account. Therefore the financial controller or manager should be well versed of the various sources of relevant information both internal and external sources published and unpublished. Currently information is available in different printed and non-printed media which are the main sources of information to meet the information need of the industries.

In the present industrial environment, National Centre for Trade Information can constitute a base for Information Services to the Industries and can assist the industrial growth and international trade boom. For this purpose the Centre should have National Information Infrastructure pertaining to the collection, computer and communication facilities, networking environment, proper encouragement and leadership and knowledge of current Information Sources on Industry.

References

1. BROOKS (Robert M.) and Brown (Morton R.): "Financial Libraries and Collections" *In Encyclopedia of Library and Information science*. vol. 8 PP. 459-471. New York; Marcel Dekkar, Inc, 1972
2. CHANDRA (Prasanna): Financial Management: Theory and practice. Ed 3. New Delhi: Tata mcGraw Hill publishing company, 1993.
3. "Centre for Trade Information setup". *Express computer*. Vol. 5, No. 32, October 24, 1994, p. 3
4. CYERT (Robert M.): "Business Management" In *International Encyclopedia of the social sciences*. V2. pp. 249-256. New York: Macmillan, 1968.
5. MURDICK (Robert G.) et. al. : Information system for Modern Management. New Delhi: Prentice Hall of India, 1993.
6. PANDEY (I.M.): Financial Management, New Delhi: Vikas publishing House, 1993.
7. VARMA (MM) and AGABWAL (RK): Financial Management, Delhi: Forward Book Depot, 1994.

24

RESOURCE SHARING OF PERIODICAL LITERATURE AMONG UNIVERSITY LIBRARIES: A CONCEPTUAL APPROACH

E. Rama Reddy

Introduction

There are around 226 Universities and 8000 Colleges in India, big and small. Of these over 70 are in the area of Agriculture, Engineering and Technology and Medical Sciences. The remaining Universities include Central Universities, State Universities, Open Universities and Deemed Universities. There is considerable informal co-operation among these libraries. However, there has been no attempt at formal networking until *INFLIBNET* was established involving the use of computer and communication technologies.

There is little doubt that for development of a modern library, information network would enable easier and wider access to the rich collection of documents and information. Further a well planned network would enable operational economics for the participating. Libraries and optimal cost effective use of information, finances and staff resources across institutions breaking down the barriers of time and space.

On an average each University Library is spending around 30 lakhes on periodical subscriptions and cumulatively it works out around Rs. 45 crores. Even after spending such a huge amount the libraries individually are not able to meet the minimum requirements of the end users within an organization. There has been always been a demand for more funds from each university. The solution lies in effective resource sharing among the libraries. The libraries may be grouped into five Zones (East, West, North , South and Central) and made to develop effective mechanism for pooling the available periodical resources for effective utilization among the universities. The present available Information Technology meets the needs for effective and efficient resource sharing.

Scope

This paper concentrates on resource sharing of current periodicals among participating libraries. Subscription to a periodical is not a one time affair as in the case of books. It makes the libraries to commit themselves in the years to come. Most of the libraries spend more than 80% of their grant for subscriptions. Over the years, the libraries are finding it impossible to renew the subscriptions of periodicals due to the following reasons:

i. Financial crunch at the institution level
ii. Slashing of allocation to the libraries
iii. Escalation of basic subscription rates and postal charges and
iv. The dealing of rupee against major foreign currencies.

The above factors have greater impact on the subscriptions of periodicals in the libraries. Hence, the need for systematic utilization of the scarce funds leading to resource sharing.

Objectives of Resource Sharing

Resource sharing can be between two or more libraries. The objectives include:

i. To facilitate sharing of periodical resources in an efficient, timely and cost-effective manner.
ii. To facilitate utilization of periodical resources, which enhance the readers ability to meet the informational and educational needs.
iii. To increase users knowledge of the range of services available from the libraries.
iv. To provide communication among the libraries.
v. To promote expansion of direct library services to all the members of the system.
vi. To support co-operative programs and services of libraries with adequate resources.

Advantages

i. Access to more number of periodicals.
ii. Avoidance of duplication
iii. Conservation of scarce funds

iv. Increase in subscriptions
v. Conservation of foreign exchange
vi. Identification of core journals
vii. Linkages, understanding among libraries
viii. Creation of information environment among users
ix. Improvement in information services

Requirements

Materials

i. A complete list of holdings of periodicals of each participating library
ii. A complete list of current subscriptions of each library
iii. A union catalogue of complete holdings of all the participating libraries
iv. A directory of the current periodicals of all the participating libraries.

Equipment

i. Computer
ii. Direct Telephone
iii. Modem
iv. Scanner
v. Photocopy equipment
vi. Fax machine
vii. CD-ROM equipment
viii. E-mail facilities
ix. For effective and efficient data an image communication, the university libraries need to use VSAT Antennae instead of item Nos. ii, iii,v,vi, vii and viii of above

Resource sharing-Pre-requisites

i. Each participating library should agree to the concept of resource sharing of periodicals.
ii. The libraries should facilitate mutual use of current subscriptions in a cost effective manner. Services that enable mutual use of costly periodicals should be

viewed as an integral part of each library's services.

iii. Each library should prioritize list of current subscriptions. A title which is second or third priority in a library but first priority in another library is a periodical that could be shared by the library instead of subscribing it.

iv. As a general rule there should be a free exchange of photocopies between libraries.

v. Adequate initial and recurring costs must be provided to ensure the quality of services.

vi. A central database with efficient manpower is a minimum requirement for resource sharing.

vii. Activities need to be identified and necessary rules and regulations governing the activities may be codified

viii. Discontinuation of any periodical by a member library should take place only after informing the member library in advance or with mutual consent.

ix. Librarians should see themselves and should be seen as managers of the resources of that they help to build. They should be vested with powers to take final decisions concerning sharing of costly resources with other libraries within a frame work of an approved policy. Each library should take all actions necessary to obtain administrative and policy support from their respective universities to enable them to participate effectively in the sharing of resources with other libraries.

Services

i. The Central Resource Centre should consolidate the current periodicals list after receiving the lists from all the participating libraries to identify the extent of duplicate subscriptions and the number of unique titles available in the central resource centre with location code of the participating libraries.

ii. The central resource centre should create the current

periodicals and content pages database and make it available for accessing by the participating libraries.

iii. The participating libraries should send the list of periodicals subscribed and scan the content pages of the periodical issues as soon as they are received in their library

iv. The participating libraries may go through the multiple subscriptions of periodicals and take a decision to retain or drop the journals in consultation with the other library subscribing the same journal.

v. The participating libraries may search the central resource centre to locate the required periodical and the content pages of the periodical. The libraries. if necessary may request for a full text article directly from the library or through the central resource center.

vi. The participating libraries should ensure that the full text article be sent to the requesting library as quickly as possible. If required Fax, speed post or courier service may be used apart from normal postal delivery depending upon the requesting library.

vii. The libraries may charge for the photocopy at agreed rates only.

Plan of Action

As on today quite a few libraries have introduced automation in their libraries. For a feasibility study, it is planned to identify, 12 libraries in the Southern Zone (covering: Andhra Pardesh, Karnataka, Kerala, Pondicherry and Tamil Nadu) who have basic computer facilities, who have finalized and paid their subscriptions for the year 1997 and who are willing to participate in this study.

Indira Gandhi Memorial Library would like to act as Central Resource Centre i.e. Central Node (CN). This node will consolidate, create and maintain a database of Current Periodicals and a database of Content Pages of periodicals. It will analyze the extent of duplication of library subscriptions in these 12 libraries. They are called as Participating Libraries or Local Nodes (LN). The Central Node will make available a list of unique titles to all the Local Nodes for their information. They can use this list to take a decision at the timing of finalizing the renewals (around August 1997) for the year 1998. They can correspond with other libraries before a periodical is dropped from the renewals to ensure inclusion or such periodicals by the other library

The Local Nodes should contribute to the "Content Pages database" at the Central Node by scanning the content pages of periodical issues received every day through fax. The Central Node will maintain the database and make it available for searching by the Local Nodes. After identifying the required material in the Central Node, the Local Node may contact the library for the full text articles directly or thought the Central Node. As soon as a request for a full text article is received, the library on priority should send the requested article by fastest possible method to the requesting library. It can use fax, E-mail, speed post or normal post etc. The libraries may maintain accounts and send consolidated bills, quarterly or other agreed frequency for settlement of payments among the libraries. This will facilitate free flow of required articles among the libraries to fulfill the demands of users.

Once this activity stabilizes with fine tuning of procedures, operational costs, database updation and maintenance, other libraries can join to widen the base. Success of resource sharing depends on the willingness to share resources voluntarily with other libraries. Rules, regulations, memorandum of understandings etc. are secondary for the success. Librarians and authorities of parent organization need to discuss among themselves before they participate in this activity.

Indira Gandhi Memorial Library is fully geared up to shoulder this responsibility to create and maintain the "Current Journals "and "Content Pages" Database with the cooperation of the other participating libraries.

Inflibnet may provide the basic infrastructure to the Local Nodes and the Central Node apart from whatever is already made available under modernization program. The Local Nodes may require: Flatbed scanner and *VSAT* dish. Antennae for efficient data communication in place of telephone, modem, photocopy equipment, Fax machine and CD-ROM and E-mail facilities.

25

STUDY OF INDUSTRIAL INFORMATION USERS : PROBLEMS AND PROSPECTS

C.P. Ramasesh

The use of information, current and retrospective has become an essential phenomenon for industrial development. Though the users gather bare facts, as well as, organized and evaluated information from various sources such as colleagues, engineers, technicians etc. are reluctant to the use of printed sources like books and journals. The use of books and journals are often found essential for the basic knowledge of the field, rather than problem solving information. These printed sources provide comprehensive and systematic knowledge.

In the real of practical settlement, for sudden arousal of technical problems in small industries or marketing often the entrepreneurs seek the advise and assistance of mechanics, personnel involved in the field for years, engineers. This trend clearly depicts that personalized information service by a competent technician/ expert available around the region is most significant for small industries.

To have a clear idea of the information seeking behaviour and the actual use of information in small industrial sector, several techniques are being employed. Some of the important techniques are being employed. Some of the important techniques adopted for the study of the information users are critically examined below.

Questionnaire and Interview

Questionnaire and interview techniques can be employed if the investigator is able to contact the respondants personally. This is a feasible technique if the number of samples selected is few and not geographically wide-spread. Getting answers by post unless the respondants are quite intimate to the investigator. It is observed that majority of the entrepreneurs do not take the burden of filling up the questionnaire and return. Often they are found afraid to give the details in writing because of various personal false-feelings of safety.

Many a time the usual replies at the industries are: "we do not have the statistics right now; permission of our owner is necessary to answer these questions." The owners hesitate to give the reply and try to redirect the investigator to some other industry or official outside stating "I am very busy with all these, please contact.....". Because of these constraints in obtaining unbiased replies from the persons choosen according to the sampling techniques adopted, many a time, investigators have to shift to the other respondants randomly. Therefore, systematic sampling technique is a difficult task especially in respect of data and opinion gathering relating to small industries.

Diary-keeping

On the other hand, diary-keeping technique may be employed. Here, the selected information seekers of small industries are asked to note down in their diaries the details in respect of (1) information needed; (2) sources sought; (3) sources which give precise and relevant, information; (4) time taken for the search and (5) the personal remarks. Here, the investigator can trace the knowledge and intelligence of the information users in seeking information at the minimum loss of effort and time. He can understand which sources are important and where they exist. He can suggest the seekers about how best they can seek relevant and pinpointed information expeditiously. The procedure of diary-keeping method may also be applied for the expert technicians and consultants of industries to get the idea pertaining to the use of sources of information and the means adopted to trace their location, how and on what basis they advice the small entrepreneurs. Related to this technique, is another that eliminates the work of making the notes by the users themselves. This is the critical incident technique.

Critical Incident

The technique is commonly adopted for the user studies during the informal discussions. Large population cannot be examined by these techniques of 'diary-keeping' and 'critical incident. A selected users of information as samples can only be subjected to pass comments and narrate incidents.

In the case of critical incident technique, the user will be asked to narrate in detail the difficulties encountered during his search procedures and also the means and methods adopted for information retrieval. Here, the investigator can understand about the ability of the user, his personal drawbacks in information use. He can come to know about the prejudice of the staff of information store, prejudice of the experts in advising and the delay caused by various factors like geographical distance and inadequacy of finance and so on. For instance, a user states: "you see, I wanted the periodical Newman's Indian Bradshaw Sept. 1983 to know the Railway distance between Bangalore and Surat. I enquired at the Mysore Branch of Karnataka State Small Industries Development Corporation. The man incharge there curtly said 'it is available at the university library, but only for the members.' I returned forgetting the 'Bradshaw.' On the next morning my neighbour told me that anybody could refer the books in the university library with permission. When I went to the library in the evening, the staff in the section asked me to come in the morning as there were no sufficient electric lights to search Sept. 1983 issue. I was quite fortunate that the staff could get the issue easily. You see this is my tedious search for this information, wasting several hours on this, ultimately for nothing as the obtained information is outdated."

In diary-keeping and critical incident techniques the user must remember the search procedures in order to note down or narrate. Industrialists often neglect to note down the procedure as it consumes their precious time and it is boredom on their part. Oral narration is unavoidable as the investigator sits with him and requests according to the needs of the user. However, the demerit in both the cases is that only a few intellectually obliged users must have to be selected for responses.

Observation

Another important user study technique is observation: Participant and non-participant. Participant observation leads to the most authoritative and valid facts and figures. However, it consumes lot of time of the investigator. He has to involve in the industry with the technicians and work with them for a longtime to know their means and methods of information seeking behaviour. For a case study, this could be most suitable but, for the study of many industries, the procedure is time consuming and practically unperceivable.

In participant observation one gets the actual behaviour of information users and their responses to the problems. Investigator can also come across the experts and technical and who advice on the spot for various problems. It is however worthwhile to be a participant observer in few industries during the course of the study because, it fetches a good knowledge of industrial information use on the whole. A manager suggests, "you work in our industry and get to know our usual problems and by what means we try to solve the problems. Then, if you have got anything to say out of your professional knowledge, try to suggest us what best could be done within our reach."

Delphi Study

Delphi study is not directly in contact with the industries or the industrial entrepreneurs but, with those who render advisory services, consultation services, trainers in information processing and management and the administrative staff of the organization.

(1) Here, a group of few experts in information science, industrial personnel trainers, consultants, popular technicians and administrators will be selected.

(2) A set of questionnaire will be mailed or contacted for interview to each of the selected persons, inviting their precious answers.

(3) The results will be tabulated and interpreted to get statements of opinions. These are authoritative as they are from those who actively take part in the field of information system for small industries.

(4) Again these statements will be sent to the same persons for further comments and criticisms.

(5) The result of the opinion will again be interpreted systematically to form a detailed report on the field.

This is called 'Delphi Study . As the number of small industries are more, geographically wide-spread and the nature of industrial entrepreneurs vary, it is difficult and practically tedious to get systematic and authoritative data, information and opinion. The delphi study coupled with participant observation is the suitable technique to study the industrial information users in modern trends.

References

1. Brittain, J.M. : Information needs and application of the results of user studies. In: Perspectives in information science, ed. by Anthony Debons and W.J. Cameron. Wales, Noordhoof - Leydon, 1975, p. 437.
2. Flanagan, J.C.: The Critical incident technique. *Psychological bulletin*. Vol. 51, 1974, pp. 327-58.
3. Parker, E.B. and W.J. Paisley: Research for psychologists at the interface of the scientists and his information systems. *American Psychologist*, Vol. 21, 1966, p. 1061.
4. Ramasesh, C.P. Characteristics and problems of information systems and services required for small scale industries in Southern Karnataka. Unpublished Ph.D. Thesis submitted to University of Mysore, 1985, p. 219-221.
5. Weisman, H.M.: Information systems, services and centre. New York, Wiley-Baker, 1972, p. 100.

26

INFORMATION SOURCES IN ARCHITECTURE

B. Ramesh Babu
K. Kaliyaperumal

Introduction

Architecture may be defined as the art and science of building. According to Parmer, architecture is the conscious creation of utilitarian spaces constructed from materials in such a way that the whole is both technically and aesthetically satisfying. Webster's *New Twentieth Century Dictionary* defines architecture as "an art, profession or a science of designing and constructing buildings".

Architecture as a Discipline

Architecture is an art like music, painting, sculpture and poetry. But it is little different from them as well. For example, a poet can express his own feelings such as joy and sorrow whereas an architect cannot use architecture as a suitable vehicle for self-expression of the kind appropriate in poetry. Le Corbusier's idea about architecture is that a house is a machine for living. A house is of course much more than a machine, but like a machine, it must work. This is true of all buildings, and architecture considers every aspect of the proper functioning of a building from water supply, heating, lighting and drainage to the design and convenient placing of door handles and the best sectional shape for a hand-rail. The field of architecture has ben considered as an academic discipline.

The architect is a master builder who depends upon a wide range of reference sources. Before designing a building, he has to consult a wide range of design guides, regulations, standards, catalogues in conjunction with official data files and sets of drawings.

Literature in Architecture

There has been a continuous expansion of information and increase in,the number of information sources. The growth reflects not only of information but also the recorded forms and channels of communicaticn. the architect is dependent on a variety of information sources in his fields of interest. Therefore the user of literature in architecture necessitate a sound knowledge of the sources, both primary and secondary in order to pursue one's career, as an architect.

Primary Sources in Architecture

Journals

There are quite a number of journals in architecture. Among them, prominent journals are listed below.

a. *Architecture and Design*, Bimonthly, Published by Media Transasia (p) Ltd, New Delhi.

b. *Inside outside, The Media Design Magazine*, Monthly, Published by Business Press, Bombay.

C. *Marg*, Monthly, Published by National Centre for performing Arts, New Delhi.

d. *Architects India*, Published by Architecture Publishing corporation of India, Bombay.

e. *Interior Design*, Monthly, Published by Whitney Communication Corporation, New York.

f. *Interiors for the Contract Design Professional*, Published by Bill Board Publications, New York.

g. *Residential Interiors*, Bimonthly, Published by Bill Board Publications, New York.

h. *Architectural Digest, The International Magazine of Fine Interior Design* (Nine per annum), Knapp Press, Los Angeles.

i. *Canadian Interiors*, Monthly, Maclean-Hunter Ltd, Toronto.

J. *Interior* (Semi-annual) Swedish Furniture Manufactures Association, Stockholm.

k. *Architecture Interieure*, Bimonthly, Society' d' Elinon et de Press, Paris.

l. *Japan Interior Design*, Monthly, Interia Shuppan, Tokyo.

m. *Landscape Architecture*, Bimonthly, Published by The American Society of Landscape Architects, Kentucky.

n. *Landscape Planning*, Quarterly, Published by Elsevier, Amsterdam.

o. *Landscape Research New*, Thrice a year, published by Manchester University, Manchester.

p. *Garten und Landschaft*, Monthly, Published by the German Federation of Landscape Architects, Munich.

q. *Journal of Garden History*, Quarterly, Published by taylor and Francais, London.

r. *Mimar*, Quarterly, Published by Islamic Arts Foundation, UK.

s. *Progressive Architecture (P/A)*, Monthly, except semimonthly in October, Published by Reinhot Publishing and Co.. Cleveland.

t. *Japan Architect (JA)*, Monthly, Published by Japan Architect Co. Ltd., Tokyo.

u. *Architecture and Urbanism*, Monthly, Published by Architecture and Urbanism Publishing Co. Ltd., Japan.

Standards

British Standards

Today, there are number of standards relating to every aspect of the building process. These have developed from the application standards to housing design in rebuilding London after the Great Fire in 1666. In 1774. They were consolidated into the *Building Act* and since then have been augmented by various local by-laws, *the Public Health Acts* of the Nineteenth Century and, since 1901, coordinated and developed by the British Standard Institution. During the twentieth century, the process of standardisation, development and coordination was extended in many countries, in different ways, towards the wider approach of the European and International Standardisation Movements. As international professional commitments increase so also must the architects know the standards of other countries. The important standards are listed below which are very relevant in architecture.

All British Standards are identified by its unique Alpha numeric codes.

British Standard Institution issuing numerous standards with alpha-numeric code, under five broad heads such as

1. Building for specific uses
2. Building elements
3. Products and components define by Form
4. Materials
5. Activities, Requirement

Indian Standards

For building construction and structure different standards are issued by the Bureau of Indian Standards.

A few standards are listed below under appropriate headings

Development control Rules and General Building requirements

IS:8888 - 1973 Guide for requirements of low income housing.

Fire Protection

IS: 8757- 1978 Glossary of terms associated with fire safety.

Building Materials

IS: 383- 1970 specification for coarse are five aggregates from natural sources for concrete.

Structural Design

IS: 3935 - 1966 Code of Practice for composite constructions.

Constructional Practice and Safety

IS: 1904-1978 Code of Practice for structural safety of buildings: shallow foundations.

Building Services

IS: 4666 - 1980 Specialisation for electric passenger and goods lifts.

Plumbing Services

IS: 3196-1982 specification for welded low carbon steel gas cylinder exceeding 5 litre water capacity for low pressure lignetiable gases.

Signs and Outdoor displays structures

IS: 3803-1966 methods of test for non combustibility of building materials.

Government Reports

Government agencies are publishing building bye-laws.

development control rules etc. These publications are very essential for the practising architects. The agencies involved in these activities and their publications are as follows:

a. Council of Architecture in India. This body was established according to the *Architects Act* of 1972 and it has a registered office located at Delhi.

b. Madras Development Control Rules, 1990 and Madras Metropolitan Structure Plan brought out by Madras Metropolitan Development Authority, Madras.

c. Delhi Master Plan, Published by the Delhi Development Authority.

d. Articles of Agreement and Conditions of Building Contracts; Code of Professional Practice; and Rules of Architecture Competition, brought out by the Indian Institute of Architects.

In Britain Her Majesty's Stationery Office (HMSO) and Building Research Establishment (BRE), Property Service Agency (PSA) are publishing many, sources specifications etc. Among them, a few have been listed below.

a. *The PSA Standards Specifications on mechanical and electrical installation.* Published by HMSO and PSA.

b. *The Schedule of Rates for Building Works 1980*, HMSO 1981.

c. *Estimating Handbook for building maintenance (PSA).*

d. *The PSA Volume of Common Defects in Buildings* by H.J. Eldridge, HMSO, 1976.

e. *Health Building Notes*, HMSO, London.

f. *Hospital Design Notes*, HMSO, London.

g. *Health Equipment Notes*, HMSO, London.

h. *Hospital Technical Memoranda*, HMSO, London.

i. *Structural Fire Precautions*, HMSO, London.

j. *Sound Installation*, HMSO 1975, London.

k. *Conservation of Fuel and Power in Buildings other than Dwellings*, HMSO, London.

Secondary Sources in Architecture

Encyclopedias

There are many encyclopedias available relating to different aspects of architecture such as design and construction engineering, urban planning, landscape architecture, history of architecture etc. A few of them are listed below.

a. *Encyclopedia of Architecture Design, Engineering and Construction*/edited by Joseph A. Wilker, New York; John Wiley. This encyclopedia lists the terms which are related to Architecture design, Engineering construction etc. and detailed account of each such terms is presented.

b. *The Macmillan Encyclopedia of Architecture and Design*/edited by P.Guedes, 1979.

c. *Whittick's Encyclopedia of Urban Planning*, McGraw Hill, 1974.

d. *Encyclopedia of World Architecture*, 2 Vols. Macmillan, 1977. It has many building plans.

e. *Hatje's Encyclopedia of Modern Architecture*, Thames and Hudson 1963.

f. *The Macmillan Encyclopedia of Architecture and Technological Change*, Macmillan, 1979.

g. *The Macmillan Encyclopedia of Architects*, edited by Adolf K. Platzek, London: Macmillan, 1982.

The Macmillan Encyclopeadia of Architects (1982) includes twenty four hundred biographies of architects from ancient times to the present and from all geographical regions. It consists of four volumes. The biographies in the encyclopedia are presented in alphabetical sequence. It has approximately 15 hundred pictures, drawings, engravings, wood cuts, plans, models, etc. It includes architecture glossary. Two computer generated indexes are provided one of names of individuals and the other for architectural works.

h. *Encyclopedia of Architectural Technology*/edited by Pedro Guedes, McGraw-Hill, 1979.

It consists of six sections:

Section 1 History and styles architecture in various countries

Section 2 Building types and built forms

Section 3 Structural aspects of building

Section 4 Services of the building system

Section 5 Building materials

Section 6 Tools, techniques and materials

Dictionaries

The numerous dictionaries on architecture are listed below:-

a. *Dictionary of Architectural Science*, Penguin 1973. It gives clear, concise description of architectural terms.

b. *Dictionary of Architecture, Building Construction and Materials*, H. Buksch, Macmillan and Evans, 1983, is a German-English, English-German Dictionary.

c. *Harris' Dictionary of Architecture and Construction*, McGraw-Hill 1975. It is a well defined alphabetical list of glossary, with numerous diagrams as well as illustrations.

d. *Dictionary of Architectural Science, Applied Science 1973*. It provides clear, concise entries and offers brief literature survey in the field of Architecture.

e. *McGraw-Hill dictionary of Scientific and Technical Terms*, Ed. 2, 1978.

f. *International Dictionary of Building Construction*/ Edited by A.C. Schwickers, McGraw-Hill, 1972.

g. *Dictionary of Architecture and Building Trades in Four Languages*, Pergamon, 1963.

h. *Cowan's Dictionary of Architectural Science. Applied Science*. 1973.

i. *Illustrate glossary of Architecture 850-1830*/by John Harris and Jill levs New York: Clarkson N. Potter. Inc. 1966.

It is a very good source for history of architecture as well as it has alphabetical list of architectural terms and detailed description about each term. It also has 224 photographs of famous historic buildings and styles.

j. *New international Dictionary of Heating, Ventilating and air conditioning*, 1983.

It provides terminology in 10 languages namely English, Dutch, French, German, Hungarian, Italian, Polish, Russian, Spanish and Swedish, with main entries in English giving translations and nine indexes for the other languages which refer to English sequence.

k. *The Manual of Photographer*: Published by American society of Photographer, 1980.

It is an advanced and comprehensive tools. It provides information on the terms and symbols used in the field of architecture and photography.

Indexing Periodicals

a. *The Architectural Periodical Index*, Qtly, 1971-Published by Royal Institute of British Architects, The articles are selected from about 450 architectural journals received at Royal Institute of British Architects (RIBA). It is aimed at the practising architect and covers in the main artcles that have been published on new buildings, conservations and design technology etc.

b. *Avery Index to Architectural Periodicals*, Qtly. 1930-It is a complimentary to the *Architectural Periodical Index*. It covers international WORLD periodicals on architecture, such as *American Architect, Architectural Record, Progressive Architecture, Architectural Forum* etc. These periodicals have been indexed from first issue onwards. The index consists of 15 volumes supplements are issued:

First supplement in	1975
Second supplement in	1977
Third supplement in	1979

c. *Current Information in the Construction Industry* CICI, Fortnightly, Property Services Agency. Half yearly cumulations under the title 'construction References.'

It aims at the architects, surveyors and engineers who work for the Property Services Agency. A wide range of materials are covered, includes periodical articles, books, reports and standards (both British and Foreign). Entries are arranged in a classified order.

Abstracting Periodicals

a. *RICS. Abstracts and Review*, monthly, Royal Institution of Chartered Surveyors.

It aims to cover the information needs of the surveyors, Architects. It provides abstracts of periodical articles, books and pamphlets, arranged in about 20 broad subject areas, Eg. Arbitration, Building and Construction, Compulsory purchase and compensation, Housing and Property Management, Its Associated Publication is RICS weekly briefing.

b. *Building management Abstracts*, Bimonthly, Chartered Institute of Buildings, UK.

It provides abstracts for books and reports in addition to the periodical articles on building management. The abstracts are arranged according to the special scheme of classification designed for this purpose.

This is useful for the references of site and project organisation, estimating and costs, Education and practice management.

c. *Building Science Abstracts* is published by Building Research Establishment (BRE). Unfortunately, however, the publication has ceased at the end of 1976.

d. *Institution of Civil Engineer Abstracts.* ICE Abstracts, Monthly, Published by the Institution of Civil Engineers, UK.

e. *International Building Services Abstracts: BSRIA, UK.* Formerly known as the Thermal Abstracts. The monthly issues covers aspects of building services with lengthy abstracts articles. Photocopy supply services are offered for members.

f. *Photographic Abstracts*, Bimonthly, 1921-. Published by the Royal Society, UK.

g. *Urban abstracts*: monthly, by Greater London Council Research Library.

The monthly issues are being published separately under two series:

Series 1: Covering Government publications, management, planning and land use and transport.

Series 2: Covering building construction, housing, Science, Technology, environment and pollution.

A cumulative subject index and corporate author index is produced for each annual volume and is issued about six months after the December. From the middle of 1981 the data base has been available on on-line as ACCOMPLINE.

h. *The Department of Environment and Transport Library Bulletin:* Published in UK.

It provides informative abstracts from a wide range of periodical articles, books, pamphlets and reports. Abstracts are arranged under broad headings like, Architecture, housing, construction, urban play land use, environmental protection, water etc.

Handbooks

Listed below are handbooks which are very important and quite useful for the practicing architects. They give detailed information about each aspect of building design, executing design etc.

a. *Planning: The Architects handbook/* edited by Edward D. Mills, London: Butterworths, 1985.

   This consists of basic Building planning data and building services. This also includes the codes of practice, BS standards, legislation and the like.

b. *Architectural Handbook/*by Alfred M. Kemper, New York: John wiley, 1979. This consists of climatic data to construction measurements which are quite useful in designing a building.

c. *The Architects Handbook*, David Kent Ballast, New Jersey: Prentice-Hall Inc., 1984. This handbook offers architects a wide range of business and financial management knowledge.

d. *Time Saver Standards for Residential Development/* edited by Joseph De Chirra, New York, McGraw-Hill. It is a comprehensive source of architectural design data for housing and residential development.

e. *Time Saver Standards for Site Planning*/edited by Joseph De Chirra, new York McGraw-Hill, 1984. it is useful for those who involved in the planning, designing, programming of individual buildings, complexes and out door facilities. It provides basic design criteria, analytic methods, and construction details for all places of site development.

f. *Time Saver Standards for Architectural Design Data*/ edited by John Hancock Calendar, New York: McGraw- Hill.

g. *Handbook of Sports and Recreational Building Design*/edited by G.John and H. Heard. London: Architectural Press.

It is a four-volume set and aims to provide practical advice and guidance on the design of sports buildings and conversion and adoption of existing buildings.

h. *Handbook of Speciality Elements in Architecture*/ edited by Andrew Alperm, New York: McGraw- Hill ; Useful reference tool for interior and exterior design of buildings.

i. *The Atrium Library of Architecture Today* 5 vols./ edited by Francisco Agensio, Spain: Atrium, 1989.

It almost covers all types of buildings data. It presents a series of examples of architectural work being carried in Europe. It portrays the different projects, groups under financial headings.

j. *Hand book of Solar Radiation Data for India*/Compiled by Annamani, New Delhi: Allied Publishers (P) Ltd., 1980.

The greater part of the hand book consists of tables of sun shine solar and terrestrial radiation and climatological data measured in 18 stations which will be useful for Architects for designing the buildings.

Directories

a. *The Architectural and Building Directory of India.* Annual, Bombay: Business Press. It is a source directory for architects, estate owners and contractors in

India.

b. *Directory of Builders and Contractors*, Architect Publishing Corporation of India, 1970. It provides upto date addresses of builders, estate developers and contractors.

c. *Indian Architects Directory, including Who's Who./* edited by A.K. Gupta. Bombay: The Architects Publishing Corporation of India.

It gives detailed list of Architectural Schools in India, code of professional conduct, architectural competitions, general conditions of contact, specifications for civil works. It also gives a detailed list of approved architects in India.

Bibliographics

The available major bibliographies in different architectural aspect such as building, climatology, conservation, landscape architecture and planning are listed below.

a. T.J. Chandler's *Selected Bibliography of Urban Climates*, The World meteorological Office, 1963.

b. Griffiths and Griffiths, *A bibliography on weather and architecture*, US Department of Commerce, 1969.

c. T.J. Peterson's *The Climate of Cities: A survey of recent literature*, US Department of health, 1969.

d. *A Critical Bibliography of Building Conservation. Historic towns, building for their furnishings and fittings*/John F. Smith, London, 1978.

e. *A Bibliography of Historical Organisation practice* F.L.Rath and M.R.O. Cornells, American Association for State and Local History, 1975.

f. *Guide to Historic Preservation. Historical Agencies and Museum Practices: A Selective Bibliography/* ;by Cooperstwon, New York: Historical Association. 1970.

g. *Conservation of Old Buildings: A Selective Bibliography*, by John H. Harvey.

h. *The Space Around Buildings: an Annotated Bibliography*, Property Services Agency 1975.

i. *Landscape: guide to Sources of Information,* property agency Services, 1978.

j. *The Brenda Whites, The Literature and Study of Urban Planning,* Routledge and Kegan Paul, 1974.

k. *A Guide to Sources of Information in Planning*/by G.M.K. Beek and S.G.M. Snowball, Information Paper No. 12, Centre for Environmental Studies, 1973.

Yearbooks

a. *British Standard Yearbook*, published by British Standard Institution.

b. *Royal Institute of British Architects. Institute of Builders Yearbook.*

c. *Hospitals and Health Services yearbook*, Annual, Institute of health Services Administrators.

d. *Annual of Architecture: European Masters* (2 volumes) published by Atrium, Barcilona - spain. it is a annual publication providing detailed description about the work of famous contemporary Architects. It is published in Spanish and English.

Conclusion

Architecture is a mirror of the civilization. Several number of reference sources are being published all over the world.

It is not possible to list every type of ephemera, but many sources are covered in this paper.

References

1. *Brad Field* (valeria J), *Ed.* Information Sources in Architecture. London: Butterworths, 1985.

2. Indian Standards Institution. National Building code of India, New Delhi: ISI, 1984.

3. Mills (Edward D), *Ed.* Planning: the Architects handbook. London: Butterworths, 1985.

27

SURVEY ON THE INFORMATION NEEDS OF FARMERS IN NELLORE DISTRICT (A.P.)

K. Veeranjaneyulu

In the third five year plan much emphasis was given for communication of new technologies to farmers, but it failed due to holistic view reaching the farmer and consequent impact. India being a developing country with wide diversity in climate and farming systems including farmers, centralised systems of communication such as Radio, T.V., News paper could not play the expected role.

Significance and role of agricultural information for agricultural development was realised after independence when the agriculture changed fast and new techniques were being used in Indian agriculture. Farm information was regarded as one of the inputs in agricultural production and farm information was made available through various sources including print media.

Among mass media, news papers, radio and T.V. are the most commonly used media. News papers are primarily a means of disseminating news and influencing the public on the current events. These days television is greatly used for educating, informing and entertaining the masses. The purpose of any communication medium is to put the ideas, make the meaning clear to get them accepted. The motivated people will adopt and practice them. Television can, therefore, be assumed to be a powerful medium.

Farmers are the ultimate users of the agricultural research findings through proper extension media. The farming category in the information communication process is likely to include illiterate as well as the literate strata. The extension workers and rural libraries have a significant role to play for communicating new ideas and practices to the farmers. For progressive educated farmers the best means of communicating research results for the library is through publications.

Objectives of the Study

The objectives of the study are as follows:

1. Finding out various type of information sources of farmers regarding seeds, fertilizers, pesticides and marketing.
2. Knowing the various ways through which the farmers seek their information.
3. Analysing the role of Radio and T.V. informing the latest developments to the farmers.
4. Assessing of farmers preference regarding news papers and farm magazines published in Telugu.

Methodology

The data required for the study was collected from primary as well as secondary sources. The primary data was collected through questionnaires by interview method.

The secondary data was collected from district hand book and agricultural abstracts available with Chief Planning Officer. Nellore.

Selection of Samples

The study was conducted in Nellore district of Andhra Pradesh during the year 1995. 150 educated farmers were selected from Nellore district for the purpose of this study. As the Nellore District is having three Revenue Divisions, 50 samples were selected from each Revenue Division.

Profile of Nellore District

Nellore district has three Revenue Divisions consisting 46 Mandals which were categorized with effect from 25 May, 1985. The three revenue divisions are Nellore, Kavali and Gudur covering 12, 18 and 16 Mandals respectively. Soils in the district are Black soils, Red soils and Clay loamy soils constituting 23%, 43% and 34% of the total area respectively. The main rivers Pennar, Kandaleru and Swarnamuki drain the district by traversing through West to East of the District and flow into Bay of Bengal. Normal rainfall of the district is 1041 m.m. which is more than State average by 141 m.m.

The total geographical area of the district is 32, 52, 006 acres of which 23.17% are under cultivation. 7.15 lakh acres are irrigated which form 78.95 percent of total cropped ares. The principal crops raised in the district are Paddy, Jowar, Bajra, Chillies, Groundnut and Tobacco.

India's principal rocket launching station SHAR of ISRO is located in the Island of Sriharikota in Nellore district. The well developed physical and financial infrastructure facilities, availability of adequate raw material offer good scope for the development of agriculture, its allied activities and the promotion of wide range industries in the district.

Analysis of Data

Table No. 1: Farmers' Source of Information about seeds, Fertilizers, Pesticides and Marketing

Sl. No.	Source	Total Respondents	Responses	% of response total respondents
1.	Friends	150	93	62
2.	Relatives	150	87	58
3.	News Papers	150	69	46
4.	Radio	150	72	48
5.	T.V.	150	39	26
6.	Govt. Agencies	150	79	50
7.	Wall Posters	150	9	6
8.	Representatives of private company	150	6	4

The above table reveals farmers' source of information regarding seeds, fertilizers, pesticides and marketing. Majority of the respondents i.e. 62 percentage are getting required information from friends, 58 percentage of respondents are getting required information from relatives and 50% of respondents are seeking from government agencies.

The above analysis concludes that farmers were getting agricultural information mainly from friends, relatives and government agencies.

Table No. 2: Source of Information from news papers & farm magazines

Sl. No.	News Papers/ Farm Magazines	Total Respondents	Respondents	% of Respondents by source total Respondents
News Papers				
1.	Eenadu	150	69	46
2.	Andhra Jyothi	150	26	39
3.	Andhra Prabha	150	—	—
Farm Magazines				
1.	Annadata	150	27	18
2.	Mapally	150	—	—

It is evident from the above table, that majority (46%) of farmers are getting required agricultural information by reading *Eenadu*, and 39 percentage of respondents are reading *Andhra Jyothi*, 18 percentage of respondents are using *Annadata*, farm magazine as a source.

The above information shows that the farmers are getting agricultural information only from two news papers (*Eenadu* and *Andhra Jyothi*).

Table No. 3: Farmers and Air Broadcasts

Reply	Respondents	% of respondents
Yes	63	42
No	87	58
Total	150	100

The above table shows that only 42% of farmers are hearing AIR broadcasts and remaining respondents are not hearing.

Table No. 4: Types of Popular Programmes

Sl.	Programme	Total Respondents	Respondents	% of No. Respondents
1.	Polampanulu	63	09	14.29
2.	Padipantalu	63	05	7.94
3.	Pallesecmalu	63	56	88.89

The above table shows that most of the farmers are hearing *palleseemalu programme*. Hence it is clear that the *palleseemalu programme* is convenient programme for farmers, because it is being broadcast in the evening times.

Table No. 5: Farmers' Programmes on T.V.

Reply	Respondents	% of Respondents
Yes	31	20.67
No	119	79.33
Total	150	100.00

It is evident from the table that more than 75% of the farmers are not watching T.V. programmes. Only 20.67% of respondents are watching agricultural programmes on T.V.

Table No. 6: Reasons for not watching T.V. Programmes

Sl. No.	Reasons	Respondents	% of Respondents
1.	Non-availability of T.V.	102	85.71
2.	Non-availability of time	17	14.29
3.	Other reasons	—	—
	Total	119	100

The above table shows that percentage of the farmers not watching the T.V. programmes, because of the non-availability. Very few respondents replied that they have no time to watch T.V. programmes.

Findings

1. Majority of the farmers are getting agricultural information regarding seeds, fertilizers, pesticides and marketing mainly from friends, relatives and Government agencies.
2. It is clear from the analysis, that the respondents are reading only two news papers (*Eenadu* and *Andhra Jyothi*) for agricultural information.
3. Half of the respondents are not able to hear AIR broadcasts because of financial problems.
4. The analysis shows that the "*palleseemalu*" programme is convenient programme for farmers,

because of its being broadcast in the evening time.

5. Nearly 80% of the farmers are not watching T.V. programmes. The main reason for non-observation is because of the finance to buy T.V. sets.

Suggestions

1. Most of the farmers are not able to hear AIR broadcasts and watch T.V. programmes. This situation can be overcome by providing Radio and T.V. to villages.
2. All India Radio and Doordarshan should broadcast agriculture related programmes only in the evening times and not in the day time, as the farmers are busy with their work.
3. The Agricultural University should establish agricultural information communication centres for fulfilling the information requirements of the farmers.
4. There is an immediate necessity to build up the Rural Information Centres as integral part of the public library system with the help of Agricultural University and ICAR.
5. The Information and Public Relations Department and Agricultural Department should open information centres in every Mandal and screen regularly film on the latest developments in agriculture.
6. The Government should start Krishi Vighan Kendras and Farmers Training Centres in every district.

References

1. Bhagat, Rekha and Ramachandran, c. Trends in Agricultural communication research. *Communicator* xxviii (4). 1993.
2. Gangadhara Rao, p. Rural Information centres. National seminar on assessment of public library development in India, 1986.
3. Mohan, Surendra. Agricultural Information Systems and Services. *Journal of Library and Information Science*, 2(2) 1977.
4. Nonjappa, D and Ganapathy. News paper reading habit of farmers of Bangalore district in Karnataka. *Indian Journal of extension education* xxii (1 & 2) 1986.
5. Raina, Roshan. Libraries in agricultural research communication. *Lucknow* Librarian 15(2) 1983.

Section IX
Technical Report Writing and Standards

28

TECHNICAL REPORT-WRITING : METHODS AND PROCEDURES

A.L. Moorthy
C.R. Karisiddappa

Introduction

Communication is the process of transmission or exchanging or interchanging of ideas, thoughts, feelings, information etc. through a common system of symbols, signs, gestures or language. This progress may take place between individuals or groups. Various types of communication include oral, visual/audiovisual, written and electronic communication.

Technical communication had its origins during World War II when the Royal Air Force Officers felt the need for an operation manual explaining the procedures and techniques of maintenance of various systems and sub-systems of aircraft engaged in the War. Since a lot of technical details were included in them, these came to be known as technical manuals. Thus, a new career specialisation, 'Technical Communication', typical of technical jargon has emerged. This branch of knowledge received attention from R & D scientists, science administrators, top management in business and industry [1]

Necessity of Technical Communication to L IS Professionals

With increased R & D activities in each and every field of human knowledge, it has become necessary to have working knowledge about technical communication. Professionals in Library and Information Science (LIS) field may have to write project proposals, for example, starting a new professional service or purchasing an equipment or development of a machine readable database of library holdings; research and review papers for publication in scholarly periodicals or presenting in conferences; chapter in a book; project report, say, automation of library operations; periodical progress reports on activities, plans and ongoing projects; brochures or promotional material for marketing professional services like consultancy, SDI and CAS; and state-of-the-art reports for management for helping in decision making. All these activities obviate good understanding of technical writing for effective handling of the tasks undertaken.

What is a Technical Report ?

A report is defined as a definitive document which provides information about a task or exercise. As R & D report states the results of or progress made with a research and development investigation [2]. A report is an organised, factual and objective information brought out by a person who has experienced or accumulated (information) and communicated to a person or persons who need it or want it or entitled to it.[3].

A technical report usually is more detailed than an article published in a journal or a paper presented at a conference. It contains sufficient data to enable a reader to evaluate the investigative process of original research or development. It is an end product of an investigation, survey, research project etc.

Technical report, the primary recording medium for R & D work, has become an important source of information in recent years. This is mainly because of the time consuming routines of publication procedures of journals and their preference to publish completed research as against research in progress. But many a time, the nature of communication does not require wide dissemination and so a technical report is brought out. Further, the government-funded research results in the areas of space, nuclear sciences, and defence is generally shrouded under secrecy and national security and so are circulated to a very limited people. All these factors have resulted in the emergence of the technical report, which is issued in different sizes and formats [4].

Technical reports are characterised by their objectivity and targeted audience. They define the problem, analyse and assess the current and future conditions, describe the method/experiment to solve a problem, discuss the results, draw conclusions and recommend future course of action.

A technical report is prepared for various purposes. Project proposals are submitted to get grants; periodical reports are made to inform the status of and progress made in a project; state-of-the-art reports are prepared to make the top management abreast of the latest developments in a specific field; technical papers are published to inform the outside world and those working in the field about the new findings and so on. Whatever may be the form of the technical report, it is written with three main purposes: (a) to inform readers about the outcome of a study, (b) to record the research findings and test outcome for posterity, and (c) to recommend appropriate future course of action.

Although, of late, the get-up of the technical report has improved a lot mainly due to the computers and DTP techniques, it is quite common to duplicate/mimeograph the typed report. Generally, limited copies (not more than 50 in majority of cases) are made for circulation, though many reports are issued in large quantity. Though a small per cent of reports are prepared from published papers, a majority of the reports find their way to primary publications like scholarly journals, conference or symposium proceedings, books, etc.

It is difficult to answer a question if a report is published; a technical report is supposed to be 'published' (for limited circulation), however, it is 'unpublished' for practical purposes as it is not available easily!

Types of Technical Reports

Technical reports include technical papers, memoranda, proposals, progress and status reports, feasibility reports, technical manuals, investigation reports etc. A technical report may be a letter, an article, a research paper, an operational manual, a news bulletin, a company brochure, a book review etc. [(5)]. Passman [(6)] includes preprints, institutional reports, and committee reports also under technical reports literature. Depending on the purpose and information content, reports can be classified as informal and formal reports.

Informal reports usually present the results of investigations and convey information of products, methods and equipment. The informal nature makes these more accessible, and easy to be adapted to any situation. These are generally meant for immediate superiors and colleagues in an institution. These include memoranda, brief analysis reports, trip reports, laboratory reports, field reports, inspection reports, etc.

Formal reports provide information which is needed by the management for decision making. Thus a formal report will have a larger target readership as compared to the informal report, and serve as a main source of information. Formal reports include project proposals, progress or status reports (half-yearly, annual etc), state-of-the-art reports and review reports, trend or critical evaluation reports, feasibility reports, etc. Types and characteristics of some of the above mentioned reports are briefly described in the following paragraphs.

Committee Reports

Many a time when a major decision is to be taken, the government or its department constitutes committees to go into various aspects of the issue (for example, the Abid Hussain Committee of CSIR, Committee on Bhopal Gas Tragedy etc). These issues include policy formulation, restructuring the organisation, prevention of losses due to hazards, etc. Usually, all the members in such committees will be experts in their fields and these reports provide very valuable information, including the pros and cons of an issue and a plan of action.

Feasibility Reports

These reports discuss the practicality, in physical and economic terms, of a new project (for example, feasibility reports on the establishment of DELNET, CALIBNET etc), new product development of a new program, purchase of a new equipment/plant or machinery, or reallocation of a factory site. A feasibility report generally includes explanation of the problem, present standards on criteria, subject-items to be analysed, examination of the scope of analysis, presentation and interpretation of the data, and conclusions and recommendations (ref. 5, p. 29). Feasibility reports may also include cost-effective analysis, alternative routes available to complete the project and a minimum time required to achieve a break-even point in cases where returns are expected.

Institutional Reports

These reports describe the activities and progress of projects undertaken by an institution or establishment. These include technical information on programs, details of infrastructural and manpower resources, and summaries of research undertaken during the period of the report. As such these reports provide valuable information not available elsewhere. The annual reports of the government departments and agencies, private and public R&D laboratories, and professional societies belong to this category of reports.

Preprints

These can be taken as the informal reports of individual authors. These are circulated to the colleagues or professionals who are working in the same field for their comments. The relevant comments made by them, if any, are incorporated and then submitted to a primary journal or presented in a conference/symposium. The format of the preprint will be that of a research paper published in a professional periodical.

Project Proposals

Project proposals are chiefly prepared for getting sanction of projects or approval of a developmental works or getting grants and contracts. These are not circulated before or after the purpose for which they were prepared. Most of the times, the information included is proprietary in nature. These are different from other types of reports because they deal with future plan of action and method of implementation of a project. The main characteristics of a proposal are the statement of intention, willingness, and qualifications and expertise to accomplish a task as per a definite time schedule. This may also include information about the capabilities of existing facilities, financial, infrastructural and manpower considerations. As these are to be professionally credible, subject knowledge is necessary to prepare project proposals. Convincing the peers to obtain financial support or sanction of project is a hidden function of a proposal. Generally, proposals include a letter of transmittal, title, executive summary, table of contents, introduction, overview and analysis of the problem, statement of the problem, methodology, infrastructural facilities needed to complete the project, financial and manpower considerations, duration and summary [7].

Project Reports

In any R&D organisation, project reports are the most frequently written documents. Once sanctioned, the project leader is bound by the schedule mentioned in the proposal. Often, one has to submit periodical progress reports-half-yearly or annual—to the institution or sponsoring or funding agency for evaluation purposes. By the time the project is completed, a few technical papers would also have been published. At the end, a detailed project report including the results and outcome of the project undertaken is to be submitted. This is a valuable source of primary information on the project. This may include a letter of transmittal, title, abstract or executive summary, contents, background material including introduction and objectives, methodology, results and discussion, conclusions, acknowledgements, references, appendices and list of abbreviations used in the report, if any.

State-of-the-Art Reports

These are prepared to keep the management or project leaders abreast of the latest developments in a subject field. These are similar to review articles and can be prepared by a person having general knowledge in the field. Here the relevant literature published in a specific subject during a particular period is collected and is grouped into the various sub-topics of the subject. This grouped material is presented after careful study of the different facets and arranging them in a logical sequence. Generalisation of the treatment of the contents and delimitation of the time are main characteristics of this report.

Status Reports

These are written to contain specified topics for a select and definite group of readers; hence it is very timely. A status report describes overall subject areas or problems for enquiry and breaks it down into component areas or problems. Conclusions are given leading to future course of action which also serve as a spring-board for the introduction of succeeding status reports. These are also known as preliminary reports, interim reports progress reports (daily, weekly, monthly, yearly) and so on (ref. 5, p. 29).

Trend Reports

These are value-added documents. The main characteristics of this kind of report is the evaluation (of published research) component, assessment of present status and prediction of the future trend the research may take. The positive aspects and shortfalls of the research already reported are also identified by the author. As such a trend report can be written by subject experts or peers only. A trend report includes title, abstract or executive summary, introduction, review of published literature, critical evaluation of the R&D, conclusions, and references and appendices.

Format of Reports

Like many publications, technical reports also have a typical format, although all the elements of the format may not necessarily be included in each and every report.

The informal reports have five basic elements, viz. preliminary material (background), introduction, discussion, conclusions and recommendations, and summary. The background material gives the reader an idea of the history of the project, and thus orients the reader towards the report. In the introduction part, objectives and the context are discussed; the reader is initiated to the problem, the necessity of writing the report, purpose of the report and general overview of the contents. Detailed and full information along with discussion of the method adopted, materials used, and the outcome, the conclusions drawn are presented in the body of the report.

While writing a formal report, the author employs a number of basic elements to orient the reader to the topic of the report and its organisation. Some of the formats used to arrange these elements include SIDCRA (summary, introduction, discussion, conclusions, references and appendices) or IMRAD (C/S) (introduction, materials and methods, results and discussion and conclusions/summary).

Format Analysis of Technical Reports

Whatever may be the arrangement of basic elements, a formal technical report should have the letter of transmittal, cover and title, summary and/or abstract, table of contents, list of illustrations, introductions, materials and methods, analysis and discussion of results, conclusions, recommendations, acknowledgements, references and bibliography, appendices, abbreviations, and symbols used in the report. A few of these elements are discussed briefly in this section.

Letter of Transmittal

This is correspondence (usually a letter) which directs the report to some one. It may contain the information regarding the title of the report, a general statement of the scope and purpose of the report, explanation of problems faced, if any (for example, non-availability of facilities which might have delayed the project), and acknowledgements.

Preliminary Material

This includes title page, preface, if any, abstract or executive summary, table of contents, list of illustrations, tables, etc.

Cover and Title

Simple, plain cover page and title layout are used for technical reports. Many a time, an institution uses same type of cover layout for all the reports it brings out (for example NASA, RAND Corp, etc). Thus the reader is able to recall and link the institution as soon as the distinct layout is seen. Bibliographic details of the report like the title name(s) and address(es) of author(s) or corporate author, contracting agency (if any), the publisher or issuing authority, and month and year of issue are included in the title page. Many report issuing agencies, for example, NASA, NTIS, RAND Corporation etc, use a unique report number for each and every report. This number is included on both the cover and title pages. Most of the reports can be identified by the library if this report number is correctly provided by the reader. An attractive, well balanced title page makes an everlasting impression on the reader.

Preface

This is usually written by the project leader or head of the establishment and includes the historical background to the project. This is excluded when a detailed introduction including the genesis of the project is provided in the document.

Table of Contents

This is an index which lists titles of all sections and the pages on which they start. The contents page provides an overview of the report's organisation, depth and emphasis of the subject dealt. When a report is large, only two levels are used in the contents. The levels of the divisions, sub-divisions, etc are maintained by following indenting, numbering or typography styles (caps, bold, italics, etc). The list of illustrations includes all the figures, flow charts, and tables included in the report.

Abstract

A short account of the contents of a document is called an abstract. It is consulted by a reader before attempting to read the whole text, and so, is expected to stand alone. Two types of abstracts are used: indicative and informative. The former is generally short in length (150 words) and as the name suggests, outlines the contents of the document. The latter is long (250 words) and includes the methodology, results and main conclusions, albeit in brief.

Summary

Summary is a restatement of the major findings and conclusions of a document. This is placed after the text of the body and is intended to help readers comprehend and review the text [(8)]. However, in technical reports, summary is placed before the text of the body. Summary should include the problem, purpose, major facts, conclusions and recommendations. Executive summary, provided some times with a report, is a digest of information intended to provide salient points which generally help in decision making. These include the financial, material and infrastructural implications, major findings and the recommendations for further action.

Both abstract and summary are meant to help readers to find out the relevancy and to ascertain if the document is to be read without actually reading the entire document, keep abreast of current developments and to get an overview of the document [(9)].

Body of the Report

Introduction, materials and methods, analysis of the data, discussion of results, conclusions and recommendations form the main body of the report.

Introduction

This forms an important part which orients the reader to the contents of the report. Introduction includes brief literature survey, the statements of objective and scope. A brief survey of literature is included to establish the status of the ongoing research on the topic. In case the report deals with experimentation, the materials and the methodology including alternative methodologies, if any, are described in detail. If the report deals with surveys, investigation, etc, the nature of population, the method used for survey and the reasons for selecting the method are to be described. The data which was collected during the study will be analysed using various statistical principles. While the objective statement clearly states the purpose and aim of the report, the scope statement reveals the topics covered and the boundaries of the study. The methodology describes the procedure or process followed in the study to meet the objectives of the report. This section is followed by the problem and background statements, which introduces the reader to the problem and the circumstances in which the problem originated. A well-written introduction arrests the attention of the reader and established the tone, subject and its limitations.

Conclusions and Recommendations

Based on the analysis and facts, the conclusions are inferred and recommendations are suggested. The conclusions section emphasizes the most important, significant data and ideas in the report. So, all the conclusions should be related to the facts and data presented in the report. The conclusions should be written in a brief manner devoid of lengthy commentaries. When the conclusions are precise and clear, the main recommendations are obvious. Each recommendation is numbered and the first recommendation should deal with the problem of the report and also its solution.

End Material

Acknowledgements, references/bibliography, abbreviations used in the report and appendices are regarded as the end material.

Acknowledgements

Author receives help from many sources while writing the technical report. These include grants from institutions, material, infrastructural and laboratory facilities from parent or other collaborating establishments, useful discussions with colleagues, suggestions from peers for improvement, and help from staff members in data collection or analysis, typing etc. Author may with to thank all those who helped and these are included in the acknowledgements. However, care is to be taken to include only those who have actually and significantly involved in the preparation of the report.

References

A scientific study is based on already published material, which is used in problem formulation. These intellectual debts will be paid through citations (in text) and references (at the end). Some times author wishes to suggest documents for further reading, a bibliography is included. Whereas the sources listed under references are all necessarily consulted, those listed under bibliography need not necessarily be consulted while preparing the report. A section discusses later in detail about citing and listing references.

Abbreviations

Abbreviations used are listed at one place, usually at the end. However, the author should keep their usage to a minimum and avoid using non-familiar and non-standard abbreviations and symbols.

Appendices

Supportive material like legislative laws and acts which do not form part of the text but is needed for better understanding of the concepts; long and complicated tables, flow charts, and questionnaires, the placement of which will not affect the readers' understanding of the report; computer algorithms, long extracts from other reports, notes, glossaries, and mathematical proofs which were used in the text but do not hamper the readers comprehension of the ideas are included as appendices to the report. It is presumed that the inclusion of these in the text would distract the attention of the reader and so are excluded from the main text. However, these are to be kept to a minimum; otherwise it would be construed that the original report has very little content. It should be borne in mind that the best written report is one which includes only a few or no appendices.

Technical Report Writing Process

Effectiveness of a technical report depends on many factors. These include knowing the target readers, quality of the contents, structural organisation of the report and clarity of the communication. These are briefly described in this section.

Audience Analysis

The writer should know the readership of the technical report. Depending on the target readers, the tone and the contents of the report can be modified to suit the purpose. For example, a proposal is to be written in a different manner compared to a feasibility report or a final report of an R&D project. The contents and the style of presentation of a technical communication will surely be different when it is intended for well informed research community from that of a document written for neo-literates and public at large. In other words, the level of understanding of the audience would decide the 'technicality' in writing.

Planning a Report

Before venturing actual writing, the author must first make an outline of the topic and various sub-topics. This skeletal framework helps in delimiting a topic, i.e., identifying only those facets which must be dealt in the report and avoiding those which are peripheral to the topic. Also, additions and alterations are possible when the author is clear about what is to be included in the document.

Once the skeleton is decided, the next step is the literature survey and data collection. The sources could be formal publications (journals, patents, monographs, standards, reports, electronic databases etc), informal communication (personal letters), and non-scientific literature including trade catalogues, house bulletins, etc.

Quality of Contents

The intrinsic value of a technical report depends upon the quality of information contained, which in turn depends upon the subject expertise of the author. The currency of information, the adequacy and authenticity of the data and the facts, the reliability of methodology followed, and the originality of research enhance the effectiveness of a technical report.

Clarity of Communication

Clarity of communication depends on two factors, viz. the structural organisation of the report and the command of the author on the language. Logical organisation of a report according to a set pattern (say, IMRADS or SIDCRA), effective usage of illustrations and style of presentation will have a greater impact on the reader.

Drafting and Revision

To make a report readable, a writer has to make drafts and revisions. When the planning and outlining of a report is completed, the writer has to explain the ideas in a coherent and logical way. This is very difficult as it demands author's command over the language and also expertise in the subject field. Thus the first draft may be refined and revised over and over again until the final draft is ready. At this stage, the writer may add headings, sub-headings, illustrations, tables, etc for clarity of communication. References and appendices are also included while revising the draft.

Style of Presentation

While clarity of expression, elegance of presentation, and simplicity of format are powerful means of enhancing understandability, consistency of format and style of presentation enhance readability. Mathew Arnold said "The secret style is to have something to say and say it as clearly as you can".

Text

Usage of simple sentences (with a maximum of 20-25 words), parallel structure for coordinate elements, and active voice enhances effectiveness of a writing. Accuracy in style results from precise use of terms and proper sentence structure precision in expression would eliminate redundancy leading to brevity and clarity [10]. This makes the author use, to a certain extent technical terms and formal standardised sentence structures. However, over usage of jargon would result in poor presentation resulting in unreadable and incomprehensible text. Use of icons, special symbols like bullets, and special typography enhances elegance, clarity and readability. Abbreviations are to be kept to a minimums as these distract the attention of the reader.

Language

Confucius said, "If language is not correct then what is said is not what is meant: if what is said is not what is meant then what ought to be done remains undone". Surely proper words in proper places makes the communication understandable.

The general principles governing technical writing are avoiding superfluous words; choosing familiar, short and precise words;

avoiding abstract expressions, double negatives and dangling modifiers; and ensuring the agreement of subject with verb and pronouns with their antecedents. The author's command over the vocabulary, grammar and diction would help in achieving better results.

Apart from this, consistency in the use of spelling (for example, American and British spelling) and punctuation is also important. Improper punctuation makes the text incomprehensible and confusing. Usage of capitals, bold or italics are to be kept to a minimum as they affect the readability of a document. Acronyms and abbreviated names of institutions are written without full stops (for example, UNESCO, NATO, USA, IISc, IIT, etc and not U.N.E.S.C.O., N.A.T.O., U.S.A., I.I.Sc., I.I.T., etc).

Tables

A table is a simple tool for listing exact data for comparison and analysis. Tables should supplement, and not duplicate the data and figures. While constructing a table it should be noted that the information always reads down from the boxhead to the end of the table; information controlled by stub heads reads across [11]. Also, independent variables should be taken in the first column (stub). The other columns are taken to denote dependent variables (column heads).

The essential elements of a table include the stub, stub head, and boxhead (for single column table). It may have different column heads and spanner heads (a common head for two or more columns) and field spanner (a common sub-head for all the columns, see Figure 1). Tables should be mentioned by their numbers and not as the below given Table, or the following Table etc. They should be typed on separate sheets and arranged in the same sequence as they are referred to in the text.

Usually, numerical data is aligned on the decimal point (when decimals are used) or units. Zero is before decimals less than unity (for example, 0.35 and not .35). Do not add zeros on the left side of decimals. It is advisable to use Indo-Arabic numerals and lower case typography to enhance readability.

Figures and Illustrations

It is said that one picture is worth a thousand words. Visuals are used for better communication and understanding. These include line diagrams and photographs. Line diagrams comprise line graphs, bar charts, pie charts, drawings, flow charts, special illustrations, etc.

Line Graphs

Line Graphs are used to illustrate trends over a period of time or data with many successive values, comparison of similar type of data over fixed or variable time period, and frequency distribution. *Bar charts* or histograms can be presented to provide a three-dimensional view. These are used when one wishes to compare two or more items having at least one common parameter, or a single item at different points or many items at a single point.

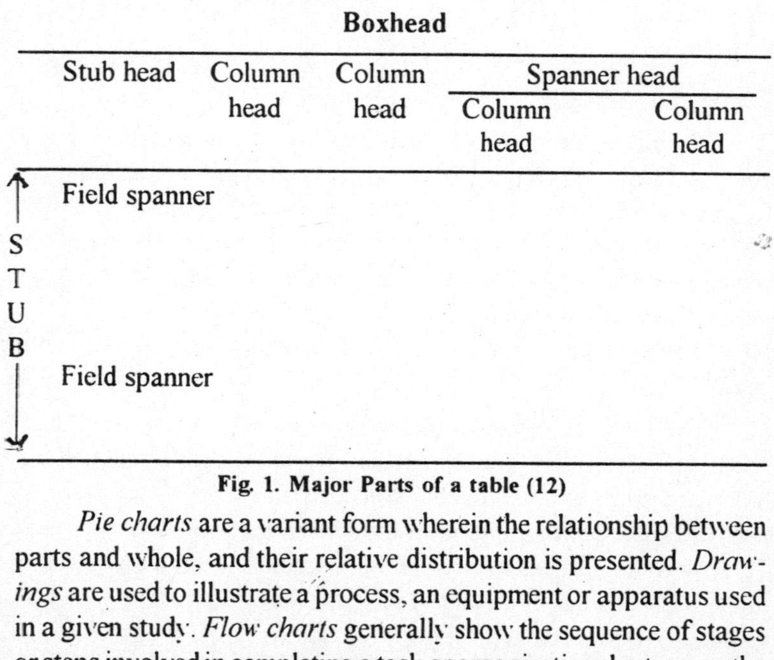

Fig. 1. Major Parts of a table (12)

Pie charts are a variant form wherein the relationship between parts and whole, and their relative distribution is presented. *Drawings* are used to illustrate a process, an equipment or apparatus used in a given study. *Flow charts* generally show the sequence of stages or steps involved in completing a task or organisational set-up, or the sequence of operations in a computer algorithm. Apart from these, *special figures* such as NMR, IR, ECG charts or structural formulae of chemical compounds are also used. Colour or black and white photographs are used for beauty and esthetics. These are reproduced as half-tones.

Care is to be taken to label each of the figures, providing them with a caption and adding index or key when abbreviations, etc are used. While preparing the illustrations, the final reproduction size of the figures is to be kept in mind and accordingly the size of letters, text, symbols and units used are to be drawn in the original figure. It is important to draw the figures in India ink. The figures are sequentially referred in the text of the report and numbered accordingly. They should be cited in the text as Figure 1, Figure 2, and Figure 3 and 'not as the Figure above, the following Figure' etc.

While table caption precedes the table, figure caption follows a figure and ends with a full stop. When a table or a figure already published is taken for reproduction in a report, proper acknowledgement is to be made. Even when author modifies or prepares a new figure or table out of the already published material, it is important to add, as a footnote, the statement 'based on data from XYZ' or 'modified version of figure from ABC' and list the citation under references.

Standard Style for References

According to the Bureau of Indian Standards, a bibliographic reference is "a sequence of items of information needed for enabling a reader of a work to identify, locate and ascertain the relevance of a document referred to" [(13)]. International Standards Organisation (ISO) defines it as "a set of data sufficiently precise and detailed to enable a publication or a part of a publication to be identified" [(14)]. British Standards Institution (BSI) defines it as "a set of data describing a document or a part of a document, and sufficiently precise and detailed to identify and locate it"[(15)].

The main purpose of providing a reference is to identify, locate and to ascertain if it is relevant for further study. Therefore, care should be taken that references contain sufficient information necessary to retrieve a cited document.

Need of References

A research report builds its base upon earlier scholarly work which is done by linking the reporting paper with related work in the same subject area or field of research which was reported earlier. This linking is usually done through references, which are designed to guide readers of new work to sources they may want to consult further. References are designed to repay intellectual debts through open acknowledgement [(16)]. Authors refer to previous material to support, illustrate or elaborate on a particular point. They may also be referred to contradict or negate the conclusions or findings of a reported article. The basic idea in referring an already published work is its relevancy and usage.

References play an important role in the life of a technical report. They will enable readers to understand and decide whether they should read the original publication which is referred to in the text. If the users want to consult/study it, the reference should enable them to get easy access with a minimum effort. Hence references ought to be sufficiently complete, i.e., all the elements of the cited work must be given.

There is a lot of variation in providing references because of confusion over the inclusion of different elements of references, viz, author(s), title, affiliation, volume number, issue number, date, month and year, pagination, publishers, etc, their sequence of occurrence and typographical representation. There are many types of documents, i.e., journal articles, conference proceedings, monographs, simple and composite books letters, dissertations, theses, reports, standards, catalogues, etc, which make the problem more complex.

Citing References in Text

There are different practices of citing of references in the text. Some journals give author's name and year in brackets, for example, (Garfield, 1980). The year only is given in brackets when the author's name is a part of the sentence. This is known as Harvard style and also nearer to the Vancouver style followed by biomedical journals. Two or more cited documents published by the same author in the same year are differentiated with alphabetical or numerical suffixes (for example, Price 1980a, Price 1980b etc). Periodicals such as Journal of Documentation, IASLIC Bulletin, etc use a sequential number as superscript over the name(s) of the author(s); the Journal of the American Society for Information Science uses parentheses within the text for this number.

Listing of References

The listing of references at the end of the main text is usually based on the citing practice in the text. They are either arranged alphabetically by author's name (Harvard or Vancouver styles) or in the order of their occurrence in the text. In the Harvard system, the year of publication follows the author's name. In the alphabetical and sequential systems, the year of publication comes after the name of the journal or publisher. In the case of a review article, alphabetisation needs more time because of the large number of references cited.

Standards on References

Many style manuals are available for manuscript preparation which include guidelines for the preparation of references. However, the do not agree on a single style for references. The national standards on references suggest two types of references. International Standard suggests abridged and expanded references. British Standard (BS) recommends minimum and expanded references. American National Standard suggests abbreviated and comprehensive references. The Indian Standard (IS) identifies two types of elements—essential and supplementary—and leaves the choice to the user. It recommends the use of any catalogue code for punctuation. The International Standards Organisation (ISO), the British Standards Institution (BSI) and the American National Standards Institution (ANSI) do not enforce any single style but recommend to follow examples given by them.

As regards to typography for a reference, ANSI recommends the use of single type face for the sake of simplicity and convenience. IS recommends to differentiate the various items of information and highlight essential items in an entry and advises that a uniform practice should be followed in the same publication. One marked difference in these standards is that ANSI prefers to use the author's name(s) in ordinary upper/lower case, whereas IS, BS and ISO recommend capitalisation. ANSI limits the maximum number of authors of a multi-authored work to two, while ISO/BS limit to three. All the four standards recommend title of journal article to be include in the reference.

Suggestions for preparing References

Standardisation practice in citing and listing references would help authors, readers and librarians alike. For efficient and unambiguous information retrieval, the following suggestions are given to arrive at a standard style of references:

(a) The main purpose of providing a reference would not be served if the title of the document being cited (i.e., journal article, a paper from a proceedings, a chapter from book, the title of a report, etc) is not included. It is important for arriving at a quick decision whether a cited work is to be consulted or not.

(b) Dividing the reference into convenient groups or parts—say three or four—would make the references unambiguous. For example, author(s)/editor(s); title of the cited document; title of journal, volume (issue no), year of publication in parentheses, inclusive pages with appropriate punctuation or conference/symposium name (preceded by 'paper presented t'), place, month and year; title of the original work followed by editors' name (in the case of a composite book); place of publication, publisher, year, etc. are some convenient groupings separated by a full stop.

(c) Inclusive pagination also provides the information regarding the size of the document cited in terms of pages. It helps the user as the librarian in calculating the cost in case the document is to be procured from a copy supply centre such as INSDOC or BLDSC.

(d) Usage of upper and lower type faces for author's name would be simple and also easy for typesetting.

(e) Giving imprint information in parentheses avoids confusion with place and year of conference/symposium in the references of conference/symposium proceedings.

Bibliographical Control of Technical Reports

As report literature is difficult to access, technical reports are referred to as 'gray literature . This is because, unlike books and periodicals, proper bibliographical control mechanism does not exist for reports. The nature of contents—security classification like restricted, confidential, secret—also poses problems making some of them inaccessible. The policy of the government (or sponsoring agency) in certain areas of R & D (for example defence, space, atomic energy, etc) does not permit corporate institutions to publish or disseminate reports brought out in these subject fields. Further very few sources are available for knowing the existence of a report. The large number of report issuing agencies further compounds the problems [17].

Because of all these factors, it has become too difficult to procure technical reports. No vendor readily takes up supply of these reports. Though the scene has changed in recent times with the coverage of technical reports in abstracting and indexing periodicals like Scientific & Technical Aerospace Reports (STAR), International Aerospace Abstracts (IAA), Government Reports Announcements & Index (GRAI), Nuclear Science Abstracts (NSA), and to a limited extent, Biological Abstracts and Chemical Abstracts, their coverage is inadequate. Of late, exclusive periodicals covering R & D reports are being published by national bibliographical control agencies (for example, the British R & D Reports of British Library Documents Supply Centre (BLDSC). Though there are agencies (UK : BLDSE : USA : NTIS & UMI : CANADA : CISTI) dealing with bibliographical control and also supplying technical reports when demanded, in India, no such central agency is available to cater to the needs of the users. Though a national document delivery centre for technical reports was suggested to be created, no action has been taken on it yet. However Department of Science & Technology is striving to bring out reference tools in this direction. As technical report literature can promote greater industrial cross-fertilisation in overcoming the technology gap, a national centre for the bibliographic control and supply of these reports is very much needed.

References

1. Rude, Carolyn D. Technical editing. Wadsworth Publishing, Belmont, 1991. p. 311. 430 p.
2. Indian Standards Institution. IS : 8010 (Part 1) - 1976 : Guidelines for preparation of technical reports: Part 1 : Research and development reports. BSI, New Delhi, 1976.
3. Weisman. H.M. Technical report writing. Merril Books, Columbus. 1966.
4. Grogan, Denis. Science and Technology : An introduction the literature. Clive Bingley, London, 1970. pp. 163-9.
5. IGNOU. MLIS course material on technical writing: Block 3: Structure and functions of technical communication. IGNOU, New Delhi, 1995. p. 28.

6. Passman, Sydney. Scientific and Technological Communication. Pergamon, Oxford, 1969. pp. 43-67.

7. IGNOU. MLIS course material on technical writing; Block 1: Communication process. IGNOU, New Delhi, 1995. p. 25.

8. ANSI Z. 39. 14-1979. American National Standard for writing abstracts. ANSI, New York, 1979.

9. Pauley, Steven E and Riordan, Daniel G. Technical report writing today, Ed. 4. Houghton Mifflin, Boston, 1990. p. 107.

10. IGNOU, MLIS course material on technical writing; Block 2: Linguistics. IGNOU, New Delhi, 1995. p. 80.

11. Dukes, Eva. Table construction : Do's ans dont's. *IEEE Transactions on Professional Communication*, 1989, 32(1), 36-40.

12. Buecheler, M.F. Table design—when the writer/editor communicates graphically. *In* Proceedings of 27th ITCC, 1980. PP. G. 68-G. 73.

13. Indian Standards Institution. IS : 2381-1975 : Recommendations for bibliographical references : essential and supplementary elements (first revision). ISI, New Delhi, 1979. 16p.

14. International Standards Organisation. ISO : 690-1975(E): Documentation-bibliographical references—essential and supplementary elements. ISO, Switzerland, 1975. 8 p.

15. British Standards Institution. BS : 1629-1976 : Recommendations : bibliographical references. BSI, London, 1976. 11 p.

16. Merton, Robert K. Foreword. *In* Citation indexing: its theory and applications in science, technology and humanities, edited by Eugene Garfield, John Wiley, New York, 1979. p. vii.

17. Dictionary of reports series codes published by Special Library Association, New York lists over 20,000 codes.

29

STANDARDS FOR PUBLIC LIBRARY SERVICES : A STUDY

S.R. Ijari
B.U. Kannappanavar

Introduction

The main purpose of public library is to serve the reading and other related needs of a community. No other social institution can perform such a wide range of services to the entire population.

The public libraries contribute to the circulation of ideas, harnessing of leisure, the demands of democracy, the spread of knowledge and the success of commercial and industrial enterprises.

The stream of social revolution was experienced in the past and the fruits of this phenomenan are now enjoyed by the present, as it is product of human endeavours. The progress of the society is firmly based on the intellectual heritage of the past. The public library is a democratic institution as it socialies the knowledge stored in its scholarly holdings and enables a society to flourish at all levels - socially, educationally, economically and culturally.

To achieve these goals successfully the public libraries should be managed, organised on sound guidelines, and set patterns in regard to collection of books, appointment of staff, provision of buildings and liberal budgetory provisions. Such standards would ultimately help to provide effective and efficient services to the public at large.

Meaning of Standards

Many experts in library profession and administration have defined the term 'Standards' more or less in identical terms. Probably the finest and the most specific statement on standards for libraries is found in the introduction to "Standards for South African Public Libraries" as given under.

"Library standards may be defined as the criteria by which....

library services may be measured and assessed. They are determined by professional librarians in order to attain and maintain the objectives they have set themselves, standards may be interpreted variously as the pattern of an ideal, a model procedure, a measure for appraisal, a stimulus for future development and improvement and as an instrument to assist decision and action not only by librarians themselves, but by laymen concerned indirectly with institution, planning, and administration of .... library service."

The above definition of standards is the most specific and comprehensive one. Standards should not be taken to be for the library officials only who are at home in the intricacies of professional jargon, but they should make attractive, enlightening reading for the concerned laymen also.

In early part of the present century, the American library professionals introduced the library standards in U.S.A. In the words of Martin, "The first formal standards for public libraries at the national level appeared in 1933, at the depth of the Depression. Libraries were hit by the prevailing economic conditions at least as hard as other educational agencies and government services were. At the same time, users flocked to the public library; some city libraries had their peak year in circulation in 1933. People sought new vocational information and still which they expected to get them a job; or they sought to escape from a world that has become hopeless for them".

Under the American influence similar trends started in Great Britain, Canada, Germany, Japan and other industrially advanced countries. Some of the international organizations like the UNESCO and IFLA have also evinced keen interest in developing library standards.

Need for Library Standards

The effectiveness of library services is to be evaluated in relation to the quality of service and size of book collection and staff. All library standards ought to be written in lucid, forceful language. Wallace in his recent article states as follows:

(a) the need for a preliminary goal for a new or developing institutions or a new or developing service which is minimal in its requirements but which must be met for accreditation or other types of recognition (which we may designate as minimal standards);

(b) the need for statements of accepted guidelines or normative practices beyond any minimum level to provide a method of comparison with leading institutions and for self evaluation (diagnostic standards);

(c) the need for long-range goals for development which may not be met by any library now but which will challenge even first rank institutions and which will set the direction for professional development in the ensuing years (projective standards); and

(d) the need to meet the requirements of individual librarians for statements dealing with qualifications, working conditions, professional responsibilities and other personal practices as distinguished from institutional needs (personnel standards)."[3]

New Views on Public Library Standards

The following are the new views on the public library standards.

(1) The standards lay great stress upon providing library services to unserved population,

(2) The standards attempt to deal with the diverse organizational characteristics of library services;

(3) The standards project the state library agency in the principal leadership in promoting the library activities in all areas;

(4) The standards call for shared financial support from social, state and other sources; and

(5) The standards maintain the staff members as on par with other members of staff in government set up.

Indian Scene

Almost all developed countries have adopted public library standards. It is a dire need for developing countries like India also to adopt such standards. In India we have so far no such standards for collection of books, staff, building and budgetory provisions.

In 1948 the Radhakrishnan Commission had strongly recommended the financial allocations to University Libraries. And again, Ranganathan Committee (1957), Kothari Commission (1964) have stressed the need for providing liberal allocations of financial assistance to University Libraries. Where as neither the State or Central Government nor National Professional Organizations have so for ventured to suggest any standards for public library services.

There have, however, been some attempts made in the direction. One of them is the recommendations made by Prof. K.S. Deshpande Committee (1980) appointed by the Government of Goa, Daman and Diu to suggest a Plan for Public Library Structure for the then centrally administered territory. The Committee in its report has made recommendations which are in the nature of standards for public libraries in regard to planning of buildings, provision of finances and services. It is a matter of regret that even after the lapse of thirteen years the Government of Goa has not taken any steps to implement the recommendations of the Committee. The other one is concerned in a paper entitled "Guidelines for Public Library Systems and Services" by D.R. Kalia and others and published in *GRANTHANA : Indian Journal of Library Studies*. Vol. 2(1); Jan. 1991. It is hoped that the Government takes note of the Guidelines contained in the paper by appointing on Expert Committee to suggest ways and means to implement these guidelines.

The absence of public library standards and guidelines for proper functioning, our public libraries are in a pathetic condition. Some of the reasons for such pathetic conditions are:

(1) Lack of proper planning of the public library system had led to uneven growth of libraries.

(2) No consistency is maintained in bye-laws governing the various libraries.

(3) Minimum comforts like good furniture, good ventilation are not provided to library users.

(4) Experience shows that library cess is disminishing every year, adversely affecting the working of the libraries.

(5) At times unwise/indifferent decisions taken by the authorities have been responsible for the slow and lopsided growth of libraries in terms of collection of reading materials, staff and the readers.

(6) Personal assistance to readers by the library staff is non-existent in most of the libraries, because of inadequate and under qualified staff.

(7) There is lot of dissatisfaction among the professional staff as they do not enjoy due status and scale of pay commensurate with their qualifications and experience, vis-a-vis the staff working in other departments of Government.

(8) The promotional opportunities are severely limited or non-existent.

(9) Cooperation and coordination between and amongst the various libraries is conspicuously absent.

(10) Most of the libraries are situated in unsuitable and unhealthy buildings.

The remedy for overcoming all these maladies lies in formulating and implementing proper standards.

Conclusion

The library is a democratic institution. the success of democracy depends upon literate persons in the community. To achieve this goal the public libraries should have proper standards to provide effective and efficient library service to the public at large.

In the light of the above discussion, the following issues are to be considered:

(1) The Central Government should appoint on Expert Committee to formulate standards for public library services.

(2) The National and Regional Professional Associations should appoint Expert Committees to suggest to Government good standards.

(3) Research Guides and scholars may come together and evolve standards for public library services.

References

(1) Encyclopaedia of Library and Information Science. Vols. 16(1975) and 28(1980).

(2) Goa, Daman & Diu : Government of (Prof. K.S. Deshpande; Chairman): Report of the Expert Committee on the Problems and Prospects of the Central Library with a Plan for the Public Library Structure (1980). Panaji (Goa), Author, 1984.

(3) Ijari, S.R.: Development Plan for Public Library System in Karnataka : Ph.D. Thesis (Unpublished), Dharwad, Karnataka University, 1983.

(4) Kalia, D.R. & Others: Guide-lines for Public Library Systems and Services. *GRANTHANA : Indian Journal of Library Studies* 2(1); Jan. 1991, pp. 31-84.

(5) Martin, C.A.: Standards for Public Libraries. *Library Trends*. 21(2), 1972.

(6) South African Library Association: Standards for South African Public Libraries. 2nd Edn., Potchefstroom, SALA, 1968.

(7) Wallace, James, D: Two Year College Standards. *Library Trends*, 21(2), 1972.

(8) Withers, F.N. : Standards for Library Services: In International Survey. Paris, UNESCO, 1974.

Section X
Information Technology

30

EXPERT SYSTEMS APPLICATIONS IN LIBRARY AND INFORMATION PROCESSING AREAS

M.S. Subramanian

Introduction

Artificial intelligence is a subfield of computer science that focuses on understanding and performing intelligent tasks such as reasoning, learning new skills adopting to new situations and problems. Artificial intelligence is concerned with the concepts and methods of symbolic inferences by a computer and the symbolic representation of knowledge to be used in making inferences. Perhaps, the most popular artificial intelligence programmes are the Expert Systems which are computer programmes that embodies human expertise and as such help people to solve important problems.

Thus an expert system is a computer programme designed to act as an expert in a particular field of knowledge or area of expertise.

Components of Expert Systems

The important components of an expert system are knowledge based concerning with the field of expertise and heuristics (techniques) for searching strategies and in building shortents in order to get the current answers as quickly as possible for manipulating those facts. To understand knowledge based system let us compare with a data base system. Both knowledge base and data-base programmes are capable of retrieving stored information. However a data base programme connot draw conclusions by reasoning about the facts in its domain.

Although data-base programmes contain knowledge abut their particular domain, this knowledge is factual. Thus if a data-base programme has stored information about the field of expert's activities, it can retrieve the activities of experts but cannot provide facts following outside the field of activities. This means that while a user of data-base programme must draw his own conclusions, an expert system will assist its user in arriving at a conclusion.

The expert system has four basic components namely .

1. Knowledge base
2. Inference engine
3. User interface
4. Explanation mechanism

The following diagram presents the above components

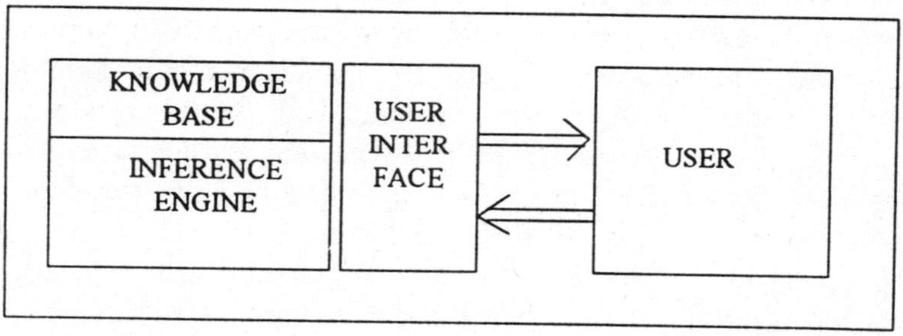

Knowledge Base

An expert system can give intelligent answers only when it has access to sufficient knowledge about the field. The contents of the knowledge base are 1. Declarative knowledge and 2. procedural knowledge.

Declarative Knowledge

The declarative knowledge concerns with the fact about objects, events and situations. Facts in the subject are represented in the knowledge base. The most complex challenge in building the expert system is the constructions of an effective knowledge base. An expert system s performance is related directly to the function and size of knowledge base. Most library expert systems developed thus far address narrowly defined subject domains. This is for the effective and correct answers to all questions it is asked. A knowledge base has the following features in representing expert knowledge.

Semantic Network: The semantic network is graphical representation of properties and relationship of objects, situations and concepts in the knowledge base. The network consists of points called NODES connected by links called ARCS, which describe the relationships between the nodes. For instance, the expression "manufacturing of teak wood chairs for abnormal children" may be thrown in the following semantic network:

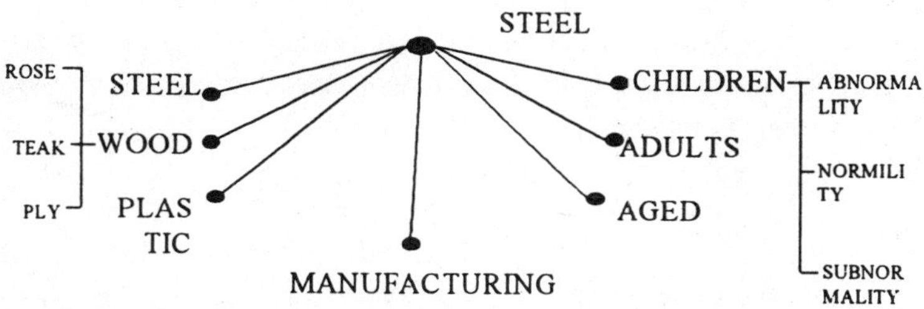

Relations are designed between nodes i.e. chairs, children and manufacturing. The lines connecting the nodes are called ARCS.

Predicate Logic: In predicate logic a proposition consists of objects, persons and concepts (arguments) about which something is stated (predicate) for example, "Manufacturing of teak wood for children" may be stated in the form of predicate logic as "Manufacturing (chair, wood, teak etc) which represent argument of predicate "manufacturing" which in this case expresses a relationship arguments. Predicates logic lend's itself well to inferences.

Frames: Frames are versatile data structure. They are meant to assemble the information about an object, act or event in recognisable entity. As with semantic networks, relationships are expressed between these entities. Frames are subdivided into slots that execute specific procedural changes. For example in a cataloguing expert system, the appearance of the word "proceedings" on the title page of book would cause the expert system to select "conference/ congress /meeting / seminars" frame and fill in the slot accordingly.

Production Rule: This method is the most commonly used technique for knowledge representation. They normally change.

Inference Engine

After the designing of knowledge base of an expert system it must be capable of using the knowledge in an appropriate manner. This systems must know how and when to apply the appropriate knowledge. For that the inference engine or control structure or rule interpreter is the component that directs the implementation of the knowledge in an expert system. In short the inference engine can be termed as reasoning electronic machine component which is responsible for applying the facts in the knowledge base in order to arrive at an answer to the question or problem under consideration. It is the structure that controls, organises and executes the processing and searches and interprets the knowledge base. For control purposes, two strategies namely

i. Forward Chaining

ii. Backward Chaining

are included in the expert system.

Forward Chaining

A forward chaining or goal-driven or top-down control starts from a potential goal and words backward to the search tree seeking facts that support that goal. If the available facts do not support the goal, the search fails, at which points another potential goal is selected and the search is tried again. The inference engine decides which heuristic search techniques are used to determine how the rules in the knowledge base are to be applied to the problem. The term "heuristic" means a "rule of thumb" that helps to determine how to proceed, without going into every detail of the problem in hand.

An inference engine is independent of the knowledge base. It is applied to interpret and search and determine how to proceed further. For this reason, the same control structure can work for various knowledge bases. A famous example is EMYCIN (Essential MYCIN) which can be used for various expert systems. This property of inference engines greatly reduces the expert system development time.

User Interface

If the expert system is to be successful, then the interaction between the human and machine should be a high priority in the construction of the system. In this a user must have a way to communicate with the system in hand. The component of an expert system that helps its user to communicate with it is known as "User Interface". its functions is a bidirectional communication in which the user describes the problem and the system responds with solutions or recommendations. For that a two-way message track has to exist in the expert system. Menus and pre-formulated questions can assist in the search of the knowledge base. One of the major weaknesses in current library expert system is the inability of the user to interpret or modify dialogue with the system.

Explanation Mechanism

The conclusion reached by the system should be explained as the users are entitled to know why the expert system reached the specific conclusion. Hence along with the user interface, a complete expert system will include an explanation mechanism. The system's explanation mechanism should display a list of steps taken in arriving at its conclusion or recommendation.

Expert system Application in Library Activities

Since library activities are confined to the trinity of reading, materials and library staff with the objectives of providing right reading materials to the right user at the right time, the application of expert system in library activities, where dialogue between library staff and users, services and guidance are required, seems to be promising in achieving the objectives. For example, an expert system will help the librarian in realising an improvement in productivity such as processing of more books, conducting more on-line searches and serving more users daily. More over, a well programmed expert system will also help to improve quality. For instance the expert system will be less likely to make human errors in answering more questions and be more consistent in providing qualitative information.

The expert system can be gainfully applied in library activities where decision making regarding the choice and rendering of personal authors, corporate etc. in the case of catalouging, and formulation of index terms, searching of database, library management and reference services are indispensable.

Expert System in Cataloguing Works

The expert system can be applied to cataloguing as much of cataloguing is rule based, that can benefit greatly in improving consistency and quality from expert system.

Several projects involving librarians and users have been tried with the expert system. In 1985, Hjerppe, Olander and Marklund conceived a project known as ESSCAPE for searching and testing the adaptability of AACR for expert systems. They performed research on the feasibility of using an expert system for testing rules presented in chapter 21 (choice and access points) of AACR2. for that two shells were used for the project work. A shell is a soft ware package designed for the creation of specific expert system. Shells are designed to handle a large number of rules presented in the "IF.......THEN" mode. More than 50 expert systems shells geared to run on personal computer are currently available-namely Tiny Einstein, I Class, Gum and Knowledge Pro. Two shells were used for ESSCAPE projects. They are known as EMYCIN and Expert - Ease. The application of EMYCIN shell to cataloguing is shown hereunder:

IF:

1. The term is not a work of personal authorship.
2. The term is not a work emanating from a corporate body.
3. The item is not a work or collection of work produced under editorial direction and
4. The Item is a work of unknown or uncertain authorship.

THEN:

It is definite that the title proper of the item is the main heading under which the term is entered in the catalogue. But they finally observed that AACR2 has many variations and inconsistencies. For instance, the terms used in AACR2 rules are poorly defined; rules are not precise; exceptions to the code appear to have been made on an adhoc basis and the relationship between general rules and specific rules is not sufficiently highlighted. Hence special attention should be paid to these concern prior to planning an expert system for existing and future edition of AACR.

In the words of Charles Finely entitled "Expert system concepts and applications. Advances in library information technology", it is highlighted that the expert system was applied at the Library of Congress for the development of a series consultant and a subject cataloguing consultant.

Series work has been described as one of the most problematic aspects of descriptive cataloguing at the Library of Congress. Series encompass rules and procedures that are complex and numerous and the practice of handling series have been undergone sufficient changes making it more difficult to work with them. For the investigation was made on how and why searches select specific searches keys during on-line database searches.

Results form this type of research will be helpful in designing expert systems that act as expert intermediaries between the user and databases, as they represent the searching behaviours of expert human intermediaries.

Expert System in the Indexing Activities

The Expert System will be profusely applied in the indexing of periodical articles so as to assist the indexer in identifying concept discussed in the periodical articles: translating the concepts into verbal descriptions; translating the verbal description into subject descriptors and their subdivisions; applying the appropriate rules governing the assignment of subject descriptors; and assigning subject descriptors including subdivisions to the periodical articles.

Susane Humphrey and Nancy E Miller conducted a computer aided project with the objectives of developing and testing a prototype knowledge-based expert system for computer assisted indexing of the medical literature in the MEDLINE database. The system was encoded in frames and was designed to interact with trained MEDLINE indexers using prompts, menus and simple commands. The indexers entered subject terms as slot values in filling in document-specific frames that are derived from the knowledge base frames. The automatic application of rules associated with the knowledge based frame produced a set of medical subject headings (MeSH) keyword indexes to the document.

Expert System in Library Management

Management expert systems are available for library management. Areas that are appropriate for library management expert systems include (i) personnel planning and recruitment (ii) collection development (iii) construction of library new buildings (iv) utilisation of existing space (v) accounting and budgeting and (vi) strategic planning. But expert system application in library management is in the infant stage due to much resistance for it by the library professionals.

Expert System in Reference Service

Connie Dowel and Crews took a project on "application of expert system technology to reference services in 1986 and found many advantages for using this system especially when the reference librarian is not available for consultation during library holidays; depending upon the architecture of expert system, there is need to provide reference service at a number of locations thought out the library, and the expert system can be designed to capture a vast amount of human knowledge based works such as the reference library collections, reference clientele; productive search strategies and out-of-the-way but useful reference sources and more users come to reference section especially during peak hours to get satisfactory responses.

Helen Brooks and Alina Vickery of the Central Information Service, University of London developed a prototype reference expert system called PLEXUS which has a well defined subject domain focusing on gardening such as guides to reference sources and directories of on-line databases. Users interact with the system to develop an effective search strategy, search the database and evaluate the results of the search.

In PLEXUS system knowledge is represented in four ways:

i. By a faced classification scheme based on both subject code and ordering system;

ii. By task-oriented rule knowledge;

iii. By referral sources contents like Walford's Guide to reference manual

iv. By semantic context of each dictionary term represented as the associated semantic category and its related same structure.

PLEXUS software is written in Pascal handling knowledge base, user interface, database management system and production rules. The system is implemented on a SIRIUS I micro computer with 850 K bytes of RAM and a 20 megabytes hard disk.

However, the inventors admit that it is not a perfect system to perform reference services as performed by manual way. In recent past, several expert systems like ANSWERMAN and POINTER ANSWERMAN were developed by Sam Waters of National Agricultural Library for helping users find answers to ready reference questions and serves as a consultant. Karan Smith of the State university of New York at Buffalo claims that his POINTER directs users to government publication for answering to a particular question.

Conclusion

When the development of expert systems and applications are becoming more and more sophisticated new phenomenon known as "Neural Networking" is evolving. Research in progress reveals the slow development of programme computer to mimic the librarian's activities. In 2001 A.D., the neural networking will share information among the interconnected neurons and performs tasks simultaneously. Neurocomputer researchers are of the opinion that neural networks will eventually prove superior because they can adjust more easily to changes in the nature of the problem to be solved.

Reference

1. Atkinson, Malcolm P: Data base systems Journal of Documentation Vol 35(1), 1979, p 49-91).
2. Crecine, John P: The next generation of personal computers (Science Vol 231, 2986, p-35-43).
3. Dowel, Connie and Crews, Philip L: Applications of expert system technology to reference service project no. 12. Chicago: IFLA, 1985.
4. Gibb. Forbes: Expert system: An overview *in* Gibb, Forbes, Ed: Expert system in libraries. London: Taylor Graham, 1986)
5. Goswami, P and Lord, E.A.: Artificial Intelligence. Delhi: Anishan publication, 1988.
6. Hayes-Ruth, Frederick, Waterman, D and Lenat, D.E.: Building expert system.: Addison-wesley, 1983.
7. Hjerppe R, Olander B and Marklund K: Project ESSCAPE (Expert Systems for Simple Choice and Access Points for Entries).

8. Humphrey, Susane M. and Miller, Nancy E: Knowledge based indexing of Medical literature: the Aid Project (JASIS VOL 38 (3), P 184-96).

9. Micco H. Mary and Miller, Nancy E: Designing an expert system for the reference function subject access to information. *Proceedings of the 49th annual meeting, 1986.*

10. Shera, Jesse: Library of the future. *Wilson Library Quarterly* Vol. 39, 1964, p 43-55.)

11. Wiig, Kari: Expert systems: A manager's guide. Delhi: Oxford and IBM publishing, 1990.

31

AUTOMATION AND PUBLIC LIBRARIES

V. Venkatappaiah
A .R.D. Prasad

The rapid and exponential growth of information has made it necessary for librarians and information scientists to employ new techniques to cope with the massive proliferation in all subject fields. Research in the sciences and social sciences has led to high productivity in document publication. To bring this vast amount of information under bibliographic control and to render it useful and accessible to potential users is a task of great magnitude which the 'information people' face. Application of communication techniques and electronic data processing of information have made a profound impact on libraries and information have made a profound impact on libraries and information centres and the computer and associated facilities have come to be recognised as indispensable for study and accurate information storage, processing, retrieval and dissemination.

Librarians can no longer be silent spectators of the computer revolution. The automation of information in the traditional activities of a library has long since shown its many advantages in the libraries and information centres of the West. It is time that we in India keep pace with the changing scenario and acknowledge and utilise the computer as an integral part of library house keeping and services. Libraries in the industrial and academic environment as well as Public libraries in the UK, USA and Japan and other countries are making full use of the computers. We in India are lagging behind especially in the area of public libraries. The public library in the West has developed into a true Community Information and Reference system with such computerised data access and facilities as Prestel and View data for providing a variety of information to the general public from housing and social security to legal and medical aid and temperature and travel schedule.

If the public library is to really reach the public and achieve the status of a national network system, the adaptation of new sophisticated techniques and technologies is a highly important prerequisite. We must change with the times and learn with them. A first step in this direction would be the introduction of micro/mini computers in a few selected public libraries in the state along with setting up of training facilities for personnel in the handling of computer equipment and software.

Areas of Library Automation

Computers are used in libraries to assist in a number of library routines necessary for efficient day to day functioning. These library tasks fall into the area of "house keeping" and consist of procedures for acquisition, cataloguing, circulation control and serials control. Computers are also used for formatting and generation of indexes.

Computer based library systems were developed in the early sixties, when several libraries in the US and UK began experimenting with using computers in information processing. These were in the main punched card data processing systems. With improvements in computer technology and libraries becoming more acquainted with computers, we find that in the late sixties the computer came to be viewed as tool for aiding routine procedures and activities. Most of these systems were developed locally in academic, special and public libraries.

The 1970's saw the development of the cooperative systems phase, when resource sharing and library networks came to be established, and many mechanised cooperative projects such as the BLCMP (Birmingham Libraries Cooperative Mechanisation Project, UK) the OCLC (Ohio College Library Centre) were started. In the eighties of course this trend towards computerised library and information network gained momentum with the highly effective and speedy communications technology coupled with sophisticated computer hardware and software developments.

Advantages of Computer-Based Library Systems

1. *Speed:* The computer can process information much faster than human beings, and this permits better work flow through the library.

2. *Accuracy:* The degree of precision and accuracy in processing information is high-however it is dependent on the accuracy of information fed into the system. (There is a computer proverb that reads "garbage in garbage out").
3. *Costs:* Operating costs can be reduced if the system is well designed and well managed.
4. Library workloads can be reduced, as the computer can do vast amounts of work and processing in keeping with the large amount of information being published.
5. Improved services to users.
6. Easier access to external data bases.

There are also arguments against computer based systems in libraries on the grounds that many of the so called advantages of using computers are only fallacies. Some of the points put forth against are that (1) Using computers does not make everything so simple or effortless (2) Computers are costly (3) They do not save time (4) Implementing systems on new computers is difficult (5) Better service is not achieved (6) Integrating systems into a network is difficult.

Perhaps there is also somewhere a hidden fear that computers may replace librarians, or prove them to be incompetent.

However it is perhaps ultimately a question of using the capabilities of the computer and electronic data processing to help librarians and information scientists in their work. The computer is an example of man's ingenuity and intelligence, and a computer system can only be as good or as bad as the persons who design, implement and operate the system.

House Keeping Activities

Housekeeping procedures in a library are those routines or tasks that are required for everyday management and functioning of the library. They are broadly:

1. Acquisition
2. Cataloguing

3. Circulation control
4. Serials control

Acquisitions

Acquisitions and ordering systems in libraries cover the selection, ordering and accessioning of items into the library's collection. Computers are used (1) to send order slips and 'chasers' for unacknowledged or overdue orders to the booksellers (2) to produce lists of books on order (3) to keep accounts of money spent (4) to produce accession lists of recently acquired books.

The detailed input to an acquisition system covers

1. new orders
2. amendments to existing orders
3. booksellers' reports
4. acknowledgements of receipt of items in the library

Selection of new books can be done from commercially available services which disseminate information about forth coming documents, or directly from MARC tapes or any local inputs.

Two files are maintained in a computer based acquisition system. One is the main file containing records of all current orders. The second is a file with the names and addresses of booksellers used by the library. A code number for each bookseller links the two files, so that bookseller information is not repeated in the order file.

The system prints out the orders addressing the appropriate supplier. Printing of orders can also be done on special pre-printed stationary that can be sent directly to the bookseller.

By checking with the date of entering the order record into the file, 'chasers' can be sent to the booksellers, if no information regarding the order has been received within a predetermined time.

When the item is received in the library the order record with the bibliographic details, becomes the basis of the catalogue record. The edited record is merely added to the catalogue file in an integrated system.

Other processes that can be performed by a computerised acquisitions system are

1. listing items on order, by author, department or subject,
2. new accessions listing,
3. notifying individuals who have recommended a particular book about the receipt of that book,
4. control of accounts,
5. production of relevant statistics to help management decisions.

Circulation Control

This is one library service that is most amenable to computerisation. The advantages are especially seen in the amount of time saved in issue and discharge routines, and the avoidance of bottlenecks which are the bane of any library. In very large libraries, users may be asked to fill up slips in duplicate at the circulation desk, and later at the end of the day these slips can be entered into the computer. Or a terminal at the circulation counter, with an operator entering the data directly is another way of doing it. Broadly, circulation systems using computers, have the details of the book issued and the person borrowing it entered on files. Dates of return are on the basis of the period of load (one week, a fortnight etc.). Daily check of the files will identify what books are due or overdue and notices can be typed and sent to the users who have borrowed them. Provision for reservation data will make it possible to pick out those books for which there is a request and user can be asked to return that particular book.

The circulation process in a computerised system depends on giving unique identification codes to books and to users. An accession number, or a call number can be used as this unique identification key for a book. Users can be given individual identity codes.

Cataloguing

Cataloguing includes the job of describing, recording and displaying details of the holdings of the library. Computers are used to aid in the production, maintenance and updating of catalogues. The quality of the catalogue depends ultimately on the cataloguer. In other words initial input data is still the cataloguer's work.

Bibliographic details are gathered from relevant sources, or from the acquisitions system. Usually there is one main or master file for the holdings of the library, and a temporary file for cumulating the additional records, because printing the master file is done only once in a way.

After initial input of the records, the computer can perform simple tests on the record structure, and errors can be located and checked. Again if a basic record structure of a package format as that of the CDS/ISIS is used (as is now being done at the Centre), entry of data becomes a very simple process. The computer can be asked to generate added entries if required, which can later be sorted into the main file. Separate listings for author, subject and key points of access can be created. A postings file and an inverted index help the computer search and display records relevant to a specific query.

Serials Control

Serials control through the use of the computer is perhaps one of the most complicated tasks of housekeeping. This is perhaps because of the literally unpredictable nature of serial publications. Some of the functions of the serials control system that can be handled by the computer are:

1. Listing of serials holdings.
2. Accessioning of serials (which includes selection, ordering, checking-in, renewal of subscriptions, sending notices when issues are not received).

1. Listing of serials holdings is basically producing a catalogue of serials. However with serials there are problems relating to change in title, periodicity etc. A listing system will depend on the bibliographic record for each serial being available in machine readable form. From a master file of such serials records, individual listings can be made based on title, subject, publishers/suppliers etc. Union lists of serials holdings of libraries within a geographic region can also be produced by computer.
2. Accessioning of serials must take into account receipt of issues, and periodicity of the serial, likely data of receipt in order to be able to send claims notices to

suppliers for items not received, and to update the holding file. To expect the arrival of periodical parts each record must contain information about the publication pattern of the serial. This relates to the number of volumes per calendar year, number of parts per volume, supplements if any, the pattern of numbering parts, and the frequency of publication. Algorithms can be written with reference to the real calendar, which use information on the details given above, to expect the arrival of each issue. Prediction cards can then be generated, and by checking them periodically 'chaser' notices can be sent to the suppliers when an issue is overdue.

Details of the suppliers and the price per volume are necessary for the system to handle subscription, renewals and accounting functions.

Information Search and Retrieval

The search process on a computerised data base has many advantage over search from a catalogue by manual methods, in terms of speed, and accuracy. Any library or information centre can create first a set of machine readable records of its holdings, based on a structured format, or using a data base package like the CDS/ISIS which is described later.

Users can search the data base through key terms of author, subject or title, which are formulated into a search expression using Boolean operators (logical connections AND, NOT, OR). Computer will display relevant terms/records, that match the terms of the user's request. Current Awareness listings and Selective Dissemination of Information (SDI) Retrospective searches are services where the computer capabilities can be used very effectively.

Index generation is another area where computers are generally of use. Computers can be used to format the entries in a permuted index, and also to generate the entries for an index. Key words can be derived from the bibliographic description, or assigned to describe the document (subject keys) and then put into the required format. KWIC indexes for instance can be produced from titles of documents, with keyword and context generation performed by the computer. Stop lists or puffword lists prevent words like 'a', 'the', 'of' etc from being used as they key terms. Fully automatic indexing can also be done through statistical analysis and word frequency counts with weighting, provided the text is in machine readable form.

Data Base Management Systems

A database can be defined as a collection of data designed to be used by different programme level. It can be viewed as a collection of interrelated data stored together with controlled redundancy to serve one or more applications in an optimal fashion; the data are stored so that they are independent of programs which use the data; a common and controlled approach is used in adding new data and modifying and retrieving existing data within the data base. A system is said to contain a collection of data bases if they are each entirely separate in structure.

S.M. Dean traces the origin of data bases from the invention of the punched card by Dr. Herman Hollerith of the US Bureau of Census in the 1880's. Further he describes the evolution towards data bases through the first electronic computer, ENIAC in 1946, the use of magnetic tape system in the UNIVAC-1 computer in 1951 and the introduction of magnetic disk in the mid 1960's. The 1960's also saw the emergence of the Management Information System (MIS) concept. One of the outstanding products of that time was the Integrated Data Store (IDS) introduced by General Electronic (now owned by Honeywell) in 1965. As the name suggests IDS was used to create large integrated files that can be shared by a number of applications. It was considered as the forerunner of modern database systems. Its pioneer, Charles W. Bachman, subsequently, played a very active role in the development of the CODASYL database proposal which incorporated many of the IDS features. It was only in the 1970's that database systems gained fame and more popularity and the CODASYL set up a Data Base Group (DBG) to provide a common frame work to all the database designs. IBM has also been keen on database systems. Most of its research in this area is concentrated on the relational model unlike the CODASYL, which emphasises the network model.

The Data Base Systems are designed around a centralised and integrated shared data file (or data base) that emphasises the independence of programs and data. In other words Data Base Management Systems (DBMS) are sets of programs that allow a user to create files, to maintain them by adding, deleting and changing records and to retrieve stored information. A Data base may have a Data definition language for defining data bases, and a query language for retrieval, a data manipulation language which usually a part of query language, and a report generation language for getting printout in a desired format.

The UNESCO is maintaining and distributing free of charge a software package to non-profit organisations. This package is called CDS/ISIS (Computerised Data System). It can be run on an IBM 370, RIAD and AMDAHS. Mainframe Computers version of this package can also be run on microprocessor like the IBM-PC and its compatibles and also on Wang-PC. UNESCO has already made CDS/ISIS available to more than 50 countries. In India it is already being used at TERI, Bombay and INCOR, Visakhapatnam on IBM-PC compatible machines. The hardware requirements for this software are an IBM - PC/XT compatible, which should have 512 K RAM and at least 10 MB hard disk and the operating system should be MS-DOS version 2.0 or more.

Minisis

International Development Research Centre (IDRC), Canada is also distributing a software package called MINISIS. MINISIS is based on the relational data base approach. Both CDS/ISIS and MINISIS are based on the ISIS software originally developed by International Labour Organisation (ILO) as a generalised information storage and retrieval system with particular emphasis on bibliographic applications. Systems in the ISIS are also characterised by certain common features: (a) similar data base structures. (b) similar record structure (Loader, directory, variable length data). (c) similar data structure (variable length fields and sub fields). (d) generalised data base definition (e) on line data entry, modification and retrieval, and a variety other basic functions such as print formating. Both CDS/ISIS and MINISIS use ISO standard 2709 format for data interchange making it possible to exchange files among installations.

Requisities of Computerisation Programme

Three important requirements which call for earnest consideration to enable libraries to switch to computerisation are hardware, software and manpower.

Availability of inexpensive, locally made microprocessor system practically reduced the problems in acquiring the hardware. There at least twenty or more well established microcomputer vendors in the country at present. Some of the brands are already tried and tested for library applications. Most of the micros are IBM PC compatible machines.

Some of the software packages for library application developed abroad are compatible with IBM PC clones. It is therefore desirable that the local IBM PC clones are to be acquired. User-friendly, portable software packages are available and to mention a few: CDS/ISIS, Scimate.

NISSAT is considering measures for development of software packages for library and information application. Software packages for library applications are also available commercially abroad. UNESCO has brought out an inventory of software packages available for library applications. However, commercial software are usually costly.

The foremost problem is the training of manpower for computer based library activities. Library professionals need not be experts in computer programming. What is required is computer literacy, that is, to know how to operate a computer with a given software for certain library applications. One must have fair knowledge of what a microprocessor can do and what kind of specifications would meet library purposes. Also one should know what are the essential characteristics of the software that should be developed for library application. All this can be achieved by sponsoring the library personnel interested in computer application to different computer application courses, training and seminars.

Design Features to be Considered for Automation

This should take into consideration the present as well as the expected say five years, growth of the library. The design features to be considered are

Means of inputting

Nature of data, one way/conventional input, input device to be used, single/multiple input, external input sources (data base on tape eg. MARC)

Types of output products

Hard copy upper and lower case, special forms display, hard copy/display (screen print) machine readable output.

File structure and size

Structure (sequential) ISAM, direct, DBMS size, (no. of characters, number of characters required at one time.

Application Characteristics

Sorting/data manipulation (numeric/bibliographic, no. of records) searching (batch, online interactive, access points, no of users) special I/O devices, response time.

A Sample Computer Configuration for Large Libraries

A sample computer configuration for LA/IR is given below. This can be used as a model while formulating the hardware/software specifications for a particular library.

Hardware

1. CPU: 16/32 bit word length
2. Memory: 512 KB, with provision for expansion to 1 MB. Minimum of 256 KB should be program addressable.
3. I/O: High speed I/O channels for handling devices like disks and tapes
4. Disk storage: hard disk: minimum 10 MB online disk. storage on 1 to 2 drives. Provision for expansion to 1 GB with additional drives.

   Two DSDD floppy disk drives
5. Tape storage: streamer tape drive for handling 800/ 1600 BPI, 2400 feet tapes. Mainly for backup/restore
6. VDU Terminals: provision to support at least 8 terminals. Two of these may preferably be PC compatible

when used stand alone, with adequate local storage for word processing and offline data entry. user terminal should have sufficient cable length to place them in actual operational point.

All terminals should have interface with dot matrix/ LOP printers for local printing. The terminals should support screen (forms) design and cursor control and function keys for forward/backward (scroll) etc., should be capable of printing screen images using a function key.

7. Printer: 600 LPM heavy duty line printer, 132 columns and 96 ASCII character set.

Software

1. Operating system: Powerful enough to efficiently coordinate the CPU with the above mentioned peripherals. It should be a multi-user, multi-tasking disk based operating system should support both menu and command (JCL) driven OS instructions for the novice and experienced user should support I/O spooling, job accounting etc.
2. System Utilities: Disk file management. Powerful sort/ merge, text editing and or processor utilities. Fast file backup/restore routines. File recovery routines. Program debugging aids.
3. File management: Sequential, direct access and ISAM file structures. Capability to support general secondary keys. Variable length field/record structures capable to supporting very large number of records.
4. Powerful DBMS with multiuser capability. Interactive query and report generating facility. Higher level language interfacing through DML Programming languages: Extensive string/text handling features. File handling capability.

Sample Computer Configuration for Small Libraries

A sample computer configuration for LA/IR is given below. This can be used as a model while formulating the hardware/software specifications for a particular library.

Hardware

1. *CPU*: 16 bit word length
2. *Memory*: 512 KB, with provision for expansion to 1 MB. Minimum of 256 KB should be program addressable.
3. *I/O*: High speed I/O channels for handling devices like disks and tapes
4. *Disk storage:* hard disk: minimum 10 MB online disk. One DSDD floppy disk drive.
5. *VDU Terminal*

   Should have interface with dot matrix/LOP printers for local printing.
6. The terminals should support screen (forms) design and cursor control and function keys for forward/ backward (scroll) etc., should be capable of printing screen images using a function key.
7. *Printer*: 600 LIPM heavy duty line printer, 132 columns and 96 ASCII character set.

32

USE OF INFORMATION TECHNOLOGY IN INDIAN LIBRARIES: PROBLEMS AND PROSPECTS

P. Venkataramana

Introduction

We are living in a society where information is a vital resource for the socio-economic development of the nation. The development of a nation is heavily dependent on its abilities to acquire, organise, store, retrieve, disseminate and use information. Information is essential for making sound decisions in all spheres of life. The higher the quality of information accessibility, the better the quality of decisions. The volume of information being published is increasing exponentially and the need for specific information is growing steadily. Availability of right information accurately, precisely and timely is of critical importance. Information has become a highly tradeable commodity enhanced by its easy access and use via Information Technology (IT). IT is the synthesis of Computers and Communications. Rapid advances in Computer and Communication technologies enable us to store, process and transmit huge amount of information easily, quickly and in expensively. The importance of IT as an instrument of progress is now widely acknowledged all over the world. A wide variety of technologies are being used for managing information to understand problems and create solutions. The abilities of these technologies to carry out information management functions speedily, accurately and efficiently make them the most useful tools for the development of a modern library.

Because of the recent economic liberalization policy of the Government of India and due to knowledge explosion changes in the nature and form of reading materials and ever growing complex information needs of users. it is impossible for the traditionally organized libraries to manage the large quantum of information. Developments in science and technology brought dramatic reduction in size and cost of IT and tremendous increase in its capabilities. Further, shrinking library budgets and escalating costs of information sources have made it mandatory for libraries to use IT in order to provide specialized, user oriented prompt library and information products and services efficiently and effectively.

Information Technology

The term Information Technology in English, 'informatique' in French, and 'Informatika' in Russia encompasses the notion of information handling[1].

According to Albert, Information Technology (IT) can be defined from the library and information science point of view as "application of various technologies for the acquisition, processing, storage and dissemination of information[2].

UNESCO definition of Information Technology:

'The Scientific, technological and engineering disciplines and the managerial techniques used in information handling and processing; their applications; Computers and their interaction with men and machines and associated social, economic and cultural matters'.

Information Technology has been concerned with the use of Computers and Communications togather, store, process and transmit information. The focus of IT has been on the speed, economy and accuracy in processing information. Information Technology used in libraries includes not just computers but a wide range of other technologies such as hardware, software, CD-ROMS, Databases, Networks, Electronic Mail, etc.,

Problems in the use of IT

Libraries use IT to increase the efficiency and effectiveness of their operations and services. Information Technology is highly dynamic, fast changing and become obsolete so quickly in such a short span that even before one technology is fully received, understood and implemented/used, an improved version or a new technology is being developed. We cannot service tomorrow's users with yesterday's technology. Constant upgradations in technology are essential for survival and success. Infact keeping up with new technologies is the biggest problem faced by the people around the world. Practically, it is becoming increasingly difficult for the libraries to keep pace with these rapid technological developments/ changes especially in developing countries where resources are scarce.

The time-gap between IT inventions and their commercial exploitation has shrunk. The personal computer market attests this continual improvements in hardware, design, circuitry, software and storage technology making machines obsolete within a year. In the case of many fast moving high technology products like computers, the product life cycles are shortening with successive innovations coming fast and increasing product obsolescence(3).

Information technology has virtually unlimited potential for variety of applications in libraries. From the experience of developed countries, we have realised the importance of IT and are convinced of its use on library operations and services. But there is a wide gap between theoretical expectations and their practical implementation for reaching results to ultimate beneficieries. Often use of IT in libraries has become more of psychological, prestigeous and publicity oriented rather than absolute necessity. In large majority of cases, the theoretical justifications for use of IT in library do not get critically reviewed, tested and evaluated after implementation. Hence large majority of our libraries are not able to adequately use modern information technologies even after several years. In other words, hardly a handful of libraries would have reached the matured operational state of using IT worth subjecting to review and evaluation(4).

In spite of substantial growth in number of computers its liberal and cheap availability in Indian market, very much has happened in the computerisation of Indian libraries and information centres(5).

R.P. Kumar(6) conducted a survey and sent a questionnaire to 300 different types of libraries which include university, public, medical, research, engineering, government and national libraries in India. He received 204 responses and said that "some of the libraries have automated their routines whereas majority of them are still in the planning stages".

Lack of management support

Librarian has no power to take decision of using IT in library. He has to depend on management for taking such decision. As IT needs heavy investment, the whole-hearted support of management is essential for its successful implementation in library. The management support depends upon the nature and level of IT awareness of the head of organisation. If the head of organisation is library oriented person having awareness about the potential of modern technologies and appreciation for modern library services, it is easy to get support for procuring and using IT in library. If the management is not willing/interested, it is difficult for the librarian to convince and get their support and cooperation. Further constant persuasion of the proposal of using IT without commitment on the part of management may get delayed without yielding desired results. Due to fast changing technology and heavy investment, any delay in taking decision and implementation may further adversely affect the modernisation process.

A recent survey revealed total absence of involvement of top management as a driving factor for adopting IT in service sector and an overwhelming majority of 75% of respondents ranked better customer service as the most important benefit of computerisation[(7)].

Top management should be persuaded, educated and convinced about the importance of IT in various library operations and services to get their support and cooperation. Top management has to take an active part in decisions concerning IT use in library. They need to be involved in the planning process of IT implementation. They should have more awareness of the trends in IT.

The responsibility of getting management support, however has to be taken by professional librarian who must demonstrate a commitment to modernisation including the use of IT in libraries for real benefits to the users. User pressure has been a significant factor leading to the applications of IT in Indian libraries as seen in many special libraries and centres of higher learning. Users at different levels should bring pressure on top management to take a policy decision for allocation of more resources. The most effective way of obtaining management support is via user groups (e.g. students, faculty, research scholars, scientists, etc.). Librarians in India need to take a more proactive approach in influencing decisions concerning resource allocation for the modernisation of libraries[(8)].

Inadequate Financial Resources

The foremost problem faced by our libraries is inadequate financial resources. Resource is a life blood of any system. IT needs heavy investment for its implementation in the library. Cost involved in hardware, software, databases, computerisation and maintenance is very large that many organisations are not able to take decisions so easily to invest in IT. At the time of allocation of funds, library is being given low priority as compared to other departments in most of the organisations. In one hand library budgets are shrinking every year and on the after and the cost of library materials are increasing regularly on the other. Budget allotted for library is not sufficient to purchase required periodicals, books and other publications and so hardly there are any resources left to be spared for procuring information technologies. As a result, libraries are not getting adequate resources required for procuring modern information technologies. Due to fast changing technologies, obsolescence in information technology is so high that it is becoming increasingly difficult for libraries to keep pace with these new technologies without adequate resources.

Top management must be made aware of the need, usefulness of IT and motivated to allocate more and more funds for procuring and using modern technologies in library management.

Lack of Trained Personnel

Most of the Indian libraries do not have adequate staff commensurating to the volume of work, to carry on routine library operations systematically and effectively. The major problem in effective use of information technology in libraries is the acute shortage of qualified and trained personnel who have adequate knowledge and skill of using IT in libraries. Without adequate knowledge. staff members working at computers have to spend a lot of time for learning, experimenting and using IT applications in real situations. Staff members feel that these rapidly changing technologies actually interfere with their job. Further, it is found that the staff experience increased stress as a result of attending to both routine as well as automation works simultaneously due to inadequate staff. Working knowledge of IT in library personnel is fundamental for its successful implementation in library. IT has immense potential for handling various library functions. To make full use of this potential in library management, it is essential that the library should have adequate personnel who have thorough knowledge of IT applications in libraries. but in practice, most of the library personnel do not have adequate level of knowledge and competence of IT applications in libraries. Working knowledge can be gained only when one is given an intensive training and gets practical hands on experience in using IT.

LIS schools in India are still following the same old curriculum of traditional librarianship. Students completing courses from these schools do not possess the required working knowledge and expertise of IT applications in libraries. Recently, though very few LIS schools have started fundamental courses on IT applications as a part of curriculum, neither they have well trained and knowledgeable teachers nor equipped with modern computers which are essential for gaining good knowledge and hands on experience in using IT. So the course curriculum should be fully revised, updated, modified and facilities should be provided according to the current needs suitable to adopt modern information technologies. More emphasis has to be put on computer applications, on line services, multimedia, networking etc. and should be included in library science education curriculum.

Training library personnel and providing facilities for hands on experience in using computers are important aspects to be given serious consideration. Continuous training is necessary to develop, maintain and improve skills. An intensive need-based practical oriented training should be imparted to library personnel to instill confidence in order to handle and manipulate new technologies. Further the staff may also be deputed to libraries which are in advanced state of automation for gaining knowledge and hands-on experience in using IT.

Lack of Consultance and Advisory Services

Libraries where decisions have been taken to use IT are confronted with several problems like what technologies i.e. hardware and databases, etc are to be procured and assessment of their performance, costs and benefits. Because of the availability of varied technologies, libraries have to consciously evaluate the different options before investing in hardware, software, and other IT products and services. Rarely systematic efforts have been made for comprehensive assessment of all the available technologies to identify key technologies suitable to a particular library[9]. There is neither single comprehensive source of published document nor consultancy and advisory council which examines available technologies, compares different options evaluates, finds possible alternatives and report the results about the implementation of right/relevant technologies in the country. In the absence of such published documents and advisory services, libraries often use either obsolete or inappropriate technologies.

IT manual has to be published which will provide information regarding selection of suitable hardware and software for different types of libraries. Further, a panel of IT experts in library automation are to be identified at national as well as regional levels to offer consultancy and advisory services to smaller libraries.

Staff Resistance to change

Staff acceptance is an important factor contributing to the successful use of IT in libraries. It is a human tendency to resist change. As some of library staff still lack knowledge of IT, they are not convinced of the use of IT and so not willing to respond positively to the change of new technologies. There is also a psychological fear in the minds of the library staff that the use of IT in libraries may lead to retrenchment/unemployment. Loss of jobs due to use of IT in library is not true and there is no such case where computers have replaced/removed library staff. It should be made clear that IT is used to introduce new services and make improvements and not to reduce either the existing library services/employees. Further they must be convinced that the rapid spread of IT use will lead to a tremendous demand for skilled personnel. Therefore they must be assured that no one is going to lose his job as a result of the introduction of IT in libraries.

The success of use of IT in library depends on the extent to which supervisory and operational staff are involved in its planning, design, analysis and implementation. The psychological barriers to change must be cleared in the initial stage involving all the staff in its implementation. Staff involved in IT implementation project need to be trained and must be made aware of the latest developments and be fully involved in the project process and provided guidelines with examples[10]. They must be sent to automated libraries for personal observation and practical experience in handling different technologies.

Library staff should be provided adequate training to have thorough understanding and knowledge of the IT potentials on library and information products and services. The knowledge, skill and interest in various aspects of IT will need to be further developed among the library staff. Due to fast changing technological developments, continuous in-service training for working library staff is essential for not only to keep them well informed about the latest developments in their fields but also to learn new skill in the use of modern information technologies.

Software Problem

India is contributing significantly in software market for industrial and other applications, but software packages for library applications are not well developed. Software package is the most important subsystem of library automation and the success of automation depends on selection of right software and its correct implementation. A few commercial software packages are available in India for library automation but no single software package can meet all the requirements of a particular library. Each package has its own unique features and limitations.. Selecting and appropriate package suited to a particular library is a difficult problem faced by the librarians today.

LIBRIS, LIBSYS, MAITRAYEE, TULIPS are some of the important commercial software packages used in India apart from CDS/ISIS. Most of these commercial packages are expensive and they are not within the reach of many small libraries. CDS/ISIS is a free package but it doesn't have in built integrated house keeping functions apart from many useful advanced facilities. It has no clear and illustrative manual which compels library staff to have training and good knowledge of computers and spare a lot of time for experimenting and effective implementation of the package.

Security Problem

The security problems faced in most of the libraries are theft, physical damage, loss of files, etc., Computer viruses are one of the most serious problem affecting the use and growth of IT. Computer viruses are small hidden programs with in a larger host programs. They have the ability to replicate themselves and to move from computer to computer through the transfer of discs or electronic communications. The effect of virus range from humorous to the catastrophe. Computer users, professionals, organisations and institutions have been seriously affected by the viruses in losing valuable data and program files. As library databases are usually huge and contain valuable data, it is necessary to protect expensive resources and data from mishandling, deletion, unauthorised access and viruses. A well planned security policy and program is essential to protect vital information resources.

Use of anti-virus programs and passwords are the acceptable means of providing this type of security. The computer room should be secure and accessible only to authorised persons. If IT has to function properly, it is necessary to protect it from environmental hazards, miserable power supply, unauthorised linkering and natural calamities. They are to be kept in a cool, dry and dust free air-conditioned environment. IT cannot give maximum service without proper environment. They should be kept in a separate room with regular electricity supply, optimum temperature, humidity and lighting. Places where power cut is more often, use of generators and UPS (uninterrupted power supply) can help to minimise the effects of the interruptions.

Lack of Standardisation

Most of the Indian libraries are not following uniform standard formats while designing databases. Each library follows its own formats there by giving a less scope for resource sharing and exchange of information. Communication, exchange of information and resource sharing will be impossible without uniform standard entries in a database. Standardization in the data elements, standard procedures of data entry and data storage is essential to ensure compatibility for interconnection, easy transfer of information and sharing of resources. Co-operation in exchange of information and resource sharing is easily possible only when there is uniformity in formats, structures of databases among the participating libraries. Development of uniform information technological standards are essential for standardisation, networking, communication and sharing resources.

Others

These are some of the important problems librarians face in the use of IT in Indian libraries but there are several others which hinder libraries to use modern technologies. They include

- Lack of proper recognition to the library as an important component in the organisation.
- Inadequate understanding of the value of information services of a good library.
- Lack of professional commitment on the part of librarians in adapting to the new culture of information technology.
- Inability to recruit either additional staff or computer professionals in libraries for using new technologies.
- Lack of reliable and cheap telecommunications system.
- Lack of published, well analysed structured practical oriented strategies for library automation.

Conclusion

Though there are some significant developments recently in the use of IT in Indian libraries, we are still lagging far behind in the development process as compared to western technological development. Despite these problems, use of IT is inevitable in libraries in the present society. Technologies pose challenges as well as opportunities before us. It is for us to use these technologies for survival/ success and to cope up with time. Librarians should take full responsibility/interest and insist on for using IT in their libraries as it is the most effective tool for managing information. Librarians should make an effort to educate policy makers, administrators and make them to understand the importance of IT and indispensability of information in supporting research, education and in taking appropriate decisions in their day to day activities.

Implementation of IT to library operations is very complex, stressful and continuous process. Most of the libraries are not following a systematic plan in using IT in India. It requires an imaginative, intelligent planning and huge investment of financial as well as human resources. Libraries intending to use IT have to plan well in advance for successful implementation and to minimize risks.

Achievement of success in using IT to library operations would enhance the rate of success of efforts made to strengthen the quality and standard of education and research activities in all areas in the country. Modern technologies would not only make existing library collections available to all as a national resource but would also enable Indian libraries to participate actively in global networks for exchange of information and sharing resources.

References

1. Zorkoczy, Peter. *Information Technology*. New York: Knowledge Industry, 1982: 3.
2. Rowley, J. *Basic of information technology*. London: Clive, Bingle, 1988: 1.
3. Ramanathan, S and S.K. Subramaniam. "Managementology: Meeting change and challenges". *Pestology Annual* 1995-96: 21-30.
4. Sridhar, M.S. Managing Modernisation of library services using IT: potentials and problems. An invited paper for the seminar on services in Automated libraries: challenges and opportunities, Dec. 4-5, 1995. ASRC, HYD.
5. Gaur R.C. and S.P. Gupta. "Problems in Computerisation of library and Information Centres in India: A case study of CRRI". *AGLIS Journal Special Issue* 11 (1995): 81-89.
6. Kumar R.P. "An overview of Modern Technologies applications in Indian libraries" (brief Communication). *International Information and Library Review* 26(1994): 327-339.
7. Radha Krishnan, V.R. "The new business chain". *Data quest* 12.30(1-15 July 1995): 89-103.
8. Haravu, L.J. Strategies for the adoption of New Information Technologies in Indian libraries. A paper presented in CALIBER-95: National Convention on Information access through Networks held during 10-12, Feb. 1995. Univ. of Hyd.
9. Ibid.
10. Msuya, jangawe. "Planning the automation of libraries in developing countries. A systems analysis approach". *Library Review* 39.3(1990): 29-32.

33

EMERGING INFORMATION TECHNOLOGIES

G. Dhanasegaran

Information

Information means the communication of knowledge about an event of a given condition. According to Prof. G. Bhattacharyya information is a message conveyed or intended to be conveyed by a systematised body of ideas. All ideas, facts and imaginative works of the mind which have been communicated, recorded, published and/or distributed formally or informally in any format.

Nature and Characteristics of Information

The following are the nature and characteristics of information:

1. Information as a commodity
2. Information as energy
3. Information as communication
4. Information as facts
5. Information as data
6. Information as knowledge

Principles of Information

Prof. G. Bhattacharyya has conceived five principles of information based on the anology of Five Laws of Library Science.

1. Information is for use
2. Every information user, his information
3. Every piece of information, its user
4. Save the time of the information User
5. The universe of information is evergrowing.

Types of Information

J.H. Shera categorised information in the following six types:

1. Conceptual information
2. Empirical information
3. Procedural information
4. Stimulatory information
5. Policy information
6. Directive information.

Qualities of Information

According to Rojas some of the important qualities of information are:

1. Accessibility
2. Comprehensiveness
3. Precision
4. Compatability
5. Timeliness
6. Clarity
7. Flexibility
8. Verifiability
9. Free of bias
10. Quantifiable.

Society

We are living in a changing society. Society has undergone many changes from the agrarian society to the industrial society, then to post industrial society followed by the information society. Library and Information Scientists such as Lancaster and Thompson have stated about the changing information environment. At present we are going through the 'technological age'.

Need for information

Information has immense value in the present day information based society. It plays a key role in todays complex economic and social environment. Information is required in every field of human activity. The value of information is now more important than ever because of the information crisis. The impact of ever growing volumes of information is a Universal Phenomenon.

Challenge for Libraries

Libraries are faced with the challenge of information deluge. Libraries have great difficulties in acquiring and sorting out the relevant information and presenting it to their users. The challenge of information handling, transfer, storage and retrieval has to be accepted by libraries. The traditional methods of bibliographic control have been put to a severe strain to cope up with the complex problem. The solution has to be sought through new information technology and services. Modern information technology has brought out sophisticated innovation such as computer, satellites and various other techniques.

Information Technology

The application of computers and other technology to the acquisition, organisation, storage, retrieval and dissemination of information. Information technology connotes an assemblage of technologies. They particularly cover the computers capability to store and process information.

Components of Information Technologies

· Some of the products and systems which form the "technology" components of information technology are as follows:

1. Computer
2. Microcomputers
3. On-Line Bibliographic Data Bases
4. Word Processors
5. Teletext
6. Videotext
7. Fiber optics
8. Electronic Mail
9. Facsimile Transmission
10. Compact Discs
11. Electronic Publishing
12. Microforms

13. Archie Services
14. Gopher
15. WAIS (Wide Area Information Services)
16. WWW (World Wide Web)

Computer

The most significant of all the new products of the technological revolution is the computer. Computers can be applied in libraries for house keeping operations and information retrieval. House keeping routines include acquisition of documents, cataloguing, serial control, circulation control and maintenance of statistics. Services such as Current Awareness and Selective Dissemination of information can also be provided to the users by the use of computers.

Micro Computers

As the name implies, a micro computer is a small computer. It uses a microprocessor for its central processing unit. The micro computers alleviate tedious activities like memorization and spending time for hunting information. Now-a-days highly sophisticated software is available to support computer usage. Micros are very user friendly. Micros have been used to automate order control, overdue control, circulation of small libraries, word processing, fund control and other accounting systems, binding control, interlibrary load etc.,

Moreover the micro computer makes an excellent computer terminal when interfaced to the computer with a modem. The major advantage of this application is that processing and secondary storage can be handled at the local level. This saves the time of the control system and also on line telecommunications costs.

On-line Bibliographic Data Bases

Information technology helps in resource - sharing by developing a small shareable database. Online searching of these databases located remotely is possible through information technology. It helps in locating and getting information. Online databases offer 'Instant Information' which is current and constantly updated. The retrospective searches are processed through computers. There are a number of commercial online search services at the international level. Dialog, orbit, H.W. Wilson, etc., are the most popular items of the commercial online search services.

Word Processors

Word processing is the application of technology to office operations. Modern word processing equipment provides text editing functions. The storage and retrieval of documents and records has become sophisticated. Word processor includes a small computer, peripheral storage devices, an alphanumeric typewriter, a printer and a CRT. These components can be separated or integrated in different combinations. The text is displayed on the CRT. Any error can be corrected on the screen. When a page of the document is complete and error-free, it can be stored on floppy disk or printed out as needed.

The machine has the capability of retrieving any document and storing portions of it in the internal memory. Words, lines or paragraphs of sections of a document can be deleted, edited, changed around or replaced using the memory. Word processors have been used in records management, administrative functions and office correspondence. Word processors may be used for maintaining user files, mailing list, overdue control, correspondence with vendors and annual reports.

Teletext

In this system the broadcast channel is one way. The user cannot ask for information. It is given from the central transmitter to the receivers. eg. Cable T.V. Network. This system is useful for news headlines, weather, sports, entertainment etc.,

Videotext

Videotext involves the transmission of display text and graphics and their reception on an adopted television set. There are two types of Videotext. Broadcast videotext and Interactive Videotext. In videotext the user has access to thousands of pages of information stored in several computers. A videotext system is useful in disseminating general informations. This system requires the user to have a telephone, to which a T.V. monitor or television set can be connected via an electronic interface. Interface has a control keyboard, a modem etc. A printer could also be connected for getting a printout.

Fiber Optics

Fiber optics is a new and well established technology. It provides extremely high bandwidth that could revolutionise cable telecommunications. It was developed as a result of laser technology. The construction of information super high ways is being aided by the use of optical fibre cabling as the transmission media. This transmission operates at a very high frequency. It can provide a larger output of data. This is mostly used in the Internet.

Electronic Mail

Electronic mail is popularly known as E-Mail. It is a general name for non-interactive communication of text, data or voice messages between a sender and a designated recipients by system using telecommunication links. E-Mail messages are from machine to machine. A message originating from the sender's machine is addressed to one or more recipients who receives it on his machine at any remote area at the global level.

The essential equipments of E-Mail are PC-AT, STD line, Modem, Software for the network. E-Mail systems permit a user to send messages to specific individual or to a group of individuals or to everyone connected to the network. Messages are entered as text files via a computer terminal i.e. connected to the network. The text file may be created and edited by using a word processor. On receiving a message the user may read the message received or printout a copy of the message or save the message in a file or forward the message to some-else. E-Mail is useful for practitioners and specialists to establish and maintain contacts to exchange professional information.

Facsimile Transmission

The systems and services such as teletext, videotext, electronic Mail etc., transmit text, data or pictures but they do not give you hard copies. To get hard copies Facsimile transmission has been introduced which enables a page of text or graphics to be scanned and transmitted via terrestrial or satellite links to a remote location. Matter of a whole page up to a maximum size of 210 x* 197 mm may be sent across the country in 4 to 6 minutes.

Compact Discs

A read-only memory (ROM) is a semi-conductor memory device used to store information which is permanent in nature. It has a variety of applications in digital systems such as implementation of combinational logic and sequential logic, character generation, look-up-table, micro processor programme storage, etc. CD-ROM, a polycarborate plastic of 12 cm size holds as much as 2.7 lakh pages of information. We can store 100 dictionaries or we can have 10 year back issues of a national newspaper on one CD-ROM. Therefore, it is very useful, efficient and economical medium for storing and publishing large amount of information with the help of optical laser technology.

Electronic publishing

The libraries now look towards different media of monographs. Information can be handled much more efficiently in electronic form than in print. Through the use of electronic technology, users now can feel that they are in control of large data banks of information. Electronic publishing can help book publishers in many ways. From now on, the author will present the information in electronic form (Including text, pictures, sound and video) and this collection will be proofed, assembled into a database and made available to the user through a variety of media-books, CD ROM's and on-line. This provides long term cost benefits.

Microforms

Microforms include Microfilms and Microfische. Saving in storage space and cost, and the ability to combine storage and display of data in one medium are the two advantages of microforms. It is a self contained medium and it is a part of computer based information system. Libraries and Information centres can increase their holdings without the corresponding increase in shelf space and air-conditioning costs. The microfilm can be viewed by means of a microfilm reader. Microfilm technology enables the transmission of images stored on the microfilm on a computerized system for video display.

Archie Services

Archie Services provide a centralised indexing information service for files distributed throughout thousands of internet public archives. Archie supports two databases. They are what is and File names.

Gopher

Internet Gopher system provides a distributed information delivery system around which a world/campus-wide information system can be built. The Gopher information is organised in a hierarchical manner. This information system can be viewed as a global directed graph containing cycles.

WAIS

Wide Area Information Services is a text-oriented information retrieval system based on the client-server frame-work. The client module translates user queries into WAIS protocol and query the Directory of Services for relevant databases. Database servers keep a fully inverted index of its stored components and execute full-text searches on them. The users narrow down to a information object based on the feedback information contained in the object descriptors.

WWW

The world wide web is an amalgamation of information discovery procedures and hypertext techniques. It is an exciting technology for developing information. WWW clients provide a hypertext-like browing interface. This system is based on Hyper Text Transfer Protocol. Each user's request is mapped on to a TCP connection. HTTP objects are identified by means of uniform Resource Locator. Documents on the WWW are written in a simple "markup language" called HTML which stands for Hypertext Mark up Language. In WWW everything is a hypertext document which may be searchable.

Conclusion

The coming decade will see newer forms and uses of communication/information technology. We will inevitably move to more information systems and linkages among systems. Technology offers greater capability with improved quality at a reduced cost. Current information is being created and stored in digited form. Libraries and Information Centres must adapt change and become leaders in the establishing of a new international information order that would provide information rights as well as privileges. The following are the essential requisites for adopting Information Technologies in Libraries and Information Centres:

a. Sufficient funds for the establishment of computer systems and purchase of CD-ROMs etc.,

b. Networking facilities and cooperation with other libraries and databases.

c. Manpower development to attend to Information Technology.

d. User education programmes to be designed to educate the user about computerised databases, on-line searches, user friendly systems, etc.,

e. Motivation of Manpower to adjust to the changing information environments.

References

1. DEVARAJAN, G. User's approach to Information in Libraries. New Delhi: ESS ESS Publications, 1989. pp 1-2.

2. ISAAC, D (Mrs). Trends in document production (Manuscript): impact on Academic Libraries. pp. 1-6.

3. JENA, AJIT K. Using Networks for Library Services (manuscript): a tutorial. pp. 1-13.

4. KHAN, H.A. Public Libraries and the contemporary Indian Society (In. KHAN, H.A. and IJARI. S.R. (Eds). Current problems and trends in Library and Information services. - Varanasi: Indian Bibliographic Centre. 1990. pp. 166-172).

5. KUMAR, R.P. Emerging technologies and the State of Health Science Libraries in India (In. Ibid pp. 261-269).

6. RAJU, A.A.N. Nature. characteristics and communication of Information (manuscript) pp. 1-6.

7. SINHA, ARUN. K. Trends in Information Technology (In. VELAGA VENKATAPPAIAH. *Ed.* Dimensions of Library and Information Science: Kaula Festschrift. - New Delhi: Concept Publishing Company. 1990. pp. 199-221).

8. VENKATAIAH, N. *Ed.* Educational technology. - New Delhi: APH Publishing Corporation, 1996. pp. 8-18.

34

MODERN INFORMATION TECHNOLOGIES THEIR IMPACT ON LIBRARY SERVICES

T. Ashok Babu
L. Venkateswara Rao

"Knowledge is of two kinds. We know a subject ourselves or we know where we can find information up on it".

Introduction

The information explosion of recent years has led to the phenominal increase in the production of scientific and technical literature. Approximately one million articles are published every year. The traditional tools and techniques proved in-adequate and slow to harness the flooding information. Innovations in computer and telecommunications technology have resulted in major changes in basic library operations.

The term Information Technology (IT) is most commonly used to mean a combination of computer and communication technologies used for information storage, retrieval and dissemination. It also covers the developments and improvements of non-print media for reordering information such as microfilms, microfiches, CD ROMs etc.

Definition of Information Technology

According to ALA Glossary information technology is the application of computers and other technologies to the acquisition, organisation, storage, retrieval and dessemination of information. Information technology is a product of information science and technology.

Moll defines IT as "various means of obtaining, storing and transfering information using computers, telecommunications and micro electronics". However it is clear that the convergence of three technologies computers, micro-electronics and communications constitute the IT.

Historical Development of IT

Prior to the development of printing in Europe there was little communication among scientists other than exchange of letters. For two centuries after the development of printing, this pattern of communication continued to be the same, small groups of scientists began to meet together to discuss the results of their research. Scientific Journals have remained a source of primary information. By 1800 there were approximately 100 scientific Journals, in 1900 approximately 10,000 and it is estimated that today there are 1,00,000 Journals that publish scientific articles.

Computers made their debut when Charles Babbage invented the difference engine in the mid nineteenth century. Developments in computer and communication technologies have brought about a new dimension process of information handling. The introduction of microprocessor and minicomputers has made things much easier. All these developments facilitate better and quicker service to the users.

Need for Information Technology

This is the era of information explosion in which large amount of information is being generated of every moment. The abilities to collect store and dissiminate of new technologies.

Information technology is a generic term used for a group of technologies. The new technologies as most relevant for application in modern library and information system can be grouped into the major areas

1. Computer Technology
2. Communication Technology and
3. Reprographic, micrographic and printing technologies.

Application of Computers

To cope with the increase in and demand for scientific and technical information, the government, scientific and technical communities, industry, and libraries began to explore and apply the technology of computers to library operations and to the development of machine readable bibliographic files.

Computer has brought in a new impact to the library and information usage. It is used in various fields of library activities. Some of the areas of automation are:

1. Acquisition
   - Acquisition/accession list
   - Order fund/report
2. Serials Management
   - serials check-in/out and claiming
   - Union/holding list
3. Cataloguing/Classification
   - Catalogue card/lable production
   - On line catalogue
   - Retrospective conversion
4. Circulation
   - Inter library load
   - Over dues
   - Reservations
5. Audiovisual Management
   - AV acquisition/cataloguing
   - AV inventory control etc.
6. Management
   - Accounting/budgeting
   - Scheduling/planning
   - Word processing/mailing
   - Statistics/report
7. Information Storage/Retrieval
   - Database construction
   - Down loading/uploading
   - On line database searching
   - Indexing and abstracting
   - Current awareness service

- SDI service

8. References/Information Services

- Bibliographics listings
- Public access/computer literacy
- Library instruction

Communication Technology

Communication technology is developing at a rapid pace. The need to communicate more quickly and more efficiently has become a central focus in our technological society. The major developments in this area are:

- Audio Technology
- Audio visual technology
- Teletex
- Video text
- Fax
- Online search
- E-mail
- Satellite Technology
- Online search
- Networking
- Teleconference
- Cellular Telephones
- Voice Mail etc.

(a) Online Technology

With the advent of the telecommunication networks also came search services. often referred to as online vendors. that provide retail access to the databases of numerous publishers. The direct impact of computer networks is the production of large number of online databases like Chemical Abstracts Service (CAS) MEDLARS. BIOSIS etc. Gaint systems like ORBIT. DIALOG. ESA. BLAISE. NASA. MEDLINE. INSPEC etc. have a global coverage of chemical medical. aerospace. engineering and technical literature with millions of entries stored.

(b) Electronic Mail

Electronic mail is an alternative to conventional postal mail service with addition of storing and processing of messages converted into electrical signal for transmission. In libraries abstract and indexes of titles are available direct from electronic databases through E-Mail.

(c) CD-ROM Technology

CD-ROM is an acronym standing for compact Disc Read Only Memory. Each disc can store approximately 600 mega bytes of information equivalent to 3 lakh pages of text or 1500 floppy disks or an entire text of 20 volumes of encyclopaedia. Some of the advantages with CD-ROM's are (1) permanent storage (2) low cost (3) more storage (4) data protection and no telecommunication lines are required etc.

Reprographic and Micrographic Technologies

Reprography includes photocopying, microcopying, duplicating and in plant printing. Micrographic technology is an out growth of photographic technology. This technology has made a big impact on the document delivery system.

Impact of Information Technologies on the Management of Libraries

The introduction of these technologies have also affected the organisation and management of libraries. Access to word processing equipment and teleconferencing is fairly common place. Software packages for budgeting, forecasting and planning are readily available. The difficult decisions for management to select suitable products and services are made easy with the help of these modern aids.

Indian Scenario of Computerisation

Presently only 3% of the Indian Libraries are using computers (272 libraries are using computers out of 8,700 libraries) and only 0.6% of the libraries are using CD-ROM's.

Since 1975 INSDOC has been instrumental in creating awareness among the library scientists about the use of computers in the libraries and information centres. In 1983 UGC set up the National Centre for Science Information (NCSI) at the Indian Institute of Science, Bangalore. The NCSI provides SDI services based on CA, INSPEC, BIOSIS, GEOREP and MATHFILE primarily to users in Universities.

Recently UGC has taken up a massive project of computerised university libraries network known as INFLIBNET. Similarly other networking programmes such as NICNET, INDONET, DELNET, CALIBNET etc. are fully based on computer technology.

Although the use of IT in libraries in our country is presently quite low, it is expected to go up in the coming years with the prices of the hardware and general software coming down.

Future Library Scenario

The application of fast developing information technologies will affect every aspect of library activities. The libraries of late 1990's will be quite different from the present one's. Prof. Lancaster predicts a paper-less library and paper-less office. Future libraries would shrink in physical size while accomodating more and more documents/publications in micro/electronic forms. Libraries will use different formats i.e. microform, online databases, videodiscs, teletex systems or even books and journals on siliconchips to provide information on demand.

Conclusion

The library environment is currently undergoing a rapid and dynamic evolution. On our side there is an increasing demand for processing of data and retrieval of information in the quickest possible time. On the other hand the publishing media which is an important field to librarianship is undergoing revolutionary changes. *With the developments of electronic media, on line text, hypertext etc. which involves the library to take advantages of information processing and dissemination.* The innovation of E-Mail and FAX facilitate the electronic document delivery. Thus the new trends of I.T. has a great impact on library and information science profession. The application of information systems and services is perhaps the only way to cope up with the information needs with speed and relative accuracy and reliability.

Section XI
Information Superhighways

35

PROTECTION OF COPYRIGHT ON THE INFORMATION SUPERHIGHWAY

Daniel Gervais

The Central role of copyright in the digital world

Copyright is the best protection for both old and new categories of works

Copyright protection is universally recognized as the best form of legal protection for computer programs and data bases. Various proposals concerning other legal systems[1], including patent protection[2], were put forward. However, it has been made clear in the GATT TRIPS Agreement[3] that both computer programs, whether in source or object code, and data bases were protected by copyright[4] subject to the fundamental requirement that they be original in the sense that they are, to use the language of EU directives in this field, the "author's own intellectual creation".

What is true of these new categories of works is also true of the more traditional ones of course, most of which are expressly mentioned in Article 2 of the Berne Convention. This article provides that all productions in the literary and artistic fields are protected by the Convention.[5] It then lists categories of works that are deemed to be literary and artistic works.

Works transmitted on the "Information Superhighway"

Protected works of all categories will be transmitted on the information highway (of the "Global Information Infrastructure—GII"). These transmissions will take place, for the most part, between, on the one hand, commercial entities operating huge data bases and, on the other hand, members of the public. Users/consumers will have access to, *inter alia*, films and other audiovisual productions, all kinds of writings (scientific and other periodical publications, etc.) and, last but not least, music. Data bases exploited in a similar fashion will offer data that are not protected as such by copyright (because they are not original) but whose compilation (or "selection and arrangement") by the data base producer will be protected by copyright. In addition, a *sui generis* may be granted to protect even non original data bases, where the investment of the data base producer justifies it[6].

All the works mentioned above are, and will continue to be, protected by copyright worldwide, under the Berne Convention, the TRIPS Agreement—and the Universal Copyright Convention. The better question to ask is thus not whether the works are protected, since copyright applies beyond any doubt, but rather which rights apply to the information highway (including whether any new rights are needed) and how they are going to be enforced/administered. Another question is what constitutes the smallest protected work, since digitalization allows the creation and transmission of very small "units".

The application of rights included in copyright to the "Information Superhighways"

Copyright is not a monolithic right. It is composed of a bundle of parallel rights, including the right of reproduction, the right of communication to the public and, although not in the Berne Convention, the right of rental.

The *right of reproduction* may be defined as the right to authorize or prohibit the making of a copy of a work or of a substantial part thereof, in any form. When a work (or other data) is transmitted on the information highway, a temporary or permanent copy is usually made at the point of reception. Since in a majority of cases a compression algorithm is used to reduce transmission time and cost, the "receiver" must decompress the copy to use/view/listen to the work. Legally speaking, the fact that a copy is made and that a mechanical device is then necessary to have access to the work seems to point to the mechanical reproduction right.

A link to *private copying* (for which a levy is provided in a number of countries world wide) is also mentioned by many commentators in this context. However, private copying was originally intended to cover *incidental* private copying, not a main mode of diffusion of works, such as the one the superhighway could become. Moreover, technology will probably allow data base operator to know whether a copy has in fact been made by the user, which is not the case currently with the private copying levy. Hence, while technical methods could prevent the making of the copy or render it "useable" only for a limited time, remuneration could be perceived base don actual usage in addition to private copying levies, which remain necessary to compensate for the substantial number of non-traceable use instances.

The *right of communication to the public* and of public performance of works is also directly involved. In copyright law terminology, "communication to the public"[7] is defined as making available of a work in any manner to persons not restricted to specific individuals belonging to the family circle. It has thus been recognized for example that transmission inside a hotel to individual rooms is a form of communication to the public. It is also well established that it does not matter whether members of the "public" are actually using/watching/listening. It is the fact that they have the possibility of doing so that matters. Consequently, a transmission, whether interactive or not, on a "public" network (even if one has to be a subscriber, of course), is a form of communication to the public—in certain countries, the act is considered as "public performance", which may be considered as a sub-set of communication to the public under the Berne Convention.

Both the right of mechanical reproduction and the right of communication to the public are exclusive rights of the author and his successors in title. They are generally administered collectively.

There have been proposals to the effect of comparing interactive transmissions to the rental of a copy of a work. Since it is true that in both cases the user/consumer gets to view/listen to a work at a time and place he or she has chosen, there may be some economic similarity (such as between marriage and simply "living together"). However, legally speaking, there would seem to be irreconcilable differences between rental and interactive delivery, since rental, in a copyright context, is defined as the "transfer of the possession of a copy of a work"[8]. No such transfer occurs during an interactive transmission which resembles much more traditional broadcasting.

Other rights apply to the digital highways when works transmitted over these highways are manipulated. Changes to a work may involve the (moral) *right of integrity* recognized by the Berne

Convention, as well as the (economic) *right of adaptation*. Where the changes give rise to a new work, authorization from the right holder in the original work is necessary to use the new work.

Finally, *compilations* of works and other data are protected by copyright when they are original, as explained above, and this protection applies when the contents are downloaded on the superhighways, even in part. In some cases, copyright protection may be complemented by a *sui generis* right.

It is thus fair to say that copyright in its present form covers all forms of exploitation, present and future, on the information highways. The real question is *how* copyright will be applied in practice.

Administration and enforcement of copyright on the Information Superhighway

The central role of collective administration

As mentioned in the previous section, the right of communication to the public and the right of mechanical reproduction are directly involved. How will they apply?

One unknown factor is which industrial sector will build and exploit the "carrier" function of the information highway: cable companies or telecommunications giants? It does not fall within the scope of this paper to examine this issue in depth, but the current battles, mergers and deregulation efforts will create winners and losers. It is my view, however, that in spite of or due to these commercial wars, a number of networks will continue to coexist for a number of years.

As regards diffusion of protected works, it is highly likely that, whoever wins the above-mentioned "war", the vast number of "service providers" on the World Wide Web and other "pre-superhighway" networks[9] will progressively be replaced by a relatively small number of "major players" that will provide access to the larger catalogues of works. Smaller catalogues probably will be grouped together on certain servers. In other words, there will be a finite number of key players.

The administration of works for this type of use is not terribly complicated. The "data base operators" will perform, in a somewhat different way of course, the function of broadcasters, coupled with mechanical reproduction. They will pay and report to collective administration organizations representing rights holders according to a negotiated (or fixed by the government if the law so provides) tariff according to the number of use instances. The collectives will then pay their members and sister organizations based on the use data.

This system will work for categories of works for which collective administration already applies such as music. It is not clear, however, to which *additional* categories of works it could apply. For example, organizations representing major computer program publishers have opposed efforts in WIPO to establish a numbering system for programs because, in their view, they are not and will not be sold on superhighways.

In the area of multimedia productions, multimedia creators will need to obtain authorizations to reuse existing material. In some cases (e.g., certain photographs), tariffs may be set by the author and then paid by the multimedia creator/producer to a collective administration organisation an "image bank", as it were. In other cases, a bilateral negotiation could be necessary. Here, central clearing houses, which will have access to information from almost all countries and also to specialized licensing sources, could search for rights clearance on behalf of the multimedia creator/producer and perhaps even negotiate on his/her behalf.

The need for a common identification and EDI systems

To work in the digital age, the identification of works and rights holders on the basis of a name will become extremely difficult, in particular if one considers the linguistic versions, character sets, etc. Common identifiers will be necessary and in this connection, digital technology affords a solution to the problems that it has created: digital sub-coding. This is important because without proper identification, the administration systems outlined above would not work properly, if at all.

Sub-codes are used to track a work, or part thereof, when it crosses a "toll station" or "checkpoint" or point of departure. The "use instances information" may then be sent to a central administration organization which in turn processes the information, collects from the "server" that has sent the work and compensates the rights holders. In the recording industry, the ISO-approved International Standard Recording Code (ISRC) is already incorporated on almost all sound recordings and identifies the particular phonogram(s) concerned (distinct from the underlying musical work). This code can be "picked up" at the point of any digital broadcast/transmission and the data thus collected used to pay the right holders.

CISAC, the worldwide umbrella for societies of authors[10], is currently developing a *Common Information System* which will include codes for musical works, audiovisual works (both for the work as such and the music it contains) and possibly also printed works and works of the visual arts. In parallel, EDI and data base standards are being discussed to ensure fast, reliable data exchange among member societies. Under the current CISAC system, when a work is performed or broadcast in a given country, a local society obtains the data, compiles it, collects from users and then pays both national rights holders (directly) and foreign ones (through the society of which the right holder is a member). The same system will be used for transmissions on the superhighway but, for the reasons indicated above, digital sub-codes and EDI standards are necessary, as is, in some respects, the co-operation of users and partners. CISAC is thus working closely with other interested organizations.

The problem of the smallest protected unit

A separate problem which will arise more often with the advent of the information superhighway and the production of multimedia products is to identify the smallest "work". This problem is different from the reuse of small parts of an existing work, which involves mainly the rights of adaptation and reproduction discussed above. The question of the smallest work concerns the definition of the notion of work and, more precisely, how small can a creation be and still embody a sufficiently high degree of originality. Before answering, it is worth noting that, here again, existing copyright law is sufficient. The question is only to see *how* it applies.

The criterion of originality is the same for all works, although its application depends, in practice, on the type of work involved. Originality follows from *the creative choices* of the author which, in the case of works of fine arts, for example, allow the author to express his/her "personality" through the work. In other cases (e.g.

computer programs, works of applied art), the creative choices are those that are not dictated by the functionality of the work, in other words, those that a given author has done differently from what another author would have produced.

How does this apply in practice? For example in the literary field, a single word is not protected, but there are cases where a single sentence has been said to be protected[11]. There is no universal answer to the question that I could give here. The only certainty is that it will most definitely remain on the agenda for the coming years. Dr. Th. Dreier of the Max-Planck Institute summed it up much better than I could:

> [...] if digital technology and networking thus have a tendency to replace the "author" with mere contributors, the dissolution of what constitutes a "work" as described above seems to work quite to the contrary, i.e., in favor of the contributors' status as authors. The reason for this is the fact that, if single parts of the entirety that was traditionally considered a work—eventually even any combination of data to which a meaning is attached—are regarded as independent "works," it would consequently be possible for independent "authorship" to attach to any of these minimal combinations.
>
> [...] the fact that what was traditionally regarded as a single work may in its digitized from have to be considered a collection of thousands if not millions of single data tends to obscure the distinction between what is protected as a "work" and what must remain unprotected as the mere "information" contained therein. The smaller the units are to which protection will be granted—the smallest unit possible being any combination of data to which a meaning is attached, i.e., arguably a byte—, the more copyright will protect not only a creative work, but mere "information".[12]

Conclusion

My conclusion is a simple one: there is no need to reinvent the copyright wheel. Over the past 109 years (since the inception of the Berne Convention), each technological change (the invention of cinema, of scratch". The superhighways are no exception. But in all previous cases, the Convention has continued to apply. And will continue to do so. The works involved are protected under the Convention and the national laws of approximately 150 countries. Moreover, the transmission of works over the information highway and their reuse are covered by existing rights.

The challenge of rights holders, including societies of authors, is to offer a fully digital, world-wide administration system for transmission of works to the public and their reproduction, as well as single sources for licensing for multimedia productions. This requires a uniform sub-coding system and global EDI standards.

Reference

1. For example when WIPO proposed a sui generis regime of protection in 1978. More recently, the US Congress Office of Technology Assessment in a report entitled "Finding a Balance" (OTA, U.S. Government Printing Office, Washington, 1992) went back to that idea.
2. V. for example, TRUDEAU, "Software Patents", in (1993) 9 *Canadian Intellectual Property Review*, p. 233; SHERMAN, Brad. "The Patentability of Computer-Related Inventions in the United Kingdom and the European Patent Office". (1991) 3 *EIPR*. p. 85; SMITH, James M. "Patentability of Software: What Can and Cannot Be Patented", in (1991) 31 *IDEA*, p. 183; BECKSTRAND, Shelley M. "Experiences Patenting Software Related Patent Applications" in (1991) 31 *IDEA*, p. 207; TACHE. "Copyrightability of Computer Languages: Natural Expansion of Copyright Law or Destruction of the Copyright/Patent Distinction", in (1990) 27 *Journal of the Patent and Trademark Office (USA)*. p. 564; STALLMAN, R. and S. GARFINKET. "Against Software Patents", in (1992) 35 *Communications of the ACM*. p. 17 and the OTA report cited in the previous note
3. Agreement On Trade-Related Aspects of Intellectual Property Rights.
4. Article 10 of TRIPS reads as follows: "*Computer Programs and Compilations of Data*
    1. Computer programs, whether in source or object code, shall be protected as literary works under the Berne Convention (1971)
    2. Compilations of data or other material, whether in machine readable or other form, which by reason of the selection or arrangement of their contents constitute intellectual creations shall be protected as such. Such protection, which shall not extend to the data or material itself, shall be without prejudice to any copyright subsisting in the data or material itself."

5. Since the TRIPS agreement has incorporated by reference Articles 1 to 21 of the Berne Convention (except 6 *bis*) in its Article 9(1), a country bound by the TRIPS Agreement has to abide by the terms of that Convention even if it is not a member of the Berne Union.

6. As proposed, *inter alia*, in the European Union in the draft *Directive on the Legal Protection of Data Bases.*

7. This term has very different meanings in other fields of law, e.g. defamation and protection of privacy.

8. WIPO, Questions concerning a possible protocol to the Berne Convention, Doc. BCP/CE/III/2-III. At p. 3.

9. These networks are, for the most part, not yet "study" enough to be considered as full "superhighways", which only widespread use of broad-band systems and new compression and tracking technology will permit.

10. CISAC has 161 member societies in 87 countries, representing almost 3 million creators and music publishers.

11. "Bereits eine such nur sparliche Kombination von Wortern und Satzen fuhrt mithin ins Individuelle. Ja oft machen Dichter jeden einzelnene Satz zur Individualitat. Etwa folgender Eroffnungssatz einer Hofmannsthalschen Novelle: "Furchtbar krummte sich dei Sperber, den die Buben ans Scheunentor genagelt hatten der hereinbrechenden Nacht entgegen."

    Dieser gleiche Satz knonnte nie unabhangig von Hofmannsthal geschrieben werden. *KUMMER, Max. Das urheberechtlich schatzbare Werk.* Berne, Stampfli, 1968, at p. 31. According to Prof. Kummer, no one but Hofmannsthal could have written the italicised sentence.

12. DREIER, Thomas. "Copyright Digitized: Philosophical Impacts and Practical Implications for Information Exchange in Digital Network", in *WIPO Worldwide Symposium on the Impact of Digital Technology on Copyright and Neighboring Rights (Harvard University, Cambridge, Massachusetts, United States of America. March 31 to April 2, 1993)*. WIPO publication 723(E), Geneva, 1993. At p. 191 and foll.

36

ON-LINE INFORMATION RETRIEVAL SYSTEM

J. Dominic
P.J. Nirmala

Introduction

What is online Information retrieval? Information retrieval using a computer is the searching for and the retrieving of selected information from the data held on a computer; the data is normally held in the form of databases: A database is a collection of related items of information held in a form intelligible to the computer (i.e. Machine - readable): these items may be the full text of journal papers: term record will be used in this book to describe an item held on a database. Records on a database may cover references to the literature in a narrow subject field, or a much more general subject area (e.g. applied science and technology); they may cover a particular type of publication (e.g.) world patent Index covers patents).

When you are 'Online' you are connected directly to the central processing unit (CPV) of a computer; today there are other types of equipment which could be used. In recent years, there has been a growth in the availability of databases on compact Disc-Read only memory (CD-ROM); When searching these databases, the searcher is still 'Online' to the database, but the database is no longer 'remote' from the terminal - the CD-ROM player is connected either directly to the terminal or via a 'local' network. The term 'Searcher' will be used here to describe the person who actually conducts the online search.

The general availability of online information retrieval systems is the inevitable technological consequence of applying computers to the processing of bibliographic and other types of information. In the field of library and information work the computer revolution has made increase rapidly and the following is a brief introduction to the stages of its development.

Development of Online Information Retrieval

Initially, computers were employed to produce printed abstracting and indexing services more efficiently. Indexing services, such as *Index Medicos* in the field of medicine, listed bibliographic details of the latest published information, which was mainly in the form of journal papers; the bibliographic details included author, title, services, such as *Chemical Abstracts* in the field of chemistry, gave bibliographic details plus as summary of "abstract" of the paper. These services are sometimes referred to as 'secondary services' as they make reference to the 'primary literature', i.e. the journal articles, conference proceedings etc.

The tremendous growth in the amount of literature, particularly in the scientific and technical fields, has been well documented. It was estimated that the total number of scientific papers begins published in 1964 was estimated to be at least 60,000. A cumulated total of all the papers indexed in the four publications *Chemical Abstracts, Engineering Index, Index Medical and Physics Abstracts* gives a figure of just under 200,000 in 1950, which had risen to about 300,000 by 1960, and to over 800,000 by 1976, in 1991 this figure was over one million. The power of the computer was harnessed to help with this marked growth in the literature. From the early 1960s the data for the production of the printed indexes and abstracting services was stored on magnetic tape in machine-readable form, but in the early stages of development the printed version of the secondary services was the sole product. Soon, however, it became apparent that, as a necessary for the production of these secondary services,. the data could be used to produce selective listings, for example current-awareness and retrospective literature searches.

The next stage of development began in the mid 1960s: online access to this data held in machine-readable form, where *forming physically* remote *form* the computer storing the data bases were used both by intermediaries (e.g. those who ultimately use the information from the search) acting on behalf of their uses and, increasingly, by end-users themselves (i.e. those who ultimately use the information from the search) to search in a conversational manner the machine - readable data stored in the computer. This was made possible by technological developments throughout the 1960, and early 1970s telephone lines capable of carrying data without corrupting it; a new generation of computers operating at higher speeds and capable of sharing their central processing unit (CPU) time with a number of searchers at once in a conversational mode; drums, discs and others direct access devices with increased storage capacity; and improvements in cable and microwave communications.

The major developments in the 1980s have been the rapid expansion of the online information retrieval industry, greater sophistication of the retrieval software used for searching remote data bases, a vast increase in the number of databases available for searching, faster working speeds, and not the least the appearance of databases on Compact Disc-Read Memory (CD-ROM).

The computer was first publicly applied to the processing of bibliographic information in 1961, when the *Chemical Abstract Service* (CAS) produced *Chemical Titles* (CT), a machine-generated alphabetical subject index to the 600 most influential journals covered by the parent journal *Chemical Abstracts*. The keyword-in-context (KWIC) format devised for CT manipulated actual keywords taken from the titles of the papers published in the journals, so dispensing with the intellectual processes involved in indexing the papers. The KWIC indexing principle thus represents a crude *form* the natural language and full-text searching facility now available in some measure in all online information retrieval systems. The KWIC index could be produced quickly and cheaply, and was readily adopted by other secondary services to alleviate the problems imposed by the phenomenal growth of the literature.

On line information retrieval systems, which enabled the user to communicate directly in a conversational mode with a computer, were being developed by the system development corporation (SDS) as early as 1965. In the same year, Drew and Summit and others, at the Lockheed Missile and space company, described the advantages of an online dialogue. Some sources of semantic distortion could be dominated by putting the user directly in contact with the systems and its vocabulary, and allowing the user to develop a highly complex search formula by a series of simple steps; the result of one search could be applied immediately to the next so that the overall search could be considered as a sequence of attempts. In the following year, the Lockheed space and Missile company, now DIALOG Information services Inc., introduced its DIALOG system. This 'on-line user directed retrieval system' for searching a database of over 300,000 NASA reports at the Lockheed Dalo Alto Research Laboratory was described in some detail by Summit. The main characteristics of the system were that the search could be constructed at the terminal, the system could be used by non specialists, i.e. the users themselves, the command language was independent of the data it searches, the online system allowed continual redefinition of the search question, and the control of the whole process remained with the user. An upgraded version of this system became operational in 1969. After a developmental period which extended into the early 1970, the use of online information retrieval systems became widespread in the united states and later in Europe. Batch processing of searches is now virtually obsolete, and even these searches can be entered online.

Online Information Retrieval Industry

The online information retrieval industry which has seen development since the early 1970 has five main sectors;

1. The producers of the data bases;
2. The online services host or suppliers some times referred to as spinners or vendors;
3. The users of the systems; libraries, information services, information brokers, and end users;
4. The telecommunications sector which provides the important networks and gateways between the other sectors.
5. Hardware and software suppliers.

Some companies provide an intelligent interface between the second and third sectors.

The Different Sectors of the Online Information Industry

The producers of bibliographic data bases are typically the learned societies and institutions which have traditionally undertaken the responsibility of organizing the primary literature covering their fields, and the various national government departments active in science based and other industries, which need to provide information services to their staffs and customers. Many of the abstracting and indexing services in the sciences are long established; for instance *Chemical Abstracts* dates from 1907 and *Physics Abstracts* from 1898. But the massive growth of the literature after the second world war, as evidenced, for instance, by *Chemical Abstracts* 100,000 abstracts published in 1957, 392,000 in 1975, and nearly 542,000 in 1991-has forced data base producers to abandon their data bases.

With the recent rapid expansion of the online information retrieval industry commercial organizations such as Data Courier Inc., Predicates Inc., Reed International plc, and DVn and Bradstreet have (also become active as online data base produces. *Information World Review* has published profiles on some data base producers.

The Overview of the Industry Development and Forecasts for Its Future

For remote online searching, the machine readable data bases produced by the first sector of the industry are leased from the producers by the online services hosts - organizations with sufficient hardware capacity who have also developed software systems to enable users to search the data bases on the hosts, computers. This interaction between host and searcher is effected by using remote computer terminals linked by standard telephone equipment over national and International communications networks to the host computers. The data base producers magnetic tapes are converted into a format compatible with the hosts retrieval system. In this process the tapes data entry format is analyzed and design specifications are developed to transfer the information from the tapes to the magnetic discs used in the hosts system. There is usually a licence agreement between the host and database producer, which gives the host certain rights, e.g. the online exploitation of the data base; in return, the data base producer receives payment in the form of royalties; where a percentage royalty applies, this can range from 10% to 85%.

In 1966, the Lockheed Missile and Space Company introduce its DIALOG system, which was used internally by the company to search a database of over 300,000 NASA reports; an upgraded version of DIALOG became operational in 1969. In 1972 it was launched as a commercial venture with just a few databases; by

1992, as DIALOG Information services Inc., Since 1982 an independent subsidiary of Lockheed Missile and Space company, the service has been offering over 400 data bases; in 1988 it was estimated to have had over 88,000 pass words. In 1972 DIALOG estimated value was $500,000; in 1981 around $ 70m, and in 1988 it was sold to Knight-Ridder for $353m. DIALOG is important for bibliographic data bases, but over 50% of data bases currently available are source databases, and the services is targeting business and financial communities as its chief market. For example, its introduction of the DIALOG Business connection (an end-user service for business), gate ways to the stock exchange etc. - While still maintaining strong ties with the general user. DIALOG first lunched DIALOG version2 in December 1984; it was then gradually introduced throughout the system in 1985; this was a major upgrade of the retrieval system. DIALOG version 1 and 2 ran side by side until version 1 was dropped, and the system is again called simply DIALOG. Fieldman says that in 1986 DIALOG had 80,000 users in 76 countries, nearly double the figure three years previously; the system used 340 gigabit of disc storage and had 150 million records on 270 database, by 1990, DIALOG had 22 offices throughout the world, in addition to those in the United States.

DIALOG has diversified in recent years as well as the main DIALOG service it has introduced knowledge Index (an offer over 70 data bases), Dialorder (document delivery), Dialmail (electronic mail service), the DIALOG Business connection and the DIALOG Medical connection (end user services), DIALOG Link (software for accessing DIALOG), dialog Image catcher (for displaying images, such as trademarks and chemical structures) and DIALOG on Disc products (databases on CD-ROM). Roger Summit, who was involved in the early development of an online system of the Lockheed Missile and Space company, and who is often referred to as the "father of on line", retired as president of DIALOG Information services Inc. on 1 January 1992.

Operations of the Seven Online Host Systems

The practical applications of the principles, with their commands and features, on the following seven online host systems:

1. DIALOG Information services Inc.

2. European space Agency Information Retrieval service (ESA-IRS).
3. BLAISE-LINE
4. National Library of Medicine (BLAISE-LINK)
5. ORBIT
6. PFDS Online
7. Data-Star

There are three self contained units for each online host system, each unit covering a number of operations with their accompanying system commands and features; the searcher can therefore concentrate on one host system without needing to refer elsewhere. Additionally, the operations are numbered similarly for each host system, so that an operation such as truncation can be found in section 2.2 in each of the seven host systems. Each of the three units introduces new commands and features, to enable the search to perform progressively more complex searchers. The searcher can delve more deeply into the complexities of a host system by reference to the user manuals and regular newsletters produced by the online hosts.

A list of the operations covered in the seven online host systems, with the appropriate section numbers, is given below.

Operations covered in each of the three units for each online host system, where applicable:

Unit one

1.1 Logging on to the system; choosing a database (file)

1.2 Entering search statements and creating sets of records; using Boolean operators; displaying records.

1.3 Receiving a search; ending the search and searching session (Logging off).

Unit Two

2.1 Displaying the index file; using both controlled and natural language terms; searching specific fields.

2.2 Proximity searching (full-text searching); string searching; truncation.

2.3 Searching using classification codes, subfiles etc; analyzing search results.

Unit Three

3.1 Limiting a retrieval set of records by some criteria e.g language, date of publication; etc.

3.2 Saving a search on one data base, changing to another data base and conducting the same search on the new database; searching a number of data bases at once (multifile searching): searching elements of records across data bases.

3.3 Printing offline; sorting records; down loading records; transferring records to an electronic mail facility.

Advantages and Disadvantages

Advantages

The advantages of online information retrieval are considerable; the following gives details of some of them

1. The amount of time spent searching the literature is vastly reduced. An experienced online searcher can conduct an online search in between 15 and 20 minutes on average, depending on the complexity of the search. Managers of information services may be concerned when they learn that the cost of searching online may amount to over $1 per minute on some host systems, but against this they must compare the total staff cost, as well as subscription charges, of extended manual searching and the recording, proof reading and duplication of search results.
2. While online it is possible to search at once the entire contents of a database, which may contain millions of records covering literature published over 20 years or more.
3. It is possible to search a number of data bases during the same search session, either together, or consecutively by saving the search on the initial data base and then processing the same search on related data bases

on the same host system. In this way a number of data bases can be searched in a matter of minutes. The state of the art search which formerly might have taken one or two days or longer to complete manually, can be under taken online in minutes.

4. The online searcher can undertàke detailed multi concept search which because of the their complexity could not be searched manually other than by extended and laborious scanning of the text of abstracts.

5. Searching online offers much enhanced capabilities over manual searching; more access points per record are available when searching manually the searcher is limited to the choice of alphabetic subject index headings provided by the indexer, which are usually limited to two or three per record; online searching gives, in additional to these headings, the full range of index terms chosen by the indexer, and the natural language of the text, e.g. title words in the abstract etc. other capabilities include searching other fields such as corporate source and language, proximity searching, truncation, searching using classification codes, analyzing search results, sorting records.

6. The manager of the online service is not usually faced with large subscription charges for using online hosts, particularly those offering bibliographic databases, although a small subscription may be required to cover the costs of regularly up dating literature. This compares favourably with the in house provision of printed for the titles needed must be placed, and these subscriptions are not variables dependent on use. Apart from purchasing printed or CD-ROM titles which are essential for the provision for a particular information services, the manager will often acquire the lesser used titles which must be available as an insurance against what may be needed; it is in accessing these online as an alternative that considerable savings may be made. As the online

information retrieval industry expands, more databases are becoming available in online form only.

7. On line searching ensures file integrity; the searcher cannot be inconvenienced by missing or misfiled issues; or by non-receipt of an issue.

8. On line research results are presented in a concise and standardized, format, where the detail can be predetermined by the searcher. The command languages of the various on line hosts allow the searcher to specify the required form of output; this may be titles only when sampling the results of an initials search, or it may be to display the bibliographic details with indexing terms of records in a set which has proved relevant from the evidence of titles displayed, or it may be to display the full records including abstracts and full text, where available. Some online hosts have special report formats for printing numeric information. This presentation contrasts sharply with the *convoluted* process involved in selecting and presenting the results of a manual search with all the inherent possibilities of errors in transcription and delays in typing and proof reading.

9. The problems of geographical location as barriers to the transfer of information are eliminated through online information retrieval particularly when the room in which the terminal is located becomes an information center in it self, giving access to millions of records on hundreds of data bases. The smallest organization in the remotest rural location can obtain accessed by citing national or larger regional libraries and other libraries with major subject collections. This has helped the emergence of the Information broker - the entrepreneur who undertakes to provide information for fee paying clients.

10. Searching databases online usually gives the searcher much earlier access to new records than when searching manually or CD-ROM.

11. Having access to online sources enables the library or information services to serve more users. As the amount of time spent searching the literature is reduced for an enquiry, the staff time saved can be used to deal with more enquiries. A survey conducted in the United States by SDC showed that in almost every case where online searching was introduced into an organization the number of literature searches under taken increased rapidly; furthermore a large percentage of organizations which previously did no literature searching at all began searching online after being persuaded of the benefits that may be obtained.

Disadvantages

1. Budgeting can be more difficult than for printed, or CD-ROM publications, as much remote online searching is on a "pay as you use basis", and it can be in a particular year.
2. Cost can seen higher than for other publications if they are looked at in isolation; however, this might not sem such a available, the staff time saved, the enhanced service provided. Initial hardware and software cost could be seen as a disadvantage if these products were not already available in the organization.
3. Access might seem more restricted than for printed publications a number of people can search a printed index at the same time, whereas there may be only one terminal for online access and the search may have to be performed by an intermediary; efficient time tabling for online searching could overcome this problem; where there was a great demand for a particular index this would probably be held in printed form and / or CD-ROM as well any way.
4. Staffing are there sufficient staff trained and available to perform online searches if and when required; Is the online service an on demand service or can it be provided only when certain staff are available? Are

end users encouraged to perform their own searches, and is training for this provided by the library staff? A particular end - user could find it a disadvantage to work through an intermediary.

5. How can the end user be sure that important records have not been missed in the search? This would depend very much on the way the search had been conducted, the databases chosen, and whether information in no way includes the whole of human knowledge. It is limited mainly to information published in the last 20-25 years; some subjects, e.g. chemistry, are covered very comprehensively, while others subjects, e.g. history covered well, but in no way comprehensively - other sources would need to be explored for a complete search. A report from the U. K. Scientific Documentation Center reviewed in online review in 1988 claims that online searching compares unfavourably with other methods of information retrieval in locating scientific and technical information.

6. Browsing, and spending sufficient time to ensure that all relevant records have been retrieved, is more difficult online than manually, because of the pressures of time and money; recent moves by online hosts such as ESA-IRS to reduce drastically the cost of connect time could make this less of a problem.

7. Online host systems could be down when required and telecommunications faults might interrupt searches or prohibit a search from even beginning. Many online hosts systems have increased the hours of availability, some to 24 hours a day, and if a host system has an unscheduled break in services which is relatively unusual, the service is normally resumed within ten minutes.

Future of Online Information Systems

The growth in the number of databases has been increasing steadily. This rate of growth will slow down as the market becomes saturated, uneconomic databases are dropped by host systems, and the gaps in subject coverage are filled. The number of full-text databases is set to increase substantially; and there will be more moves to repackage databases, in a similar way to FOXNET, BIOSIS connection and DIALOG medical connection, aiming at particular user markets.

The rate of growth in the number of database producers had shown signs of slowing down until 1991, but this trend is likely to re-establish soon. More producers may see advantages in becoming online hosts themselves, thus having more control over their products; similarly, this control is also increased by producing data bases on CD-ROM, which is another trend likely to continue at an accelerated rate. We are already witnessing substantial change in the type of producer, with powerful organizations such as large publishers, computer companies and telecommunications giants becoming more involved.

There had been a slowing down in the rate of growth of the number of online hosts also until 1991 but this trend also is likely to be restablished soon. There is likely to be more collaboration between online hosts, particularly in the area of gateways which enables a host service to be accessible via another hosts, to agreement on the use of any other hosts command languages and choice on line hosts are offering an in creating range of services as well as remote online access, such as CD-ROM and versions of databases, increasingly sophisticated software products, electronic mail services, and hybrid retrieval systems, i.e. incorporating CD-ROM and remote online access. Although there has been no rush to copy the ESA-IRS policy of pricing for information; more online hosts could introduce much lower connect time charge, with increased charges for retrieved records.

Developments in telecommunications will have repercussions for use of remote online systems. Holmes reports that electronic mail has had a marked effect upon the use of Jordans database; the introduction of ISDN, with their greater speed will help the use of full text data bases; the number of gate ways will increase giving more and easier access, and possibly altering the economics of the online information retrieval industry.

The terminal configuration will undoubtedly change, with increased use of integrated CD-ROM drives and networks to multiple CD-ROM disc drives, WORM drives, and other possible peripherals as yet not commercially available. By 1992 there were several rewritable optical disc drives available and their prices were on the way down. Software for retrieval down loading and database creation will become increasingly sophisticated, this allowing better organization of results of searches.

As regards searching features, more developments will take places in multi database searching, including more widespread adoption of the facility of eliminating duplicate records across databases, searchers one day my able to search any host with just one favorite command language. More menus will be made available.

Laser disc technology mainly at present in the form of CD-ROM, will tend to expand the market for database products, so it will complement remote online searching, rather than threaten its existence, so the two technologies should be able to exist side by side. CD-ROM may however, have an effect on printed publications. CD-ROM gives producers the ability to repackage databases.

References

1. CONVEY (JOHN): On Line Information Retrieval; Library Association Publication London, 1994.

37

LOCAL AREA NETWORKS: THE LIBRARY APPLICATIONS

B. Satyanarayana

Definition

Local Area Network is a communication network used by a single organization over a limited distance which permits users to share information and resources with any other on the network.

Introduction

Local Area Network is a system which allows microcomputers to share information and resources with in a limited area (generally less than a mile from the file server to the work station. A LAN requires that the individual workstations be physically tied together by cabling or by a wireless link and some network software resides on the workstation hard disk. This permits the sharing of peripherals, data and application programs.

Sharing peripherals equipment such as printers, hard disk, drives and plotters is the major use of LAN. Hardware represents the major microcomputer cost in most libraries. Today the networks increase savings by allowing diskless workstations.

Full media sharing LAN can carry information simultaneously from many stations over a shared high speed medium. Each PC on a LAN has to be filled with an adopter card to deal with sending and receiving network messages.

LAN based on the client-server principle with one or more computers acting as servers for the rest of the machines on the network known as clients. LAN connecting together systems of PCs and peripherals, with conventional operating systems such as Window. PC LAN can be connected to Unix operating systems and to the mainframes in big libraries.

Uses of Local Area Networks

LAN can give the following benefits to the users of the library.

* LAN enable the sharing of computing facilities. Expensive hardware such as printers, modems and CD-ROM drives can be made accessible to all library users on the network. Software and data resources may be shared.
* LAN allow files of information to be stored in one place can be accessed by each user under ensuring security, consistency and updating.
* LAN allow easy computer communication such as electronic mail, conferencing etc., between all connected users and support group working.

Networked Library Applications

There are a variety of potential uses for LAN within library services. If the library is on the same network as its user community, so that users have access to the library information from their own desks, and library staff can access information elsewhere in the organization. This situation is common in both academic and commercial organizations.

The five main categories of library LAN applications are:

Sharing Facilities and Equipment

The most important use of the LAN is to enabling the sharing of the equipment between users on the network. The most common example is the sharing of printers, so that all users can send their files for printing to a common printer rather than each user having their own. If local printers attached to each PC are the norm, the network can still be used for more expensive printing devices like laser printers or colour printers. The other equipment which can be connected to a network and shared include CD-ROM drives, Modems, Fax machines.

Internal Communication

LAN are the best solution for allowing communication by computer within an organization. This is done by electronic mail (E-mail) sending messages between individuals. All LAN support E-mail. The main communication within the library include:

* General administrative messages between library staff

* Loan requests and the notification of arrival and recall of items
* Search requests and sending of search results.

E-mail can be used for transmission of regular information such as information bulletins, SDI profiles and to disseminate mailings from outside the library.

E-mail is used to send not only the plain text but also allow complicated documents from text processing and spreadsheet packages. Multimedia e-mail featuring graphic images video clippings and voice messages is becoming available.

E-mail allows messages to be sent from one sender to one or several recipients. Other techniques can be used to "broadcast" electronic messages over a LAN: these include broadcast e-mail. In a library setting these may be used to pass on the information and publicity to a wide group of users and to receive open feedback and response.

Sharing Information

Computer users on a LAN can share common administrative systems. This to the idea of group working. This involves very close sharing of information between colleagues, integrating electronic communication, document management and office automation. LAN can also be used for joint co-operative production of complex documents and reports with several authors.

Access to Information

Information held centrally on a single computer can be accessed over a LAN by all users connected to it. The library applications include:

* Catalogues and other database
* Serials holdings and location information
* Circulation records
* Reading lists
* CD-ROM databases and other multimedia services etc.

Holding the data in this way has some advantages. It avoids the problem of having distribute multiple copies of databases to all those users at other locations. As the data is in one place it is easy to update and modify, back-up and kept secure. All users still can have access as though the information on their own machine. Virtually all library automation and housekeeping systems are designed to run in a networked environment.

External Communication

Although a media-sharing LAN is primarily used for communications between the users of the machines connected to it, it can also provide for LAN users to contact the outside world. Access to fax, Internet etc., largely via e-mail and access to information world wide.

The future of the library LAN

Libraries can use local area networks to support their activities. Developments in library services are generally set by users demand for services which are dependent on information technology. It is better to look at the trends in Information technology to predict the likely evolution of services and to gain insight into the future of library networking.

Trends in Information Technology

Computing

Tremendous increases in processor power and storage capacity and have now reached where multimedia can easily handled by personal computers. To handle the multimedia information, including the colour graphic images sound and video makes computers much easier and interesting to use. Now many people are using the computerised information resources.

We are also witnessing the miniaturisation in that more powerful features get crammed in to even smaller spaces. Laptops now rival desktops for dominance in the office environment and can include integral CD-ROM drives.

Telecommunications

We have seen an increase in the availability of high band width network connections. This is the result of the new media. eg. fibre optic cabling and improved transmission techniques. This makes it possible to send large multimedia files from computer to the other computer. Existing telephone cables can even be used to deliver video services. But in India the telephone lines are not that reliable to send such high speed transmission of video services. Now with the entry of private industry in telecommunication sector we may expect laying of high speed cables to suit these services. The move to digital mobile telephones allow users to connect them to Laptop computers to send or to receive multimedia data from any location. Many libraries are connecting into wide area networks such as Internet and compuServe to send and receive e-mail and to access and disseminate information.

Trends in Information Services of Libraries

If we combine the trends in computing and telecommunications we have the means to store, process and transmit multimedia information rather than simply the text handled by the computer systems. Multimedia including full colour graphics, sound, animation and video has powerful appeal as an information resource, learning package, entertainment or working environment. Library users require access to information in multimedia format. Increasingly wide area networks such as Internet make this possible.

The demand for multimedia information services to the user will be a significant factor in the future of Library networking. Users may prefer to use library services from their homes and offices via electronic mail and videoconferencing.

The importance of the Internet cannot be ignored. users can connect the library catalogues, bibliographic databases and full text journals through their telephone lines. The increasing use of the World Wide Web is another example of where multimedia, hyperlinked information is made available to the Internet community.

Conclusions

The need to network resources will only increase moving from a need to share resources within one location, to a need to share resources of other location. The future of the library LAN any include:

* Increased access to both internal and external services

from the library LAN

* Increased access to library LAN from outside the library building
* Increased demand for multimedia information services
* Increased electronic communication by e-mail and videoconferencing
* Increase in work group computing activities.

We live in a Digital age. The library LAN is probably just the beginning.

References

1. Fortier, Paul J (ed). : Handbook of LAN Technology. 2nd ed., New York: McGraw-Hill, 1992.
2. Hammond, Joseph L and O'Reilly, Peter J.P.O: Performance analysis of Local Computer Networks. California: Addison-Wesley, 1986.
3. Basandra, Suresh K.: "Linking Computers Through LAN" Information Technology. Vol. 3.No.2. (July) 1993.
4. Schatt, Stan: Understanding Local Area Networks. 4th ed., New Delhi: Prentice Hall of India, 1995.

38

MOVING TOWARDS VIRTUAL LIBRARY: ROLE OF REFERENCE LIBRARIANS

Sai Lakshmi Parvathaneni

".. Whenever I think of my future

I shudder like a coward...."

Parvathaneni Gangadhara Rao

I often share with my colleagues the description and concern of the ultimate reference tool of the future.

Although frequently called the "information superhighway," the Internet is actually a precursor to the multi-network that will some day provide universal access to digital communication services around the globe. It has been likened to a highway system because it functions much like a network of interstate highways. In reality, the Internet is a "network of networks," connecting a growing number of regional sites to an international electronic grid that today encompasses over 13.4 million individual servers in more than 100 countries around the world.

The Internet came about as a logical extension of the massive building campaign which took place during the 1950's when the cold war was at its height. In the name of national defense, the government underwrote the cost of constructing a system of interstate highways linking major cities across the country, and thereby allowing the military to quickly reinforce any front in case the United States was ever attacked.

The basic assumption was that, if one city was destroyed, the effect on the overall flow of supplies to the rest of the country could be minimized by the availability of alternate routes bypassing the area of destruction. Similarly, the highway network would allow the military to decentralize and avoid having to rely upon a single "command headquarters" that could be targeted ad put out of commission by the enemy.

This notion was also the driving idea behind the creation of the Internet. By the late 1960s, with the highway system in place and supply routes secured, the military turned its attention to securing its system of intelligence. It set about ensuring the safe transport of data between huge mainframe computers at different strategic locations by creating unlimited alternate communication routes in case of bomb attack and by decentralizing functions so that no single computer could be targeted as an "information headquarters."

In 1969, the Department of Defence's Advanced Research Projects Agency (ARPA) created the Internet. But it wasn't known then as the Internet; it was called "ARPA" or "ARPANet," and it had to do with security and defence. ARPANet used myriad connections to link together four mainframe computers — at Stanford Research Institute, the University of California at Los Angeles, the University of California at Santa Barbara, and the University of Utah — so that if one were taken out, information could continue to flow among the others over alternate paths. This was accomplished using a new technology called packet switching. Previously, computer networking efforts required a line between each computer on the network and data moved in continuous flow from host to host. Packet switching changed all that. It allowed data files to be broken down into chunks or "packets" of from one to around 1500 characters for random transfer to their ultimate destination. Packet switching allowed the same communication lines to be shared by many different users at the same time.

In the years that followed, the network grew. The Department of Defence concurrently developed MILNet, a network for not-so-top secret stuff, which was linked to ARPANet. In 1986, another U.S. government agency, the National Science Foundation (NSF), set up a network of five super computer centers called NSFNet. NSFNet proved so successful that it eventually replaced ARPANet, which was shut down in 1990. NSFNet provided additional networking links to academic institutions around the country by creating a system of smaller regional networks connecting universities to their nearest neighbors in chains that at some point connected to one of the five linked super computer centers. In this manner, any computer on any of the computer or any of the chains by forwarding the conversation through its neighbour. The Internet, as we know it today, had come into being.

With the creation of NSFNet, academia suddenly found itself with access to fast computers, previously available only to government employees and contractors, weapon developers and a few computer science researchers. With this connectivity also came access to newer, higher-level Internet working protocols (the language unlike computers use to talk to each other), such as TCP/IP. TCP and IP are two of the most important protocols; you don't need to know the details of how they work in order to appreciate what they do. The TCP part of TCP/IP assumes responsibility for breaking down the raw data into "packets" at the one end and resembling everything correctly at the other; the IP part takes care of transferring the data packets successfully to their intended destination.

As more and more networks, both within and outside the country, "gatewayed" E-mail access to the emerging Internet, an exchange of information on a global level flowed. One of the first gateways was to BITNet, (Because It's Time Network), an academic network of mostly mainframe computers developed in the early 1980's in response to academic researchers needs for collaborative scholarship. (the first LISTESERVS, i.e., electronic discussion groups, among academic institutions) Since BITNet connections were limited to mainframe systems and the network speeds were much slower than allowed by Internet's networking scheme, BITNet has gradually been superseded by the Internet.

Throughout the 1980's technological advances in computer hardware and software made powerful computers more accessible to the public. Better communications systems allowed more computers to link to the network. Still, during this period, computers on the Internet numbered only in the hundreds and, for the most part, were used primarily by government and scientific researchers and a few free-wheeling "teckies". Then, in 1991, Vice President Gore gave his "Information Superhighway" speech, and overnight, the "Internet" and "Information Superhighway" became household words.

These new users are both searching for information and bringing information with them. Every day, they add megabytes of data to the Internet. New addresses are created and old ones shut down. The Internet is, indeed, a vibrant, living web of interconnecting strands or links crisscrossing the entire globe and providing multiple avenues to information on a scale never before known.

Who's managing and coordinating all this activity? Actually, nobody. You'll never see complete uniformity on the Net because no central authority or governing body controls or runs the Internet. Universities, schools, governments, individuals and businesses own the hardware and the files at their particular sites. The backbones that interconnect the sites are jointly owned by hundreds of telecommunications companies, government agencies and universities, which spend tens of hundred of thousands of dollars annually for Internet connectivity.

The government originally funded the network's physical development and encouraged academic participation by providing grants through the National Science Foundation (NSF) to establish connections. Regional Internet providers sold NSF hub connections to interested industries and to institutions of higher education. In April of 1995, the government's NSFNet project was officially replaced by the NAPS (Networks Access Points) schema, with acknowledged commercial providers controlling the backbone now supporting the Net; today, the original regional providers relay costs and services from a NAP rather than from an NSFNet hub.

Internet is changing the nature of the library. Instead of being at the end of the block, the book collection will exist in cyberspace. The user (patron) is moving beyond the library's physical resources to online resources outside the library. Technology is now extending library collection and resources beyond the library hand that holds them. Library administrators across the U.S. are determined to carve out a key role for their institutions in the digital age. In addition to ferrying local citizens into cyberspace, reference librarians are counting on technology to extend their patronage beyond the immediate neighborhood, working closely with technological companies, that are digitalizing collections for delivery over the Internet to local, national and even global audiences.

In the last decade perhaps no other phenomenon has so significantly affected the provision of reference services as has the Internet. The convergence of telecommunications technology and computers has caused our profession to undergo a powerful paradigm shift affecting the manner by which we access, manipulate, and interpret data.

Reference Librarians are becoming proficient in assisting patrons access information electronically. Providing access to information will be the principal goal and activity, and coping with technology and change will be the typical driving force of the emerging information age library. Knowledge about the holdings within one's own library is not enough to quench the information thirst of today's library patron; indeed, it has become impossible for reference librarians to rely on printed pages (or other information resources) with in their own libraries. The reference librarian of the future must be proficient in using the virtual library, a system by which a user may connect transparently to remote libraries and databases using the local library's on-line catalog as a gateway. The resources on the Internet serve as the foundation of the virtual library. The use, interpretation, and evaluation of these resources are becoming important responsibilities for today's reference librarians.

The Internet has much to offer libraries and their clientele. Reference by electronic mail, specialized discussion lists, database searching in OPACs and indexes, full-text books and articles, and document delivery are just some of the services and resources available on the Internet. The breadth of these available materials require that libraries above all need the tools to filter the data, to bring them to a widening circle of users in whatever from they require and increasingly, to enable users to locate and retrieve the data themselves, easily and transparently.

Identifying, accessing and utilizing materials on the networks can be viewed as logical extensions of the reference librarian's mission. Librarians need to incorporate network resources by adapting their services and applying their expertise in this new environment. There is an added benefit in librarians learning the resources on the Internet, since these experiences will prepare them to serve as guides to the emerging infractures of machine-readable information just as they do for printed materials.

In a virtual world of Internet information, *access* becomes the *sine qua non* of the universe. If one cannot access the information, one cannot use the information. By every measure, whether you consider the number and types of information objects, the speed of their transmission, or the worldwide breadth of their distribution, computing technologies and high-speed, wide-area networks have changed radically the ways in which information is created, stored, and disseminated. To this end, the responsibility of educating the patron and rescuing him from the vicious nets of cyberspace remain on the shoulders of the reference librarian. Such education will allow both librarians and end users access the brave new world of the Internet. This brave new world, however requires adjustment to new technology and a positive change in the reference environment. With each library doing its part we should have national information mosaic, where libraries could interconnect on a bigger scale to offer a compendium of information. These global networks will allow the emergence of a global electronic reference library. *The virtual library will become a reality.*

"Trends, like horses, are easier to ride in the direction they are going..." *Anonymous*

Section XII
Internet and W.W.W.

39

INTERNET AND WORLD WIDE WEB

S. Palani
S. Ganesan
T. Rajendran

What is Internet?

The Internet is the largest computer network in the world. Just like any other computer network, it consists of a set of computers, a set of physical (or wireless) links between the computers and a set of, rules or protocols governing the exchange of information among the computers.

The speed at which information is transmitted across the Internet varies depending on the machine used to access it, the type of connection, and the volume of usage at any one time.

What is out there?

Much of the recent interest in the Internet centers on a relatively new feature the world web (the WWW or the web). This provides a user friendly method for accessing, manipulating and even publishing information on the Internet.

However the web is just one of several ways of exchanging information; others include E-mail, telnet, file transfer protocol, network news and gopher.

The World Wide Web

Given the sheer size of the Internet (more than 5 million computers in over 75 countries) how does one find the required information is literally a needle in a haystack. If you know precisely the information you need from the Computer and also its location (where it is stored) then the problem is easy to solve. There are also specific programs available on the Internet (archie, gopher, verona are examples) that will help to search the information of one's choice. But most of these tools are not adequate. Some of the machines on the Internet now provide a service called the "World-Wide-Web"

(WWW). Somewhat, WWW is a parallel network, which uses the Internet as the backbone. In the WWW network, computers are linked by information. You hop from one macdhine to another using the information links until you find what you want. The Computer programs that follow the WWW links are commonly referred to as WWW browsers. If you get an account with VSNL, they provide a simple browser called LYNX or EXPLORER. (for Windows 3.1 or 95)

History of the Web

The World Wide Web dates back to march 1989 when Tim Berners-Lee of Geneva's European Particle Physics Laboratory (Which is abbreviated as CERN, based on the Laboratory's French Name) circulated a proposal to develop a "hypertext system" for the purpose of enabling efficient and easy information sharing among geographically separated teams of researchers in the High Energy Physics community.

More than a year later, in October 1990, the project was presented anew, and two months later the World Wide Web project began to take shape. Work began on the first line browser (called WWW), and by the end of 1990 this browser and a browser for the Nextstep operating system were well on the way.

In March 1991, two years after the presentation of the original proposal, the WWW line-node browser saw its first limited network use. Two months later, WWW was made available more extensively at CERN, and the Web was effectively off and running and then several important developments came in 1994. First work expanded on the development of "secure" Web access, the kind of security needed if real corporate work were to take place across the web, and if users were ever to provide such details as credit and information.

Accessing the Consortium's Web site (http://www,w3.org/) lets you see the organization's official statements.

How the Web Works: HTTP

The most interesting feature of the web is its simplicity. Of course, that might be the reason for its use worldwide by most of the researches. You would expect a technology like this to have the complexity commensurate with its capabilities, but it doesn't.

In fact as the web document prepared by CERN (European Laboratory for particle physics) (http: //info.cern.ch/hypertext/www/ protocols/HTTP/HTTP2.html) reveals that, the transaction takes place in four basic phases, all part of the underlying HTTP (Hyper Text Transfer Protocol):

Connection

Request

Response

Close

In the connection phase, the Web client (for example, Mosaic, Net scape, Lynx) attempts to connect with the server. This appears on the status line of most browsers in the form connecting to HTTP server. If the client can't perform the connection, nothing further happens. Usually, infact, the connection attempt times out, yielding and explanatory message saying so.

Once the connection to the HTTP server is established, the client sends a request to the server. The request specifies which protocol is being used and it also tells the server what object it is looking for and how it wants the server to respond. The Protocol can be HTTP, but it can also be FTP, NNTP (Network Transfer Protocol), Gopher, or Wais (the 239.50 Protocol). Included in the request is the method, which essentially is the clients command to the server.

Searching the web

The world wide web provides a uniform, user friendly interface to the Internet. Web pages can contain text and pictures and are interconnected by hypertext links. the addresses of web pages are recorded as Uniform Resource Locators (URLs), transmitted by hypertext transfer protocol (HTTP), and written in Hypertext Mark-up Language(HTML).

The Bio-Medical presence on the web is now far too large to be surveyed by one individual. To illustrate the breadth of medical information available, if we use a key word NEURO FIBROMATOSIS, the search will be completed in two minutes and provide the links to seven web pages at four sites.

One particularly informative site at the Massachusetts General Hospital provided a description of the condition, complete with magnetic resonance scans, information about clinical services, research, conferences and the self help groups.

The rich results that can be obtained on a fairly obscure subject suggests that whatever your specialty you will find something of interest on the internet.

Let us imagine that you are giving some lectures on AIDS and want some images related to the subject. There are two ways you can try. The first is to start your search at a site that provides a hierarchical index of the web. You might begin your search on the top menu of the popular web site YAHOO. You select the link to Health, then the link to Medicine which takes you to a list of medical specialities from which you select AIDS. You find say for instance five immunology institutes. You select the Hypertext link to AIDS at Queens university. This takes you to Web Page detailing the activities and resources of the Microbiological department. Now all you need is to click on the link to the HIV image database to access department collection of slides.

Alternative approach to finding information on the web is to use one of the "search engines" that collect and index data published on the web. The most comprehensive of these is Lycos, which currently holds information on over five million web pages. You can query several search engines one at a time through the Configurable Unified Search Interface (CUSI), or in parallel, using "Savvy Search". You choose to use save search. You type the query term "Aids" into the search window and cross check the images box to tell Savvy Search what sort of sites to search for. Savvy Search then lists numerous links, most of which take you back to Queen's University.

Gathering Information of the WWW

Today the biologist will often go on the "Walkabout" to discover new Internet resources; many problems can be solved by walking the Web Maps of the Internet resources of every European Country are available on the WWW. The programs called spiders or Robots have been written which move about the web collecting information about URLs (uniform resource locators).

A particularly good tool for searching the WWW is called "Web Crawler" which specializes in biological sites.

Hypertext Markup Language (HTML)

Web pages are plain text documents, marked up in hypertext markup language (HTML), which defines the format of areas of text by "tagging" them. The tags are interpreted by a web browser so that tagged areas are displayed differently from the normal style of text (for example, in bold fig. 1). Tags usually surround the tagged area in the format <tag> text <tag>. For example, a top (level 1) heading is tagged as follows:

<hi> This is a top level heading </h1>. Tags are usually defined functionally, rather than visually, so that the way in which a given tag is displayed varies from browser to browser. Take, for example, text tagged with <h1> </h1>. Both Mosaic and Netscape would display this text in a large, bold font; Win Web would also underline the text: Lynx would center the text and then capitalise all the letters. Hypertext links are marked up in a special format:

<A HREF* "URL">hypertext</A>

For Example:

<A HREF* : http://WWW. qmw. ac. uk/~rhbm001/ index.html">The Microbial Underground</A>

Links marked up in this way can be used to take the reader elsewhere in the same document, to other marked up documents, or to completely different types of file.

You may include in the web pages the details of your interest or the interest of your Dept/Institution. This will depend on your position as an Official Author of your Department's or Institution's web pages or whether you are acting independently. Departmental and institutional web sites usually include general information about the Department or Institution with local phone number and e-mail addresses; specific information about local research, educational and clinical interests; and links to related sites elsewhere on the web.

Publishing on the web

Although some scientists have made their research papers available through the Internet for many years, the arrival of the web presents a more attractive and powerful medium for electronic publishing. Several medical journals have now moved on to the web. Some provide only a table of contents for each issue. Others like *British Medical Journal*, publish a selection of their articles in electronic form; yet others, such as the *Journal of Biological Chemistry*, are available in a full text format.

The richness of the web stems largely from the fact that it is so easy to contribute material to it. You need no training in computer science or graphic design, just the ability to write Hypertext Markup Language and access to a web server.

Newsgroups

Network News is divided into numerous newsgroups. The largest collection of newsgroups in USENET, which contains several thousand news groups covering almost all imaginable topics, from alcohol to Zen. USENET newsgroups are arranged in a hierarchy, which originally had seven top level categories: sci (Science), comp (Computing), soc (Social), talk, misc (miscellaneous), news and rec (recreational). The addition of the alt (alternative) category to this original list triggered an explosion of often bizarre newsgroups. Each top level category is further subdivided many times, with each group conforming to a hierarchical naming convention, so that, for examples, "sci.med" is a general medical news group within the sci category, and "sci.med". aids is a newsgroup dealing with the medical and scientific aspects of AIDS.

The BIONET NEWSGROUPS is a widely available set of news groups, outside USENET, that are interest to bio-medical workers.

The Future of Medicine on the Net

The medical colonisation of cyberspace has only just begun. It is difficult to predict the future of medicine in this new world. Some have already proclaimed the death knell of medical journals, but others point out that the Internet cannot yet complete with a good library as a source of scientific information. Medical Librarians are already planning to save the Internet's wild frontier with the ambitious OMNI (organising medical networked information) project, which aims to provide biomedical workers with a gateway to high quality networked information".

Conclusion

With the fascinating INTERNET, the research environment is no longer need to be confined to a single laboratory with its limited resources but can have access to information world wide through computers connected with internet facilities. Computers may be located in different parts of the world but with modem networking they can be seamlessly linked together. That is researchers may work locally, but can compute globally.

References

1. Huntley AC, Conrad SJ. Internet tools in the medical classroom. Med Educ. 1994; 28:508-12.
2. Millman A, Nicholas I, Kealy K. The Internet, BMJ 1995; 311 : 440-3.

INTERNET AND JAVA : THE ULTIMATE FOR THE LIBRARIES

B.S. Swaroop Rani
S. Swaminathan

Introduction

Information today is the lifeblood of society. As society changes through years so also the complexity of information. One image of the Post-industrial society was the Information society. Following industrialization there emerged a society organised around knowledge for the purpose of social control and the directing of innovation and change[1]. Social control in Bell's terms calls for importance of Information and knowledge.

Information

Shera defines that Information in the sense of librarians use is a fact. "It is a stimulus we receive through our sense. It may be an isolated fact or a whole cluster of facts"[2]. Viswanathan experience that a highly sophisticated method of communication is the act of reading the recorded information in the form of printed books and allied graphic documents[3].

Information becomes meaningful only when it is transformed or communicated. Thus for speedy transformation of information the modern information technology, computer and telecommunication has helped the librarians to transform information to their clients in selected areas through network system.

Networking

Nora and Mine unequivocally stated that information technology (Telematics) would accelerate the emergence of a very highly productive society with less but more effective work and jobs very different from those imposed by industrial life[4]. The Information Technology has helped people come closer through the concept of networking. Networking is the linking of people and available resource within cohesive information unit. Networking has thrown to the librarians an intellectually challenging task in providing client-oriented services.

The networking function is to effectively and efficiently distribute information and resources to those who want it clearly, device that will have a significant impact on networking is the computer hardware and software. The computer hardware and software can effectively distribute resources in various libraries as they become available and rapidly respond to international request as they are generated. The computer is the technological marvel behind our information age and the means by which network will effect the library and the society as a whole.

Internet

The slogan "Network is the computer" is picking up and a client server strategy is expanding. The Internet which has been building up for years on the foundation of office networks where it dominates now but Microsoft and Novell believe it will extend to various other fields. It also has a booming future in the publishing industry similar to the paper based, desktop publishing market.

The head of IBM Irvine Windawaky Brger, who heads IBM's Internet division has said that once companies and libraries move Internet networks supporting a few hundred people to sophisticated WEB sites supporting thousands they will rediscover its security and reliability.

The Internet requires an entirely new software model. The software which are sold today be sold On-line for cheaper rate in the future. The modern network programme with the existing software holds good for the future specially tailored to software products. The Internet will shake up plenty of established industries service centres from telecom to libraries. Since it's cheaper it's going to be everywhere.

The Internet has the potential to become bigger and go bigger and the starting point for revising that potential is the Software Industry.

A recent networking software - Java

Conventional Web pages, convenient as they are essentially no more flexible than the old mainframe screens. In the spring of 1995 however Sun Microsystem for workstation maker came up with a computer language called Java that was designed explicitly for networks. It is a way of writing small programmes each designed to do a single task that reside in the network until needed.

Web pages are static documents, Java applicts are real programmes that one can control like any other software. Once they are downloaded they run totally on the PC's largely free of network delays.

Computer languages come and go without sparking revolution. Java is different because it is more than a language. It is also in a strange way itself a computer the appletes that zip down the line when one checks on a Java enabled page are not written in the usual sort of code that processor chips can understand. They have to be decoded by a special programme on the computer. Java virtual machine that translates them into instruction which computer can understand.

This method has two main advantages namely,

a. The first is protection from computer viruses.

b. The second is Java is a cross platform language, the same applet will work on any computer running a Java virtual machine.

However Java has its own disadvantage. For a start, some technical hitch remains to be received. Before software is shipped it is compiled into a code that a processor chip can understand. Java however is translated line-by-line, by the virtual machines as it arrives. That means it can be as much as ten times slower than conventional software. Java is not the fastest language and also it is incomplete.

Conclusion

However as years go, the software holds a bright future in all client-server oriented services including the library. Technology is marching towards globalization of Information through network. Various types of hardwares and softwares are going to affect the future of libraries.

References

1. Bell(D). The coming of post industrial society: A ventura in social forecasting. New York: Basic Books, 1973.
2. SHERA (JH). Foundations of Education for Librarianship. New York : Becker and Hayer, 1972.
3. Viswanathan (C.G.) Elements of Information Services. New Delhi : Today and Tomorrow Printers, 1976.
4. Nora (S) and Mine (A) (1980). The Computerization of Society. A report to the President of France, Cambridge, MA. MIT Press.

41

INTERNET IN THE INFORMATION SERVICES: EXPERIENCE AT THE UNIVERSITY OF ILLINOIS AT CHICAGO LIBRARY OF THE HEALTH SCIENCES

Rama Vishwanatham

Introduction

Libraries in the present day are poised at the juncture where technology is the "limits of libraries" and traditional libraries (a place that provides access to information) that can be called "primitive approximation of access to knowledge" are the barriers (Matheson, 1995). Health information explosion is the highest rate and the health information professionals are taking on the challenge by being the "agents of change" (Matheson, 1995). They are leading the way and pushing the limits of the idea that technology is the "limits of the libraries". In this current environment health sciences librarians are developing their knowledge and skills to access, organize and filter the abundant information to assist health professionals in their pursuit of knowledge. Since academic health sciences libraries in the United States are more likely to access the Internet, the health sciences librarians are "turning toward networked information" as a resource (Lacroix, Backus, Lyon, 1994; Hicks & Tedd, 1995). As resources have become available over the Internet, the role of the health sciences librarian has also evolved as new uses for the Internet are discovered. Internet provides new communication vehicles where librarians can learn new techniques. It provides improved access, retrieval and distribution of information for both traditional and electronic resources through E-mail, telnet, file transfer protocol (FTP), menu driven Gopher and hypertext and hyperlink-based World Wide Web (WWW) capabilities. With the Internet becoming an integral part of a health information professional is well positioned to apply critical thinking skills in understanding the organizational differences of the Internet, the lack of standardization of format, and the impermanence of the information. This paper will discuss how the Internet has evolved and how the Information Services librarians at the Library of the Health Sciences at the University of Illinois at Chicago (LHS - Chicago) are developing new roads to health information resources.

Internet - History and Background

The Internet started in the 1960s as ARPANET, a computer network developed by the United States Government to facilitate the flow of information between government agencies. BITNET was one such network that linked academic and research communities across the country. Internet is currently a network of networks and is based on a protocol called TCP/IP or Transmission Control Protocol/ Internet Protocol. This standard protocol allows users to communicate through tools or software such as E-mail, Listservs and Usenet news groups. It also facilitates these users to access, retrieve and distribute information through telnet, file transfer protocol (FTP) and the client/server architecture. Gopher and the World Wide Web (WWW) lend organizations and structure to this vast maze of information on the Internet and help navigate the Internet.

E-mail, a basic function of the Internet, allows librarians to communicate one on one or as groups through electronic mail messages sent over Internet. When a group of people with common interests stimulate a discussion over the Internet, they form Discussion Groups. These online discussion groups can be either Listservs or Usenet groups. Listservs automatically distribute messages sent to a central Listserv address to all the subscribers of the group and subscribers receive the messages via E-mail. Usenet, sometimes called Bulletin Boards, are similar to Listservs in that they are discussion forums serving groups with similar interests. In this case however, messages are posted to a central location, and individuals must log on to the discussion group to read the posted messages. This medium can be used by librarians to read about issues central to librarianship, such as intellectual property, copyright issues, and to send messages to a select group of colleagues or request information.

Telnet facilitates remote access to another computer on the Internet. This direct connection allows the librarian to connect to remote databases or online catalogs and "enhance their services for the new open environment" (Lacroix, Backus and Lyon, 1994).

FTP (File Transfer Protocol) permits users to transfer various types of documents and files (text, graphic and sound) available over the Internet from remote locations onto their desktop computer or transfer files from their computer to a remote machine.

In addition to these basic navigational tools for the Internet, there is a set of more advanced tools to organize, access and retrieve the information over Internet. GOPHER is a software developed in 1991 at the University of Minnesota that organizes Internet resources in a hierarchy. FTP and Telnet capabilities are included within this system. GOPHER is a system that allows viewing only textual documents in the form of a menu. This approach to organization of Internet resources paved the way for the World Wide Web (WWW).

WWW was developed at the European Particle Physics Laboratory (ERN) in Switzerland in 1989. It allows transmission and display of inter-linked documents, images and multimedia files. WWW, unlike the menu driven GOPHER, is composed of interactive hypertext links and is based on the protocols of the Uniform Resource Locator (URL) and Hyper Text Transfer Protocol (HTTP). Mosaic and Netscape are two of the graphical browsers that allow access to WWW.

The "Client/Server" method of accessing data is a fundamental change in the way networks communicate with one another. It allows one computer (a client) to get connected to another computer (a server) to access information. With Client/Server applications two or more programs can be run, with one program acting as the Main (Server) and the other Dependent (Client). A client machine is responsible for interacting with the user; a typical example is a machine that accepts input from the user and displays data.

These Internet tools are part of the daily operations of the health sciences librarians in the present decade. The current technology has paved the way for improved services through new access points.

Internet & Information Services

The Library of the Health Sciences at the University of Illinois at Chicago (LHS-Chicago) is the fifth largest health sciences library in the United States. With a collection of about 450,000 volumes and about 5,000 journals, this library serves the faculty, staff and students of the University of Illinois. It is also the Regional Medical Library for ten Midwest region states under a contract awarded by the National Library of Medicine and is part of the National Network of Libraries of Medicine. As a Regional Medical Library it provides access to bio-medical and health care information resources to health science practitioners, educators and administrators in the ten-state region.

The Information Services Department at the University of Illinois Library of the Health Sciences is juxtaposed at a unique crossroad. The Director of the University Library, also the acting director of the Campus Computer Center, put the library at the forefront of the campus initiative to access the Internet. This structure also facilitates the library's goal to provide cutting edge service in new technology. In such an environment the health sciences librarian's role is two fold: as an information specialist and as an instructor.

At LHS - Chicago, Information Services librarians follow three pathways to information delivery - research consultation, teaching and online searching. The Internet supports all three services by providing a "rich new medium" to the health sciences librarian to find new routes and unlimited access to traditional information delivery (Lacroix, Backus & Lyon, 1994). Internet access is an integral part of the daily activities of the Information Services librarians for accessing health information resources, and telnet, FTP and the web are routinely used in the daily activities in providing research consultation. Internet provides easy access to catalogs and bibliographic databases that are used extensively by the librarians at the Library of the Health Sciences in teaching health professional students to locate information to support their course requirements. The Information Services librarians telnet to various catalogs like UICCAT (UIC Library's Online Catalog), Illinet Online (statewide library catalog of about 800 libraries), and OCLC First Search system (worldwide catalog). Accessing the online catalogs of various libraries via the telnet or web is extremely helpful as a locator tool in ascertaining the location of a certain item before going to that library to pick up the item or requesting the item through Inter Library Loan service. Internet has changed the way one views a library where access of information has been positively enhanced.

A number of bibliographic databases accessible via the Internet provide convenient access to bio-medical information to support the patient-care and educational needs of the LHS -Chicago patrons. Client/Server software like Grateful Med and OVID are used at LHS-Chicago which use the Internet to connect to the databases and then download the results to view. The library of the Health Sciences at the University of Illinois at Chicago is one of the first in the nation to contract with the National Library of Medicine to provide the faculty, staff and students of UIC with the Grateful Med software. This software provides access via the Internet to databases like MEDLINE, CANCERLIT, AIDSLINE and twenty other databases available through MEDLARS (Medical Literature Analysis and Retrieval System) established at the National Library of Medicine. All these various bibliographic databases are vital in accessing health information and the Internet facilitates easy access to that information.

Besides catalogs and bibliographic databases, full text resources available over the Internet are used extensively by the Information Services Librarians when locating health information. WWW is an excellent way to obtain text and graphics over the Internet. If offers reference at the keystroke of the Information Services Librarians. Online textbooks like OMIM (Online Mendelian's Inheritance of Man)- a catalog of human genes and genetic disorders and online encyclopedias like Britannica Online (Encyclopaedia Britannica Online) on the web provide quick information right at the desktop and paves the way towards a virtual library. Government agencies and organizations like the World Health Organisation (WHO) and National Institutes of Health (NIH) have provided information on the Internet which is constantly used by the Information Services Librarians in providing health statistics, health policy guidelines and other such health information. Internet has paved the way where the key is quick access to the most current information. This also addresses the access vs ownership issue, where the information can be accessed without the library being the owner of that information.

Electronic journals are the most recent additions to the Internet resources whose advantage again, lies in easy access at the reader's desktop. Client/Server software like OVID provides the full-text, including graphics, of about fifteen major bio-medical journals. Web is also a medium by which a number of bio-medical journals are accessible. At the University of Illinois at Chicago, *Nucleic Acids Research, Online Journal of Knowledge Synthesis in Nursing and Virginia Henderson International Nursing Library Database* are just some of the online journals subscribed and available via the web for the library patrons.

World Wide Web provides access to not only text and graphics, but also provides an interactive medium which cannot be provided in a print textbook. Numerous interactive multimedia web sites are available to patrons at the LHS - Chicago through the home page of the library. "The Interactive Patient" at Marshall University School of Medicine is one such unique interactive web program that allows the user to simulate an actual patient encounter which enhances the learning process of the health professional student.

The health sciences librarian's role as an instructor is equally influenced by the Internet. The librarian has evolved beyond the traditional "Bibliographic Instructor" role. The Information Services Librarians go far beyond the role of the "Bibliographic Instructor" working with course coordinators and administrators to successfully integrate information seeking skills into the curriculum. At the University of Illinois Libraries, including the LHS - Chicago, the Information Services Librarians "teach the Internet" and also use the Internet as a "medium" of instruction.

Although services are generally described in semester orientations, curriculum integrated classes are developed to support course objectives in the university health professional schools of Medicine, Nursing, Dentistry, Pharmacy, Public Health and Associated Health Professions (Nutrition, Occupational Therapy, Physical etc.). Instruction by Information Services Librarians include faculty development and staff development courses for faculty and staff of the medical community (clinical and academic departments).

Instruction sessions are tailored to background information on the Internet, tips on navigating the Internet using the search engines effectively, resources related to specific discipline, and demonstration of resources to support course objectives. Librarians as educators teach an integrated approach to resource utilization so that these students of health professions are well prepared to apply the same in their professional world.

The Information Services Librarians at the LHS - Chicago are now teaching interactive web-based courses that foster self-paced learning. These courses are web based and include class agenda, exercises, assignments and class handouts. Exercises and assignments to do during the class, questionnaires and surveys are all available on the web and the participants complete them and send them electronically to the librarian-instructors of the session.

The University of Illinois at Chicago Library was one of the few libraries to be at the forefront in using the Internet as a "medium" of instruction. Long before the introduction of web-based instruction, a task force of librarians at the University of Illinois developed an introductory course on the Internet, to be distributed over the university's E-Mail network. This 16-lesson course was distributed via LISTSERV to students, staff, residents and faculty, some using university facilities, some using equipment at their home or office, in various locations throughout the state. Initially over 450 people subscribed. Subscribers received two lessons a week for eight weeks. Lessons were made available via FTP or GOPHER after initial distribution. Content included basic information, troubleshooting advice, and exercises to practice. Pre-tests and post-tests were conducted via LISTSERV to access prior knowledge and subsequent knowledge gain among participants. This course showed that the Internet medium provides the flexibility in instruction where the participants did not have to travel to the library for the course, but could participate at their convenience either in their office or home.

In their role as specialists who deliver information (besides reference and instruction), the Information Services Librarians at the LHS - Chicago continue to expand service options to users who wish to access information from remote locations. Librarians have re-engineered the current awareness services in the context of the electronic environment. Beginning in 1993 librarians established a partnership with the Illinois Geriatric Education Center (IGEC) a major research center at UIC. with the goal of helping researchers to better utilize information technologies. Although this initiative grew to include various workshops and research consultation sessions, one of the first collaborative projects included the provision of a current awareness service. In its infancy, this service combined elements of a traditional current awareness service with a modern approach. Today, this service, which has also been extended to researchers at the Prevention Research Center (PRC), has evolved to include customized subject search in *Current Contents*, Wilson databases, and FirstSearch's numerous databases the service being all electronic from search to the transfer of results to the user. Besides the current awareness service, the Information Services Librarians do fee based online searching. The electronic environment, especially the Internet is used while searching and transferring the results. The use of Internet has definitely enhanced the quality of the service - in terms of the speed and the timely way in which the information is delivered.

Future Challenges

As the Internet matured over the years and as navigational ease has increased, the Internet promises to foster easier communication and access to information. There are numerous challenges facing a health sciences librarian or any information professional who uses the Internet. There seem to be no boundaries to the content, no formal organization or standards on the Internet and the health sciences librarian has to both, use and teach critical thinking skills. Since all information on the Internet is not reviewed, the information professional is challenged to filter the information for quality. The multitude of resources available on the Internet requires proper selection and organizations to produce knowledge. The health sciences librarian has traditionally searched and selected print and electronic resources but now the challenge lies in the Internet environment with its lack of standardization and any formal organization. The lack of permanence on the Internet also requires the health sciences librarian to be flexible. Internet has changed the way information is transferred and the boundaries of the knowledge are not marked as clearly as they have been in the past. The future seems to be moving toward the digital library with no walls and with increased institutional cooperation in creating on-line libraries serving all of the campuses of the participating universities As Nina W. Matheson said, "In the 21st century, the idea of the library will be a knowledge server, an encyclopedic source of knowledge, ... and the organization of the universe. In the 21st century knowledge sources... must be neither privately owned nor commercially oriented" (Matheson, 1995). Thus with the traditional role changing to the modern, the health science librarian is an active participant in the challenging process of self-education and making the best possible use of modern technologies.

Acknowledgements

I would like to thank Karen Dahlen, Karen Curtis and Margaret Jones for their assistance.

References

1. Corn, M, and FE Johnson. "Connecting the Health Sciences Community to the Internet: the NLM/NSF Grant Program." *Bulletin of the Medical Library Association* 82.4 (1994): 392-95.
2. Hicks A, and Tedd LA. "Networked Information Resources for Medical Librarians: an Overview and Some Case Studies in the UK." *Journal of Librarianship and Information Science* 27.4 (1995): 199-208.
3. Hollander SM, and Lanier D. "Orientation to the Internet for Primary Care Health Professionals." *Bulletin of the Medical Library Association* 83.1 (1995): 96-98.
4. Lacroix Em, Backus JEB, and Lyon BJ. "Service Provides and Users Discover the Internet." *Bulletin of the Medical Library Association* 82.4 (1994): 412-18.
5. Lindberg DAB. "The Modern Library: Lost and Found. " *Bulletin of the Medical Library Association* 84.1 (1996): 86-90.
6. Matheson NW. "The Idea of the Library in the Twenty-First Century (Janet Doe Lecture on the History of Philosophy of Medical Librarianship; Presented at the 1994 MLA Conference)." *Bulletin of the Medical Library Association* 83.1 (1995): 1-7.
7. Powsner SM, and Roderer NK. "Navigating the Internet." *Bulletin of the Medical Library Association* 82.4 (1994): 419-25.
8. Tennant R. "Internet Basics." *ERIC Digest EDO-IR-92-7* (1992).

42

THE INTERNET INITIATIVE AT THE ATLANTA-FULTON PUBLIC LIBRARY

Grace B Agnew

Agnew - Internet Initiative

In November 1994, the Atlanta-Fulton Public Library (AFPL) began offering Internet access to approximately 300,000 registered patrons from its 34 branches and through remote 24-hour dial-up communication equipment. In addition, the library implemented a special partnership with all twenty-three of Atlanta City and Fulton County high schools through which it provides Internet access to the library's commercial information databases and electronic mail (e-mail) accounts. This Internet initiative was begun to address the two most critical Library long-range goals: To support adult independent learning and schools. The Fulton County, which encompasses much of Atlanta, is one of the largest and most diverse counties in the United States.

The Internet initiative was developed as a key component of the library's ongoing three-year technology plan. The technology plan was developed by the library administration and was approved by the Library Board of Trustees to reflect the library's goals for patron service. It is revised annually to incorporate advancements in technology and to ensure effectiveness and flexibility in addressing the library's goals.

In 1993, as part of this plan, the library decided to become an Internet node via the South-eastern regional provider, SURANet (now known as BBN Planet), in order to provide database and e-mail access to its patrons. It was hoped that Internet access will enhance the library's telecommunications structure and provide alternate telecommuting routes to the library's resources. It became evident that Internet was becoming a major publishing medium for critical information resources. For example, it was clear that the Internet would shortly become the most important publishing source for much of the government information. In fact, in the past two years, the Internet has gone beyond government and locally-produced information to become one of the most important sources for multimedia information.

It was decided that the library's initial Internet offering would be a web server with selected text-only information databases. In addition, the library would offer Internet accounts and e-mail access to educational project in Atlanta city and Fulton Country high schools. Although many interactive Internet web-sites seemed specifically geared to middle and elementary schools, the library focused first on high schools to ensure that students graduated to higher education or the job market with a basic familiarity with the information superhighway.

The Atlanta-Fulton Public Library became an Internet node through BBN Planet and purchased a CISCO 7000 router and CSU/DSU to connect via leased T1 line to the Atlanta point of presence (POP). The CISCO 7000 router was selected for its scalability for wide area networking, as well as its packet filtering and superior routing capabilities.

The library utilised a fan-out box as a place-holder for a forthcoming high-speed switched network currently under development. A competitive bid was issued for an Internet service provider to implement the server, web browser and e-mail applications. A requirement for the Internet was that it should serve as a gateway to remote branches via the library's mainframe integrated library system-CARL.

One of the basic tenets of the library's technology plan is that technology is used to provide equitable access to resources at all library branches. All technology was therefore designed and implemented to accomplish this objective.

An Ethernet gateway card and TCP/IP were already available on the mainframe, in anticipation of the need to gateway LAN (Local Area Network) services to branches. The library's online system vendor-CARL Corporation-was awarded the bid and provided a Sun SPARC-5 workstation for the Internet server, LYNX web client/server software, and Pine e-mail.

In 1993, the library began offering its PASSPORT electronic reference service, which provided access to its online catalogue, commercial databases and reference sources such as the *Academic American Encyclopaedia, Facts on File, Company Profile*, a directory of corporations, and EBSCO's *MasterFile*, a collection of 350 full-text magazines. In 1995, *The Atlanta journal/Constitution* full-text, in ASCII format, was added to this service. In addition, the catalogues of fourteen CARL libraries around the country, primarily large public libraries, are available as PASSPORT databases.

Another tenet of the library's technology plan is ease of access. All information services are designed, as much as possible, to be available at the same workstation in a user-friendly format. The PASSPORT electronic reference service was therefore designed and developed as a 'one stop shop'. The library's Internet databases are integrated with the public access catalogue and mainframe reference databases. The library's web server or 'window to the Internet' is an option on the PASSPORT main menu on all 465 public access catalogue workstations in all 34 branches.

Adult Learning Service

The library's web server home pages were designed to provide critical adult independent learning and skill needs. More than eighty databases are currently provided in the following areas: Electronic Reference Desk; Business and Economics; Government Agencies and Information; Career and Job Market Resources; Geography and History; Health and Nutrition; Science; Literature and Biography; Recreation; and School Resources. In February, 1995, dail-up access was provided to all library patrons, who can dial-up from their homes, schools or offices, to all of the library's PASSPORT databases, including the 'window to the Internet'. The library's Internet access was heavily promoted on the library's cable channel and through press releases and front page article in the *Atlanta Journal*/Constitution. Dial-access brochures and instruction guides were posted at each workstation. The library's Internet Project Team trained library 'Internet Expert', who then trained the other library staff. The result has been a user-friendly Internet gateway which is currently accessed approximately 5,500 times per month by library patrons.

The only serious technical difficulty has been the inability of the library's graphical user interface (GUI) workstation - Everybody's catalogue-to provide Internet gateway access. The library purchased *Everybody's Catalogue* with grant money while the product was still in development. The library served as a beta tester of the product and assisted the vendor in resolving difficulties with database access and indexing. The product has evolved into a mature, user-friendly navigational tool that is very attractive to patrons and staff. Internet access, however, was the most difficult to resolve, but is currently in test for public release.

Support for High Schools

In addition to the widest possible patron access, the library installed two CISCO 516 communication servers for dedicated dial-up access to the Internet server by Atlanta and Fulton Country high schools. The Atlanta and Fulton County school systems, in 1994, were mostly entry-level computer users. To ensure smooth, efficient installation and access, the library made several hardware and process decisions.

The Telebit WorldBlazer modem was selected for communication between the schools and the library's Internet server, for several reasons. The modem supports many speeds and protocols and cap step down to slower phone lines, but can also step up when a faster line is encountered. Fulton County is fast-growing, and public utilities have not kept up with growth. Outlying areas with rapid expansion, in particular, may have poor phone service. In addition, the modem's two-year warranty, extendable to four years at minimal cost, has resulted in reduced ongoing equipment maintenance costs. Ongoing maintenance is always a major consideration with any hardware and software purchase for the library, for reasons of cost effectiveness and reliable, uninterrupted performance.

To ensure smooth functioning with minimal technical support to the schools for Internet connection, the library required a standard modem and standard communications software package. This greatly reduced the number of variables to be tested, and assured familiarity with hardware and software for remote troubleshooting at the library computer room.

Although the schools purchased their fax/modems, the library installed the modems and the ProComm Plus software at the schools. This eliminated start-up problems due to faulty installation and setup. Twenty-one schools were connected online within three weeks. School support has not required more than three on-site hardware service calls monthly since the project began.

The WorldBlazer modem also assures smooth, stable, secure telecommunications traffic through the use of a proprietary protocol to provide callback service to the dialling stand-alone school modem, for only those phone number programmed into the rackmount modems at the library computer centre. Each school's phone number is programmed on two rackmounts, to ensure flexible access. Each school knows which others share its modems, so that as use becomes heavy, or if a class is scheduled, schools can negotiate with each other for dedicated access. To date, no availability problems have been reported by the schools, although schools average between 58 and 77 login sessions daily. As a result, the dial-in service as designed approximates the security and reliability of leased-line access at considerably less cost. The CISCO 516 communications servers fully support all functionalities and protocols of the CISCO 7000 router and the WorldBlazer modems.

A key component of the school partnership was the involvement of school administrators, teachers and students in every phase of project design and implementation. A decision was made to offer Internet access in the media centre of each high school. The media centre co-ordinators for the city and the county participated in initial project design and in database selection for the web server School Resources home page, which provides interactive learning experiences, on Kidlink Gopher, NASA SpaceLink and Classroom Earth and access to the Library's PASSPORT electronic reference service. Teacher and media specialist resources such as AskERIC and Empire Internet Schoolhouse, are also provided on the School Resources home page. A focus group of students and teachers pre-tested and critiqued the training program and web server. As a result, the library provided an intensive 'training the trainer' workshop for six people-media specialist, students and teachers-at each school. These six people then became the trainers and resource staff at each school.

Each school was provided with Pine e-mail access and an e-mail address for interactive education projects. One class immediately began to participate in a project with Tufts University. A high school German class began and e-mail correspondence project with an English class in a high school in Germany. The library's Internet project manager encourages Internet use through promotional contests, regular e-mail communication, surveys and visits to schools to meet with students, media specialists and teachers.

Internet use in the high schools is a stable, reliable service that provides access to the library's selected Internet resources and to the library's PASSPORT electronic reference service. Providing secure access via Internet to PASSPORT helps to prevent bottlenecks on the public dial access lines.

There were several challenges that emerged in the high school Internet project. The greatest challenge was the lack of computer expertise in the media centres, which was resolved by requiring standardised hardware and software and providing installation and ongoing support. An unanticipated concern has been the difficulty in understanding and working with school structures for ongoing enhancements to the project. Technology co-ordinators are being appointed for the Atlanta high schools and appear to be a better resource, along with existing curriculum committees in both school systems, for encouraging active classroom use for educational projects than the school media centres. On the other hand, the school media centre provides centralised access to Internet and PASSPORT databases for student independent study and research.

Another issue currently under discussion has been the library's interim policy of allowing access only to databases selected by the library. This is accomplished by disabling the Lynx 'Go' command, which opens URLs. This was a feature requested by the city and county Media Centre Co-ordinators. As teachers and students become more familiar with Internet, however, they are increasingly requesting unrestricted access to the Internet. The library is also currently the only public library in the metropolitan area to offer Internet access. To date, the public has not clamoured for unrestricted access but, as other metropolitan public libraries offer unrestricted Internet access via PeachNet, the Atlanta-Fulton Public Library can expect that its patrons will begin to ask this capability. The library's interim policy is that Internet materials are selected, just as other library materials are selected, just as other library materials, to meet patron information needs, but this policy is currently under review.

Conclusion

The library is continuing expansion of its Internet initiative through several new projects. Local databases are currently in development to provide such as bibliographies and frequently asked reference questions. These databases are primarily designed to support school projects and assignments. Fulton County government databases, to be offered in a Fulton County home page tentatively.

References

1. Ian Winkworth. "Stock Management and Disposal : Collection Building and Demolition". *In Academic Library Management*. Edited by Maurice B. Line. London, Library Association, 1990. p. 54.
2. Brian J. Enright. "Concept of Stock : Comprehensive vs. Selective". *In Academic Library Management*. Edited by Maurice B. Line, London, Library Association, 1990. p. 43.
3. R.N. Sharma. *Indian Academic Libraries and S.R. Ranganathan*. Delhi, Sterling, 1986.
4. S.D. Vyas. *Backlong Management of Cataloguing of Cataloguing in University Libraries of Rajasthan*. A Survey Report. p. 16. A U.G.C. Research Project.
5. Brian J. Enright. "Concept of stock: Comprehensive VS. Selective". *In Academic Library Management*. Edited by Maurice, B. Line, London, Library Association, 1990. p. 47-48.

Bibliography

1. Haines, Helen E. *Living with Books: The Art of Book Selection*. 2nd ed. Newyork, Columbia University Precis, 1950.

43

WORLD WIDE WEB AND THE WEB PAGE FOR AIDS

Ṡ. Palani
Manorama Srinath

This article is based on the research work carried out for a Ph.D programme in the University of Madras. It provides a detailed description about WWW and the HTML. Further it also lists the major objective of the study.

Objectives

The Major objective of this research work is to create a database regarding the various aspects of AIDS with special reference to India in Hypertext environment. Further an attempt will be made to create a Web page in the INTERNET.

Need for the Study

Several million individuals throughout the world are currently believed to be infected with human immunodeficiency virus (HIV), the causative agent of the acquired immunodeficiency syndrome (AIDS) and it is estimated that more than 40 million people will have been infected by the end of the millennium.

Hence it becomes dire necessity to have a AIDS web page to provide information to people of all walks of life on the prevention and treatment of HIV infection.

Authority of the Internet

The Internet has no headquarters nor any central authority. The central standards body, the Internet Engineering Task Force (TETE) works on-line, meeting face to face only three times a year. The Internet collects no fee nor pays any charge. The Internet has no nationality either. Born in U.S.A. but flew fast across the American borders and has found nest in 150 countries. It speaks English but can switch to Japanese in Japan or German in Germany. It is virtually above all law though several Governments try to tame it.

World Wide Web

The world wide web provides an uniform, user friendly interface to the Internet. Web pages can contain text and pictures and are interconnected by Hypertext links. WWW is a Client/Server information system. The World Wide Web is the crowning glory of the Internet, providing a uniform user friendly interface to the net. It allows information to be presented in a sophisticated and attractive format, interlacing pictures with text, simply by clicking on highlighted terms, the user can surf the net or search for information.

Networks like "Compuserve", "Prodigy", "American On-line" offer connection to the Internet. They are not called "SPIDER" but "PROVIDERS" and they provide a connection to the Internet. In India, the Department of Electronics (DOE) links the entire academic and research community in India through the Education And Research Network (ERNET). India's Videsh Sanchar Nigam (VSNL) became a spider recently.

Programs that allow the user to use the Web are available for most operating systems. Powerful On-line search engines make it relatively easy to find information on the web. Browsing through the "web-net surfing"-is both easy and enjoyable. Contributing to the web is not difficult, and the web opens up new possibilities for electronic publishing and electronic journals.

The web page is the basic unit of information on the web. Four elements are needed for its creation viz., transmission, or retrieval;; hypertext; uniform resource locators (URLs); Hypertext Transfer Protocol (HTTP); and Hypertext Markup Language (HTML)

Hypertext

Hypertext is a system in electronic form which facilitates non-sequential reading and writing and it has a great advantage over the traditional printed media. it consists of fragments of texts 'Chunks' which are interconnected by the 'links' or cross references. These links create a web of related matters which facilitates the user to browse the data base in non-linear fashion and to retrieve any piece of information from any source. In its most basic form, hypertext functions like an electronic footnoting system, where a hypertext link takes you to more detailed information about the issue in question.

However, hypertext links on the world wide web, unlike conventional footnotes, may lead the user to information held any where on the Internet in another city, country or even on another continent and the information you received may be a text, graphics or sound file, or even an movie. Hypermedia is an extension of hypertext with a difference. Hypermedia documents contain links not only to other pieces of text, but also to other forms of media sounds, images and movies. Images themselves can be selected to link to sounds or documents. Hypermedia simply conbines hypertext and multimedia.

Hypertext transfer Protocol (HTTP)

Hypertext transfer protocol (HTTP) is used to transfer information on the web. All Web clients and servers must be able to speak HTTP in order to send and receive hypermedia documents.

Uniform Resource Locater(URL)

A universal resource locater is a computer address that identifies the location and type of resources on the Web. A URL consists of four separate parts that, when combined, completely define the location of any file or service located anywhere on the Internet. These parts are the protocol, domain name, path and filename, a completed URL will usually look something like this: http// home.micom./home/internet-search.html.

Hypertext Markup Language (HTML)

The standard language the web uses for creating a recognizing hypermedia documents is HTML. Web documents written in HTML are usually named with the suffix ".html". HTML documents are nothing more than a standard ASCII files with formatting codes that contain information bout layout (text ;sytles, document titles, paragraphs list). Tags inserted into the text identify its component parts-headings, paragraphs, references etc., The tags are interpreted by a web browser so that tagged areas are displayed differently from the normal style or text. Tags usually surrounded the tagged area in the format <tag> some text</tag> For example, a top level (level 1) heading is tagged as follows: <h1> level one heading </h1>. tags are usually defined functionally so that the way in which a given tag is displayed varies from browser to browser. The mechanism for creating hypertext links is part of HTML. There is a tag called 'anchor' that the browser interprets as a link to another file.

<A HREF = "URL"> link </A>

Here all the material within angle brackets is instruction to the browser and will not be visible in formatted display. The "A" denotes the start of an anchor and "/A" marks the end of it. "HREF" stands for hypertext reference and it is followed by the name of the file to be opened when the link is selected. "Link" is displayed with appropriate highlighting to identify it as a link.

But HTML is limited, even with HTML + (which is underdevelopment) it's barely possible to place graphics where you want them, and simple items like font selection are constrained as well. Nothing in HTML even approximates the sophistication of the desktop publishing capabilities of today's word processors and it's a long, long way from offering the design tools of a desktop publishing package such as pagemaker or QuarkXPress. The Web in its current state is still well short of the interest of professional page designers and as a result many of the pages are amateurish, garish or just downright ugly.

Setting up a Home Page for Aids (Acquired immunodeficiency syndrome)

Treatment of AIDS and AIDS- related complex, potential developments in treatment, General features of associated infections, subtypes of HIV-I and the various attempts made by the researches to find a vaccine for all the subtypes. It becomes essential to unite all the research centers which are all actively participating in AIDS Research.

Here is an example of document on AIDS webpage:

Human Immunodefiency virus

** CDC Classification of HIV infection*

- * GROUP 1 : Acute HIV Infection
- * GROUP 2 : Asymptomatic Infection
- * GROUP3 : Persistent generalist lymphadenopathy
- * GROUP 4: Other HIV associated disease

* ***HIV Infection***

  * Pathogenesis
  * Clinical manifestations
  * Prevention and Treatment of HIV Infection
  * Vaccine

* ***Drugs***

  * Aclclovir

  .

  .

  .

  .

* ***AIDS in India***

  * Statistical Information
  * Research Centers
  * Treatment Centers

* ***Other Systems***

  * Ayurveda
  * Homeopathy
  * Siddha
  * Unanai

The Webpage starts with an introduction followed by many information on HIV and AIDS with hyperlinks to various files and images. External weblinks may also be included in AIDS webpage. All the terms listed above are Hyperlinks and the selection of any one of these links will lead to the corresponding information.

It is expected that the study will prove to be a very useful contribution since it will provide a detailed panorama of information on AIDS in India. This will be a very valuable source of information for the scientists and doctors who are involved in the on-going research on this dreadful disease and as well as for the human society to increase their awareness about the symptoms and prevention of Aids.

References

1. pallen, Mark: Introducing the Internet *British Medical Journal*, Vol. 311, 25th Nov 1995. P. No 1422-4
2. Workshop on Internet for Educational and Research Organisations: Institute of mathematical Sciences, Madras- 600 113. 9th March 1996.

Section XIII
Prof. Gangadhar Rao: Bio-glimpses

44

THE MAN AND THE PROFESSOR IN PROF. P.G. RAO

Abbas Ibrahim

Pro. P.G. Rao had two distinct personalities:

1. P.G. Rao as the Man.
2. P.G. Rao as the Professor.

I joined my M.LI.S. course in the University of Madras, we both not met each other. But we knew well each other as players in the Library and Information Profession in Tamil Nadu for more than two decades. How we both had missed each other to meet, though actively in the same profession, in the same state in India, I don not know.

But after knowing me as his student, Professor P.G. Rao did not hesitate to confess that he was having a wrong picture in total about me so far.

When I organized the 3rd Tamil Nadu Librarians Conference, assembling librarians in thousand, during the period of my studentship under him, he was thrilled to see so many librarians sitting together and deliberating. Prof. P.G. Rao started admiring me, from that occasion.

He was my guide also for the preparation of my dissertation for the M.L.I.S. But he was great enough to leave me independently to do the same and refused to oversee the draft even. When I insisted, he told "Why you want the formality. You can be the better guide for yourself". When I further compelled him out of respect for my Professor, he has asked Madras I.T.I. Deputy Librarian Mr. Deenadayalu only to see it and again was sticking on his stand.

I was melted to see the unquestionable faith and regards he showed to me in this matter, where he had a right to oversee my work.

As a typical information scientist his advice was available on all terms changing from cinema to serious academics. I personally witnessed many such occasions in which he has taken so much pain to convince the visitor on the modus operandi required to get a thing done perfectly.

We can witness most men with negative characters only. I have come across in my professional walk with so many scholars. Most of them I can classify under one of the following categories only.

- Those who want to prove their calibre.
- Those who want to prove their capacity to harm the interest of any other person they know already.
- Those who want to form a group for hiding their weakness.

But Prof. P.G. Rao, as the man, was above all types of short-comings of such average persons.

He showed real leadership quality, by encouraging every one, he has handled.

This is not an academic strength of Prof. P.G. Rao.

It is God given gift to him, since God only decides whom. He wants to make good and whom. He wants to go astray. Prof. Rao though looked small in figure, he is international in his out look. He always planned things ahead. He worked hard to achieve his aims and goals. He was always a friend and philosopher to his friends, Students and Colleagues.

45

PROFESSOR P. GANGADHARA RAO: THE ARCHITECT OF OPEN LEARNING EDUCATIONAL SYSTEM IN LIBRARY AND INFORMATION SCIENCE

B. Ramesh Babu
V. Kasi Rao

Introduction

Professor P. Gangadhara Rao - Popularly known as 'PGR', used to recall quotations/ proverbs in the class room . We can recall some of the following:

* Time and tide wait for none
* To do hardwork, the reward would come in appropriate time.
* Knowledge is power
* Mistake makes man wise
* Blessed are the meek; for they shall inherit the earth
* Haste makes waste
* Brevity is the soul of wit.

i. His constructive ideas are the instrumental in building an open learning educational system for Library and Information Science in the Madras University,

ii. His sayings as cited above are the basement to the student community for their professional career development. With these pre-face remarks, the paper attempts to give a brief sketch of the life and work of prof. P. Gangadhar Rao, which falls into the follows three phases:

1. Early life and education
2. Professional Career Development

3. Professional Career Achievements

Early Life and Education

Professor *PGR* was born in an agriculture family on 2nd February, 1929 at Panadipadu in Krishna District which is 12kms from Vijayawada in Andhra Pradesh State. After his secondary school education, he entered Andhra University, Waltair. Where he obtained B.Sc. (Hons) in Geology in 1952 and Diploma in Library Science in 1954.

Professional Career Development

Soon after his post-graduation, he started his professional career as Technical Assistant in Andhra University Library and served for a period of one year from 1954-55. It was fortunate for him in 1955 that he was awarded a scholarship to pursue higher studies in Librarianship in the United States. Consequently, he joined in the Minnesota University (USA) for his M.A. Degree in Library Science and obtained the degree in 1956. During his course of studies and thereafter, he worked as a part time employee in the Minnesota University Library. Subsequently he joined in Kansas University Library (USA) as Librarian Gr. I and served between 1957 and 1959.

Having visited USA during 1955-59 for higher studies and gained rich experience, he returned to India. Soon, he joined the University of Madras service in 1959 as "bibliographer" in the University Library and served in the same capacity till 1962. In 1962, he switched over to the teaching profession and joined in the Department of Library Science, University of Madras as "Reader" in which capacity he worked for more than 17 years. In 1979, he was elevated as "Professor", to the prestigious Sarada Ranganathan Chair of Library Science, University of Madras, the first and foremost in the whole of South East Asia, created by late Dr. S.R. Ranganathan, National Research Professor in Library Science himself, by contributing Rs. One lakh from his own funds.

Professional Career Achievements

During his academic career, he conducted personal research as well as guided the scholars. Besides, teaching in the department, he also delivered extension lectures at Annamalai and Andhra

Universities, during 1981. He guided more than 20 projects leading to MLIS Degrees and 10 Scholars undergoing Ph. D.

He was a prolific writer in general and in professional field. He had published more than 50 research papers in Indian and foreign journals of high repute. He had participated and presented papers in more than 20 National and International Conferences. He had written two books in Library Sciences and a few novels in Telugu. These received wide popularity and won recognition for him. He is one of the pioneers in Dewey Decimal Classification and conducted many case studies which received much attention and appreciation from the Editorial Board of Dewey Decimal Classification, Library of Congress, Washington D.C.

His association with professional bodies and journals is remarkable. To mention a few, he was the founder President of *MULISAA* (Madras University Library and Information Science Alumini Association). He also had close connection and played an active role in *MALA* (Madras Library Association). He served as a Chairman of the Editorial Board of '*RILISAR Bulletin*'. He had edited and published "DELISUM Report", an in-house magazine of the Department of Library and Information Science (DLIS) till his retirement in 1989. He served as one of the members of the Editorial Board of '*Library Review*' (UK) and also of the *Madras University Bulletin*. He served on selection panels in many Indian Universities, Government bodies and R&D Institutions. He also served as Chairman and Member of the Board of studies as well as on the Board of Examiners of various universities.

His vital role in the planning, organizing, coordinating and conducting of CLIS, BLIS and MLIS courses through open learning system for the first time in the whole of India is the worth mentioning achievement. Soon after his retirement from the *Department of Library and Information Science (DLIS)* in 1989, he was absorbed by the Institute of Correspondence Education, University of Madras, as Professor where he strengthened the Library and Information Science programmes at national levels.

He was a popular speaker in All India Radio and other forums and a convincing writer in English and Telugu and always eager to share his rich personal experiences with his colleagues. His prodigious memory had always been an asset to him, probably that being a reason why, he had a wide circle of friends and admirers.

Conclusion

Prof. P.G. Rao, a vivid personality, attained his eternal bliss on 29.10.1990. It is an irrepairable loss to the world of librarianship. But, Prof. P.G. Rao will always be remembered as the initiator and implementor of correspondence courses in Library and Information Science in Tamil Nadu in particular and in India in general.

Thus, in short was Prof. P.G.R., the man, the friend, the philosopher and the guide to many. If he has not paid the nature's debt, if he has not gone to that far off place, "From which no body returns", he would have been not out with a century.

Let us offer our salutations to Prof. P.G.R. and bow our heads to him in respect and regard,

Lives of Great men all remind us.
We can make our lives subbing,
And, departing, leave behind us,
Foot prints on the sands of time.

INDEX